BUILDING
A BETTER
WORLD

DAVE ANDREWS

BUILDING A BETTER WORLD

AN ALBATROSS BOOK

© Dave Andrews, 1996

Published in Australia and New Zealand by
Albatross Books Pty Ltd
PO Box 320, Sutherland
NSW 2232, Australia
in the United States of America by
Albatross Books Pty Ltd
PO Box 131, Claremont
CA 91711, USA
and in the United Kingdom by
Lion Publishing plc
Peter's Way, Sandy Lane West
Oxford OX4 5HG, England

First edition 1996

National Library of Australia
Cataloguing-in-Publication data

Andrews, Dave
Building a better world

ISBN 0 7324 1033 9

1. Community life. 2. Public health. 3. Social isolation.
4. Social justice. I. Title.

302.545

Cover photograph: Phil Andrews
Printed and bound in Australia by Griffin Paperbacks, Netley, SA

Contents

For Evonne and Navi

Foreword

Even if one were only to read Ange's poem, 'Who of you will join me?', on page 203, reading this book would be worthwhile. But, of course, there is more, much more. . .

I work in one of the most dysfunctional communities in Australia — the federal parliament. Within this community, respect for people — of a different political party, or faction within one's own party — is rare. Character assassination is common. Childish tantrums, head-kicking and point-scoring are applauded by one's own side, deplored by the other side and met with more childish tantrums, head-kicking and point-scoring.

Some of the best people in the Senate are devalued because they actually try to debate issues in the hope of trying to achieve worthwhile outcomes for all Australians.

One of the most sobering experiences I've had was to be invited to dinner at the US Embassy. I sat down with about twenty people around two oval tables. On one side was an American senator and on the other was

11

an Australian senator.

The Australian senator (who shall remain nameless), in a loud voice that could not have been ignored by any of the other guests, completely monopolised the conversation during the hour-long meal. The main topic of his monologue was how his party had run the country, his faction had run the party and he had run his faction. 'If anyone got in my way,' he said, 'I crushed them!'

I sat there wondering who the tirade was directed at. The American? Me? Who knows? Perhaps he was simply behaving as he always did!

There are many people in the federal parliament who wish the atmosphere of politics in Australia could be different. I am one of them.

In *Building a Better World*, Dave Andrews challenges the model of anti-community I have described above and proposes a way forward in terms of developing communities of hope in troubled times.

I believe the key to the kind of community we hope for is to be found in this statement from the book: 'If we are to create true community groups rather than false community groups, we need to encourage one another to endure chaos and embrace compassion. . .'

As I read these words, I reflected on the two communities I have been a part of most of my life — the church and the parliament. On the one hand, the church has no lack of compassion, but cannot cope with chaos. On the other hand, the parliament has plenty of chaos, but lacks a lot of compassion. 'We need to encourage one another to endure chaos and to embrace compassion. . .'

I trust that many people will read this book and seek to create, within their own circles of relationships, true human community.

John Woodley
The Senate
Parliament House
Canberra, ACT
May 1996

Preface

THIS BOOK IS QUITE PERSONAL, because it's about people, people like you and me, and the hope we have that we may yet still be able to build a better world for those whom we love.

At one stage, I was tempted to scrap much of the book because it seemed too personal. It contained so many references to myself, my wife and my children, and the way we try to make the dream of community a reality in our locality.

But I was persuaded to keep the book as personal as it is for two reasons — first, people are sick and tired of so-called experts telling them to do things they'd never dream of doing themselves; and second, everything we are talking about needs to be grounded, for better or worse, in the reality of our own lives.

This book is full of quotes and anecdotes, incidents and illustrations of people who have challenged us to do our bit to build a better world. All of these stories are true. Where they are positive, real names are used. But where they may be negative, pseudonyms have been used — I introduce it by 'We'll call this person. . .' —

to avoid any unnecessary embarrassment to anyone. Except, that is, to ourselves.

I see this book as part of a continuing conversation as to how we can go about the task of developing a community society together, and I trust that we will be able to take this discussion further when we meet.

I would like to thank the many people who contributed to this book: my wife, Ange, and my daughters, Evonne and Navi, who seek to achieve the aim of this book; my friends in Dilaram, Aashiana and the Waiters' Union, who have achieved it with blood, sweat and tears; my brother Phil and my sister-in-law Karen, who taught me how to use a computer to type up the manuscript; my mother and my mother-in-law and father-in-law, who let me hide out in their houses while I wrestled with the text; *On Being*, who let me draw on my regular column; *Zadok*, who let me use much of the material they published in occasional papers; Phil Andrews who took the photos; John Woodley who wrote the Foreword; Ken Goodlet who edited the draft; John Waterhouse who published the document; and, last but not least, my colleagues in Servants, Interserve, Baptist Community Services and TEAR, whose solidarity in the struggle I value more than words can say.

To those whose contributions I have neglected to mention, please accept my apologies. I owe so much to so many.

Dave Andrews
Brisbane, 1996

Part A: The reality

1

Our world is not working for us:

'The blood on the streets is our own'

ON THE SURFACE, THE WORLD WE KNOW seems to work pretty well. But scratch that surface and we bleed disquiet, distress, desperation and despair. Let us look at the cause of this pain and what we can do to respond to it.

✠ THERE IS A GROWING SENSE OF DISQUIET:
'They have everything they want, but. . .'

These days, a lot of people are laughing all the way to the bank. Many of us have far more purchasing power and far more overall opportunity than we ever have had before. We have access to an increasing range of housing options, health services, educational alternatives and both employment and unemployment benefits.

From the prosperous early seventies to the rigorous mid-nineties, Australia's gross domestic production has risen by fifty per cent and our gross domestic consumption has risen by thirty per cent. We have a very high rate of life expectancy and, along with many industrialised countries, great apparent wealth.

Yet, amid the general jubilation in the endless merry-go-round of parties being conducted on the patios of middle Australia, there is a sense of growing disquiet.

A study, undertaken by the Clemenger group, based on a series of discussions held in Brisbane, Sydney and Melbourne, asked people to describe their feelings about living in Australia.

The aim of the study, known as *Present Tense*, was to discover not objective reality, but the subjective reality of ordinary everyday life, as experienced by contemporary middle-class Australians.

They identified progress in technology, medicine, information flow, interpersonal communication and personal choice as significant gains, but identified fragmentation in the community as one of the biggest losses in their lives. They said they believed that our culture had become 'very individualistic' and 'very materialistic', that ambition had become 'aggro', competition had turned 'cut-throat' and, though the standard of living had risen, that the 'quality of life' had fallen apart.

As a result of our basic support systems breaking down, people said that not only had our level of anxiety gone through the roof, but the level of human resources available to help us deal with this level of anxiety had gone right through the floor.

Hugh Mackay, an acute observer of contemporary trends, says that the tensions caused by such fragmentation are reflected in fights that break out in households all over middle Australia:

A married couple appear to have everything they want.

They live in their own home with a mortgage they can afford; they have two young children who are healthy and happy; they have an affectionate relationship; they both hold secure and satisfying jobs.

And yet almost every night of their lives arguments break out about things which, in retrospect, always seem too trivial to explain the intensity of the anger which they direct at each other.

Sometimes the arguments are about one partner having spent money without consulting the other; sometimes they are about the sharing of domestic responsibilities; sometimes they are about relationships with members of the extended family — especially in-laws; sometimes they are about lack of sexual responsiveness.

Almost always the arguments seem to start because one partner interprets a remark made by the other as being below the belt.

Gradually, they are coming to realise that their nightly arguments are a symptom of a larger difficulty: they realise that they are both permanently tense and that their reactions to minor irritation are born of that deeper tension, but they have not yet worked out what to do about it.[1]

While we struggle with these issues on our own, in isolation, it is unlikely we will be able to solve them, because our separation from one another keeps compounding the problems we are trying to resolve.

✠ THERE IS A GROWING SENSE OF DISTRESS:
'Lying awake at night wondering. . .'
While many share in the wealth of our society, many of us have had our dreams dashed. Some of us weep

because we always dreamt of doing some meaningful work, only to wake up one day to the reality that we don't have a job — and we are not likely to ever have one, either.

Many countries, including Australia, have for a number of years had an unemployment rate that hovers around ten per cent of the population. In many areas around Australia, for certain specific sectors of the population, unemployment may be twenty, thirty, forty, even fifty per cent or more.

Those of us who are unemployed try to get by as best we can without a job, but we have to battle with the indignity of being on the dole.

The following letter, written to the editor of a major Australian newspaper, shows the anguish of soul of the average Aussie battler that we seldom ever see:

Sir:
What's it like to be unemployed and living on the dole after working for close to fifteen years?

Let me tell you how it feels. . .

It's dreading the arrival of the mailman in case he has a bill you hadn't budgeted for. It's praying your rent won't be increased or the light bill's too high.

It's trying to remember what it was like to have a phone. Contact with family and friends is almost impossible without one. So is applying for jobs.

(Not that they ever answer anyway.)

[It's] never having friends in for an evening because you can't afford to feed them or give them a drink. Never dropping into the pub for a quick one because that dollar could pay for soup for the evening meal.

[It's] walking blocks to save ten cents. It's shopping carefully, always buying the cheapest. It's envying people who buy their lunches in the shopping mall, when you can't even afford a cup of coffee.

[It's] getting all your family clothes in the op-shop.

[It's] never buying a treat for the kids. It's telling the children that they can't attend certain school functions because they cost money. And then watching the hurt in their faces. (Bless them, they never kick up a fuss. They have an understanding of the situation.)

[It's] upsetting to read in the papers about how us 'dole bludgers' are living in the lap of luxury. If this is luxury, then God help the poor.

Probably the worst thing of all is the hopelessness. . .

The lying awake at nights wondering what it's all about, will it ever change? Will I ever find another job?

For the first couple of months, I went out every day looking. Then less and less as my pride waned. Now I just check the papers every day (my neighbour lets me look through his), but I rarely answer any ads. If I apply, it's seldom that I receive the courtesy of a reply.

The people at CES [Commonwealth Employment Service] are sympathetic, friendly and helpful, but they can't perform miracles.

Our marriage is under constant strain. Some days I get so depressed I consider just walking out the door and not coming back. But I could never do that to my family. It's not [their] fault and I love them too much to ever hurt them.

Well, that's my story. Thanks for letting me get it off my chest.

Life will go on, indifferent to my situation, but we still have our health and hope springs eternal.

All I would ask for is the sympathetic understanding of the public. . .[2]

Those of us in such situations should not be dismissed as 'bludgers', as parasites, asking others to solve our problems for us. We know only too well 'people can't perform miracles'. But as 'battlers', we know we can't solve all our problems on our own. We are in it together. 'All I would ask for,' says the person on the dole, 'is the sympathetic understanding of the public.'

✠ **THERE IS A GROWING SENSE OF DESPERATION:**
'Why won't they make up and live happily ever after?'

Some of us weep because we always dreamt of having a beautiful marriage, the kind of relationship that would support us through such times of distress, only to wake up one day to the fact that our partner, on whom we depended, is gone forever.

In Australia during the 1970s and 1980s, more and more marriages ended in divorce. In 1971, it was fifteen per cent. In 1978, it was twenty-five per cent. And in 1981, it was forty per cent.

During the early 1990s, less marriages ended in divorce. A lot of couples weren't prepared to run the risk of getting married while so many marriages were breaking down around them. Nevertheless, by 1995, the figure had again risen from thirty-five to forty per cent of all marriages that ended up in divorce.

Recently, a young child whose parents' relationship was unraveling before her eyes was quoted as saying:

> I really hate how on TV shows married couples are always happy. . . as that's just not how things are in real life!
>
> My parents have been fighting endlessly lately and

it's started to make me really depressed.

My mum keeps on talking about moving out and getting a divorce from Dad and how this would be best for everyone.

But why?

My parents have had some fights before, but they've always made up.

Why won't they make up and live happily ever after this time?

Things always work out on TV, so why don't they in real life?[3]

We don't always know why things don't work out the way we'd like them to. What we do know is that some of the things we want most don't work out in real life the way they do on *The Love Boat* or *Fantasy Island*.

A lot of us deal with the loss of a spouse by trying to find another partner.

Twenty years ago, ninety per cent of marriages were first marriages. But these days, sixty per cent of marriages are first marriages. And the rest represent the second, third, or fourth attempts to get it together. Eventually, a lot of us just give up on ever being able to get a partner.

Consequently, the number of single parent families doubled from 130 600 in 1969 to 282 000 in 1981, and now single-parent families constitute some fourteen per cent of all households.

Those of us who are single try to do the best we can to carry on without a spouse, but we have to struggle with the difficulty of living all on our own.

Some time ago, a woman whose partner had left her was asked if she felt she could cope with life by herself from now on. She spoke for many of us when she said:

> I couldn't.
> It's unimaginable.
> I'd be depressed all the time —
>   because I need love.
> I need someone to talk to,
>   someone who cares about me,
>   to the exclusion of all other[s].
> I think it's the most important thing
>   in life, not only for me,
>   but for every[one] I know.
> I suppose my life wouldn't end
>   if I never got married again. . .
> But I wouldn't enjoy it much.
> I'm not enjoying it now.[4]

All of us, trying to rebuild our lives amidst the ruins of family breakdown, desperately want 'someone to talk to', 'someone to listen', 'someone to care'.

✠ THERE IS A GROWING SENSE OF DESPAIR: *'They know my sorrow, yet I bear it alone'*

Some of us weep because we always dreamt of having a wonderful family, the kind of relations that would sustain us at such times of desperation, only to wake up one day to the fact that the relatives, to whom we turn for the greatest help, often do us the greatest harm.

The Public Policy Research Centre in Australia sent shock waves round the country when its survey showed that twenty per cent of people (twenty-two per cent of men and seventeen per cent of women) actually approved of men using force against women to coerce resolution of conflicts in their favour.

With this attitude in mind, it's not surprising that, on average in Australia, ten per cent of women report being threatened, battered and abused by the men in their family. Over any given six-month period in Queensland, the state where I live, more than 1 300 women have to flee the violence in their homes.

One Brisbane woman I know, who turned up at a refuge after a terrible row but was turned away because her injuries were not considered serious enough to merit her admission, wrote the following poem to express her desperation:

I came here for help,
Sure I'd get it somehow;
I was once more the loser
In a violent row;
There is none here can help me —
Though they'd like to, I know —
But they need more proof
And the scars don't show.

When I married my man,
I was the happiest bride.
I was so full of love
For the groom at my side.
Too soon came the sorrow
That has seen me laid low
And I've long had to bear it,
For the scars don't show.

My health has suffered
From long years of stress
And our children, dear children —
Dear Lord, what a mess!

I tried to keep their lives normal —
Such a hard row to hoe! —
For they've felt his wrath,
Though their scars don't show.

Many know of my sorrow,
Yet I bear it alone.
I've been advised by police
And counselled by 'phone.
I feel so shut off — remote —
From the people I know. . .
Lord, I'm so weary,
But the scars don't show.[5]

The Australian Abused Child Trust has it on record that almost sixty-five per cent of the Australian parents interviewed believe that how they treat their own children in their own home, whether good or bad, is their own business and nobody, but nobody, should interfere, still less intervene.

With this attitude in mind, it is not surprising that, on average in Australia, almost ten per cent of children will be abused in some way before the age of sixteen, and twelve-and-a-half per cent of boys and twenty-five per cent of girls are likely to be sexually abused before the age of eighteen.

Over any given six-month period in Queensland, the state where I live, more than 2 000 children have to flee the violence in their own homes.

One Brisbane girl I know of, whose stepfather was later found guilty, wrote the following poem to express her despair when he was earlier acquitted on charges of sexual assault against her and her sisters:

Daddy, don't touch me again —
I really can't handle the hurt.
Daddy, please don't undo my blouse,
Please don't lift up my skirt.
Daddy, think of me when I grow up —
Can't you see what you're doing isn't right?
Think of me when I'm all alone,
Crying in the middle of the night!

Mummy, why don't you listen?
Mummy, why don't you believe
That what I'm saying is true?
For I am what you conceived.
Surely, you must know
That I would never lie to you
About something as important as this,
Something which is very true.

This is the cry of a little girl
Who is scared out of her mind,
But nobody seems to be listening,
Nobody seems to be kind.
Kind enough to listen
To the things that have occurred,
Kind enough to do something
About the things that have happened to her.[6]

This is the cry that echoes in the cry of all of us who
have been battered, broken and abused. It is a cry not
to be abandoned by society, but to be embraced by a
community that cares enough to treat us considerately
and take our stories seriously.

✠ HOPING AGAINST HOPE FOR SOME SUPPORT: *'Are there groups that will create a sense of belonging?'*

Our pain may be different, but our hope is the same. We are desperate for 'some sympathetic understanding', for 'someone to talk to', for 'someone to listen', for 'someone to care', for someone — as social worker Tim Corney says — 'to share our stories, the journey of our lives':

> I belong to Generation X — the children of the most mobile, most divorced parents this century. I live in a time of exceptionally high incidence of youth suicide and drug-induced trauma, of child abuse and violent crime. Hope, for my generation, has gone missing. I have accepted the global media's paradox of macro-homogenisation and micro-fragmentation.
>
> The result is that I no longer know who or what I am supposed to be. Gender distinctions have been blurred; national cultures appropriated and dismantled; normative values have been turned on their head and societies' structures are. . . breaking down.
>
> This is not an ideological revolution. The only blood on the streets is my own. The old has not gone; it has been de-constructed, the guts surgically removed leaving only the great external shells at which to gaze. . . As a child, I was promised a future — a future full of hope. I hoped for racial equality, gender balance and economic justice.
>
> I am the child of a generation of counter-culture parents. I watched as they grew their hair, took their clothes off, sang songs of peace and love — and then orchestrated the largest global recession in recent history.
>
> Instead of hope, we received greenhouse gases, ozone

holes and the bulldozing into extinction of the humble tree.

The dreams. . . were replaced with technology and then force-fed to us by the siblings of the summer of love. Technology is no substitute for the future that was promised. The key to our survival must be the sharing of hope, the experience of hope, the realisation of hope, the incarnation of hope.

Douglas Copeland, in his book *Generation X*, writes simply that hope is contained in the sharing of our. . . stories, the journey of our lives.[7]

That being so, as Hugh Mackay says, it is not surprising that 'many Australians. . . search. . . for a group. . . to which they may belong'.[8] He goes on to say: 'For young Australians, . . . "the gang" provides one option for satisfying the urge to belong to a. . . group'[9] and, 'in precisely the same way as teenagers gravitate towards. . . "gangs". . . so adult Australians are searching for groups which will create a sense of belonging'.[10]

In *Reinventing Australia*, his bestselling account of the mind and mood of Australia as we move towards the twenty-first century, Mackay says, 'the signs are already beginning to emerge of [the] desire to pay more attention to personal relationships, to re-connect with each other, to re-establish the sense of belonging to a neighbourhood, [to develop] community'.[11]

As our way of life is breaking down, there is a growing recognition of the need for us to rebuild our world.

Part B: The dream

2

Our dream of an ideal world:
'Dignity, integrity, harmony and joy'

THE DANGER IN DREAMING is that our dreams don't come true. And it's hard for us when things we envisage don't work out.

But the danger in not dreaming is that, without our dreams, we don't know what to do. And though it's hard for us when things we envisage don't work out, it's even harder for us to work for things we can't envisage.

✠ DREAMTIME IS VITAL:
'Those who lose their dreaming are lost'
The indigenous people of Australia have struggled for survival in the harsh conditions of this often quite inhospitable continent for over 40 000 years, battling everything from flood and drought to genocide. They have a saying about survival that we all would do well to listen to:

Mordja Amari Boradja.
(Those who lose their dreaming are lost.)

Unless we seek the dream of who we are meant to be, they say, we will never find out what we are really meant to do. And unless we seek the dream of what we are meant to do, they say, we will never find out who we are really meant to be.

Maureen Watson, a respected Aboriginal elder in the same area I stay in, tells a dreamtime story that illustrates this point perfectly. It's the story of the Willy wagtail, a very common and very cheeky little Aussie bird:

The Willy wagtail and the hawk lived by this big wide river and Willy wagtail used to look across the river and try to fathom out what was going on on the other side. But whenever she talked about crossing, flying across the wide river for a visit, [the] hawk would clip her wings so she couldn't make the journey. So she'd spend her time planning and waiting for her wing feathers to grow so she could make the journey.

But every time she started to fly, she'd get her wings clipped again. So she laid her eggs and she hatched them out. Taught the babies how to fly. Showed them from the tops of the high branches the big wide world around them and the world across the water. And she waited for them to grow so their wings would be wide and strong and they could all fly across the river. And time went by and she waited and there were more eggs and more babies and more times when she got her wings clipped.

One day, a pelican who used to live on the river stopped by and said, 'I often see you looking over the river.' She said, 'I'd love to fly over there.' And the pelican said, 'Well, you can.' She said, 'No, whenever my wings grow long and strong enough, they get clipped and I couldn't make the journey.' Then the pelican said, 'You can do anything you want to do. If you want to do it bad enough, then you will find a way.' And she said, 'Well, that's very nice of you to tell me that, but,' she said, 'I haven't been able to find a way.' And pelican said, 'You will.'

Some time later, pelican stopped by again and said, 'Are you still wanting to cross the river?' And she said, 'Yes, I do.' He opened up his beak and said, 'Well, there is enough room for you and your babies to hop in and hide.' The Willy wagtail gathered up her babies and they settled themselves comfortably in the pelican's roomy beak and they flew away. And over the other side with all the adventuring and. . . the wonderment of new discoveries, her wings grew big and strong and to this day nobody has ever clipped her wings again.'[1]

All of us can relate to the story of the little Willy wagtail. Like the Willy wagtail, we want to be ourselves, realise our potential and, in spite of the opposition we may be up against, grow big and strong, stretch our wings and fly as far as we can into the adventure of our future.

It was a dream like this that kept slaves going through centuries of grinding captivity, inspiring not only the faith for the struggle, but also the focus of the struggle.

It was a dream like this that kept activists going through decades of agonising conflict, empowering the people to rediscover their identity and their destiny, to recover their liberty and their equality.

It was a dream like this that Martin Luther King articulated eloquently in terms of specific personal, social and political aspirations that many of us share:

I say to you today, my friends, that, in spite of the difficulties and frustrations, I still have a dream. I have a dream that one day this nation will rise up and live out the true meaning of its creed:

> We hold these truths to be self-evident — that all [people] are created equal.

I have a dream that one day on the red hills of Georgia, the sons of former slaves and the sons of former slaveowners will be able to sit down together at the table of brotherhood. I have a dream that one day even the state of Mississippi, a desert state sweltering with the heat of injustice and oppression, will be transformed into an oasis of freedom and justice. I have a dream that my four little children will one day live in a nation where they will not be judged by the colour of their skin, but by the content of their character.

I have a dream that one day the state of Alabama, whose governor's lips are presently dripping with the words of interposition and nullification, will be transformed into a situation where little black boys and black girls will be able to join hands with little white boys and white girls and walk together as sisters and brothers. I have a dream that one day every valley shall be exalted, every hill and mountain shall be made low, the rough places will be made plains, and the crooked places will be made straight, and the glory of the Lord shall be revealed, and all flesh shall see it together.

This is our hope. This is the faith I shall return to the South with. With this faith, we will be able to hew out of the mountain of despair a stone of hope. With this faith, we will be able to transform the jangling discords of our nation into a beautiful symphony of [fraternity]. With this faith, we will be able to work together, pray together, struggle together, go to jail together, stand up for freedom together, knowing that we will be free one day.

This will be the day when all of God's children will be able to sing with new meaning:

My country 'tis of thee,
sweet land of liberty,
of thee I sing.
Land where my [ancestors] died,
land of the pilgrim's pride —
from every mountainside,
let freedom ring.

When we let freedom ring, when we let it ring from every village and every hamlet, from every state and every city, we will be able to speed up that day when all of God's children. . . will be able to join hands and sing in the words of the old Negro spiritual, 'Free at last! Free at last! Thank God almighty, we are free at last!'[2]

When James Baldwin heard these words, he said: 'That day, for a moment, it almost seemed that we stood on a height and could see our inheritance; perhaps, we could make [it] real, perhaps the beloved community would not forever remain [a] dream. . .'[3]

They killed the dreamer, like they killed the dreamers who came before him. But they couldn't kill the dream of 'the beloved community'. The words that were heard that day are still heard today, echoing encouragement in the conscience of each succeeding generation as we consider the challenge to 'make [it] real'. . .

I have the audacity to believe that peoples everywhere can have three meals a day for their bodies, education. . . for their minds, and. . . freedom for their spirits. I believe that what self-centred [people] have torn down, other-centred people can build up. I still believe that one day humanity will bow before the altars of God and be crowned triumphant over war, and nonviolent redemptive goodwill will proclaim the rule of the land. And the lion and the lamb shall lie down together and everyone shall sit under their own vine and fig tree and none shall be afraid. I still believe that we shall overcome.[4]

✠ DREAMING TOGETHER IS VITAL:
'Everyone at peace with another'

If we are ever going to be able to build a better world, we need to be able to *dream* of a better world.

We need to think about it. We need to see it and hear it, smell it, touch it and taste it.

We need to talk about it. We need to read it and write it, relate it, sing it and dance it.

After all, as Emma Goldman once shrewdly observed, 'If you can't dance to it, it's not my [kind of] revolution.'[5]

Our children can help us to start to dream again by putting us in touch with the child inside us who has never stopped dreaming.

Lorraine O'Sullivan, age thirteen, tells us:

My ideal world would be to live in a beautiful stretch of country. . . I would live in a little cottage with roses creeping up the wall. . . Food would be nearby waiting for you to pick it. . . Animals would be all around for company. . . Best of all, though, everyone would be at peace with another, in harmony — no wars, no fear of losing your loved ones. . . This is my dream. . .[6]

Our parents, who have not lost touch with the child

inside us, can help us find a way to understand this dream as adults.

Bill Mollison, the elder statesman of the environmental movement in Australia, who has become so well known for being able to translate visions like Lorraine O'Sullivan's into viable alternatives such as the successful permaculture community at Crystal Waters, says:

> For myself, I see no other solution to the problems of mankind than the formation of small responsible communities. . . I believe that the days of centralised power are numbered and that a re-tribalisation of society is an inevitable, if sometimes painful process.
>
> Unwilling as some of us are to act, we must find ways to do so for our own survival.
>
> Not all of us are, or need to be, farmers and gardeners. However, everyone has skills and strengths to offer and may form ecology parties or local action groups to change the politics of our local and state governments, to demand the use of public lands on behalf of landless people and to join internationally to divert resources from waste and destruction to conservation and construction.
>
> I believe we must change our philosophy before anything else changes. Change the philosophy of competition (which now pervades our educational system) to that of cooperation in free associations, change our material insecurity for a secure humanity, change the individual for the tribe, petrol for calories and money for products.
>
> But the greatest change we need to make is from consumption to production, even if on a small scale, in our own gardens. If only ten per cent of us do this, there is enough for everyone.
>
> Hence the futility of revolutionaries who have no gardens, who depend on the very system they attack,

and who produce words and bullets, not food and shelter.

It sometimes seems that we are caught, all of us on earth, in a conscious or unconscious conspiracy to keep ourselves helpless.

And yet it is people who produce all the needs of other people — and together we can survive. We ourselves can cure all the famine, all the injustice and all the stupidity of the world. We can do it by understanding the way natural systems work, by careful forestry and gardening, by contemplation and by taking care of the earth.

People who force nature force themselves. When we grow only wheat, we become dough; if we seek only money, we become brass; and if we stay in the childhood of team sports, we become a stuffed leather ball. Beware the monoculturalist in religion, health, farm or factory. He is driven mad by boredom — and can create war and try to assert power because he is in fact powerless.

To become a complete person, we must travel many paths and, to truly own anything, we must first give it away. This is not a riddle. Only those who share their multiple. . . skills, true friendships and a sense of community and knowledge of the earth know they are safe wherever they go. There are plenty of fights and adventures to hand: the fight against cold, hunger, poverty, ignorance. . . and greed; adventures in friendship, humanity, applied ecology and sophisticated design — which would be a far better life than you may be living now and which would mean a life for our children.

There is no other path for us than that of cooperative productivity and community responsibility.[7]

✠ DREAMS CAN COME TRUE:
'Declared impossible before they were done'
If we are ever going to be able to build a better world, we need to not only dream of community, but also

make that dream a reality in our locality.

We must not be put off by the scoffers who say it is impossible. For as Lois Brandeus says: 'Most of the things worth doing in the world had been declared impossible before they were done.'[8]

It doesn't matter how small a group we may be, nor how great the odds we may be up against. As Margaret Mead reminds us: 'A small group of thoughtful, committed citizens can change the world. Indeed, it's the only thing that ever has!'[9]

What does matter is that we are able to articulate the dream, demonstrate the dream and celebrate the dream in our own lives and in the lives of those around about us.

❏ Dreams need articulating

It helps to put some time aside to write out our own dream as clearly, concisely and cogently as we can. Our 'dream' statement can then serve as our mission statement.

Some time back, I felt the need to write out my own dream. At the time, I felt a bit embarrassed about putting down my dream alongside the dreams that others had put up. But I knew I needed to articulate my own dream, regardless of how it compared or contrasted with others.

My dream statement has since become my mission statement — a vision which I share with groups of people who want to build a better world. And it seems every time I share it, it strikes a chord which puts people in touch with the beat in their own heart:

I dream of a world in which all the resources of the earth will be shared equally between all the people of the earth, so that even the most disadvantaged will be able to meet their basic needs with dignity and joy.

I dream of a great society of small communities cooperating to practise personal, social, economic, cultural and political integrity and harmony.

I dream of vibrant neighbourhoods where people relate to one another genuinely as good neighbours.

I dream of people developing networks of friendship in which the private pain they carry deep down is allowed to surface and is shared in an atmosphere of mutual acceptance and respect.

I dream of people understanding the difficulties they have in common, discerning the problems, discovering the solutions and working together for personal growth and social change according to a visionary agenda of sustainable, holistic justice and peace.[10]

☐ Dreams need demonstrating

Once we have been able to articulate the dream, we need to do anything we can to demonstrate the dream.

The hard task of building a better world doesn't begin with changing others, but with changing ourselves. If we can make some changes in our own lives, it not only makes it easier for us to believe that we can change; it also makes it easier for others to believe they can change, too.

Every act of truth is a reason to believe we can overcome lies. And every act of love is a reason to believe we can overcome hatred. Every act of justice is a reason to believe we can overcome brutality. And every act of peace is a reason to believe we can overcome bloodshed.

If we want to believe we can build a better world, we must stand by the needy, with integrity, against the cruelty in our locality. For it is only by standing by the needy, with integrity, against the cruelty in our locality, that any of us will have a reason to believe we can build a better world.

To do so will always involve a risk of some kind. Sometimes, all we may have to risk is putting up with a bit of embarrassment. Sometimes, we may actually have to risk putting our bodies on the line. But not to do so involves a risk of another kind — the risk of making a mockery, rather than a reality, of our dream.

I was living in Delhi when Mrs Gandhi was assassinated by her Sikh bodyguards. People went crazy. They took to the streets. Wherever they could find Sikhs, they would grab them by their long, uncut hair, hold them down, pour petrol over them and set them alight. Mobs stopped buses and stormed trains, searching for Sikhs, pulling people off at random and cutting them to pieces as they struggled to escape their captors.

Within a period of less than twenty-four hours, more than three thousand Sikhs were killed in the place where I lived. I thought then, as I do now, that I had to make a stand. But at that time I felt totally inadequate and terribly afraid. It's one thing to talk about the risks we need to take when we don't need to take any. It's another thing to actually take the risks we talk about when we need to take them.

This, I knew, was my moment of truth. Yet, at that very moment, I was tempted to do anything but take the risk I knew I had to take to make a stand. To my shame, I must admit, I was so terrified that to me, doing nothing seemed infinitely preferable to doing something that might be very scary.

However, I knew that if I didn't do something, then and there, to stand by my Sikh neighbours against the Hindu backlash, it would be a complete contradiction of everything I had ever said about my dream of 'neighbourhoods where people relate to one another genuinely as good neighbours'.

I discussed it with my wife, Ange, and we decided we had to do something. We didn't know what to do. All we knew was that we had to do something.

To start with, we organised some houses in our locality to be made available as sanctuaries for Sikhs seeking refuge. As the word spread, Sikhs fled to us. We closed the windows, drew the curtains, locked the doors and prayed the mobs would pass us by. Then, I hopped on my motorbike with my mate Tony and went in search of Sikhs under siege whom we could rescue. As we rode around a corner, we drove straight into a mob of over a hundred people wielding knives and swords and an assortment of wooden clubs and iron bars. We stopped the motorbike, took a deep breath to calm our nerves and stepped over to talk to them.

'What are you guys doing here?' I asked them.

'We're here to kill some Sikhs!' they said. 'What are you doing here?' they asked me.

'Well, believe it or not,' I said, 'we're here to stop you.'

They just laughed. I laughed, too. It was rather ridiculous to think that there was anything a couple of unarmed men could do to prevent an armed mob going on a rampage.

'Well, let's see what happens,' they said. 'We are going to wait here for a bus, check out the passengers and, once we get our hands on one of those bastards, we're going to cut him to pieces. It'll be fun to see what you're going to do about that!'

A bus came along. They jumped aboard. Searched high and low. No Sikhs. They got off, disgruntled. Another bus came along. They jumped aboard. Searched high and low. Still, no Sikhs. So as they got off, their anger turned to rage.

They marched off to a shopping centre, smashing into the shops and setting them on fire. But they quickly abandoned the shopping centre and rushed up the road towards a housing estate. It was blood, not loot, that they wanted.

We jumped on the motorbike again and raced ahead of the mob to try to organise some neighbourhood resistance to the invasion.

'They are going to kill the Sikhs!' I cried.

'Serves them right!' the Hindus replied.

We were pacing up and down in a panic, wondering what to do next, when a shout rang out and seemed to grab us by the scruff of our necks.

The mob had come across an address that indicated Sikhs in residence, had broken into the house and the family had fled to the roof, calling for help. So we raced to the spot, pushed our way through the crowd and took our stand at the bottom of the stairs between the mob and the family.

There we turned to face the mob and, with our hands held together in a gesture of peace, we pleaded for the lives of the family. The mob broke down the door, busted up the furniture and threatened to butcher us if we didn't let them through.

We waited. And as we waited, for a moment, our fate hung in the balance. They hesitated. And as they hesitated, the moment of danger came and then went, as quickly as it had come. One by one the members of the mob broke ranks, spat curses at us, turned their backs on us and walked away.

When the family clambered down from the roof, we greeted each other, hugged one another and wept together.

A little while later, the army arrived, deploying squadrons of armed soldiers all over the troubled area. There was no need for us to stay around any more, so we decided to go home for a quiet cup of tea.

In times such as these, when we feel least able to make our dream come true, there is most need for us to do so. We may be tempted to think there is nothing we can do. But there is always something we can do. We may be tempted to think that anything we can do won't make a lot of difference. But the little difference we can make may make the difference between life and death.

❒ Dreams need celebrating

Once we have demonstrated the dream, we need to do everything we can to celebrate the dream in our own lives and in the lives of those around about us.

We alone can build a better world, but we cannot build it alone. We need to make changes in our own lives, but others need to make changes in their own lives, too. We can only build a better world if all of us do all we can all the time. We need to encourage one another to take a stand for the needy, with integrity, against the cruelty in our locality, right here, right now, today.

Each of us who feels inadequate needs to be helped to realise our capacity to act. And each of us who feels afraid needs to be helped to realise our courage to act. Each of us who feels impotent needs to be helped to recognise the potential of our actions. And each of us who feels insignificant needs to be helped to recognise the consequences of our actions.

We can do this by *commemorating* every act of truth as a victory over lies and every act of love as a victory over hatred; *consecrating* every act of justice as a victory over brutality and every act of peace as a victory over bloodshed; and *celebrating* every risk a person takes, no matter how small, to make a stand as a victory in the battle to build a better world.

The other night a loud fight broke out next door.

I live in inner city Brisbane, an area with a high crime rate, and it seems that there's always some guy breaking in or some fight breaking out.

Thefts don't annoy me that much, at least not when robbery is without violence. Thieves can be in and out of your house before you know it. In fact, I actually slept right through the last time our place got burgled. But fights really annoy me because fights always involve violence. Violence means somebody is going to get hurt

— and sometimes it means somebody is going to get hurt very badly.

It wasn't very long ago that, in a domestic dispute that erupted at our local fish and chip shop, a man shot his ex-wife in the face and wounded two of her friends who tried to protect her. So when the fight broke out, I immediately felt my heart begin to pound, impelling me to intervene before our next door neighbours became the next casualties in our neighbourhood.

However, before I could move, my neighbour Ronnie sprang into action. Ronnie called out to the angry young man next door — who we'll call Leon — who, he suspected, might be beating up his elderly parents.

'Leon, Leon!' Ronnie cried. 'What's going on in there? Tell me what's going on in there!'

But there was no reply — only the pathetic sound of crashing and screaming as if bodies were being knocked about the place. So Ronnie rushed through his house, out the front and round to the neighbour's house, whereupon he started banging on the front door, demanding some kind of response.

'Leon!' Ronnie cried. 'Come here! I want to speak with you! Come on *now*!'

Again there was no reply, but soon the sounds inside the house began to subside and somebody opened the door.

As soon as the door opened, Ronnie walked straight in and, while Leon was hurling his fists about to prevent anyone from interfering in the fight, Ronnie calmly strode up to Leon, put his arm around his shoulders and carefully ushered him out of the house.

After Ronnie had taken him round the block a few times, Leon was brought over to join us on the verandah. And while I spoke with Leon, Ange my wife went over to speak with Leon's mum and dad about what could be done about his abusive behaviour in future.

As I sat there sipping my cup of tea, sharing a plate of biscuits with Leon, I reflected on the events of the evening. It hadn't turned out as I expected. It was far more traumatic than I had imagined it would be. But it was also far more momentous than I had imagined it would be.

Ronnie had made the dream of community a reality in our locality that night. He'd assumed responsibility for the welfare of his neighbours himself. He hadn't projected the responsibility to help onto anyone else. He'd understood that, in a crisis, responsibility always requires action. He hadn't prevaricated. He'd acted promptly and he'd acted appropriately, taking a great risk in the process. And, as a result of Ronnie's action, Leon had been saved from doing damage to his parents, and Leon's mum and dad had been saved from having to struggle with the rage of their son on their own.

In times such as these, when we least expect it, people make the dream come true.

We may be tempted to think nothing is happening. But there is always something happening. We may be tempted to think that there's nothing happening that's really great. But there is always something happening that's really great.

The great things are not the big things. The great things are the little things which, done quietly, gently and graciously, bring life out of death in our localities.

3

Our ideal in the real world:

'Only then will we be satisfied'

I HAVE FOUND WHEN I TALK to people about the possibility of making their dream of community come true, they respond very positively. According to the sociologists Bell and Newby, it seems 'everyone — even sociologists — has wanted to live in a community'.[1]

✠ COMMUNITY IS MORE THAN A WARM FUZZY: *'The way it ought to be'*

Some say it is because community is a touchy feely word, like 'love', 'romance', 'friendship', 'marriage' or 'family', and the concept has warm fuzzy connotations. Certainly, according to Williams in his book *Keywords*, the word *community*, 'unlike all other terms of social organisation (such as "group", "party", "network", "association" or "institution") is never. . . used unfavourably. . .'[2]

Some say that the reason the word 'community' is never used unfavourably is that we have forgotten how parochial and oppressive communities can be. According to Bryson and Mowbray: 'In drawing on the historical notion of community, the Nelsonian touch is applied by communitarians [turning a blind eye] to the tensions. . . and conflicts that were ordinary parts of their archetypal communities. Gross inequalities, rigid status. . . blood feuds. . . intolerance, bondage and ignorance are carefully forgotten, so that "real community" is seen only in terms of cooperation. . .'[3]

And, for some, that may be so.

But the reason the word 'community' is never used unfavourably by the people I talk to is not that we have forgotten how parochial and oppressive 'communities' can be. Quite the contrary. We remember very acutely the tensions and conflicts that so often have characterised our 'communities'.

Yet, for us, the word 'community' is essentially a qualitative term which refers to 'the way we ought to be', liberated from 'intolerance, bondage and ignorance', rather than 'the way we are', circumscribed by 'gross inequalities, rigid status, and blood feuds'.

According to Nisbet, our use of the word is quite typical. Whether we are talking about Confucius, Aristotle, Ibn Khaldun or Thomas Aquinas, the notion of 'community' has always been a 'normative prescription' of an ideal for the world, rather than an 'empirical description' of the real world.[4]

According to Bellah, this notion of 'community', which we speak about in qualitative terms, may be 'resisted as absurdly utopian. . . But the transformation of which we speak is both necessary and modest. Without it, indeed, there may be very little future to think about at all.'[5]

So, for us, 'community' is not merely a warm

fuzzy; it is actually a framework for building a better world.

✠ COMMUNITY IS A FRAMEWORK FOR OUR LIVES:
'A commitment to common mutual concern'

In the spectrum of social science research, the term 'community' is not only one of the most common, but also one of the most crucial concepts for the welfare of our society.

Yet there is a lot of confusion about the meaning of the term 'community'. As long ago as 1955, Hillery noted no less than ninety-four different definitions of 'community'. And more than a decade later, Stacey stated that 'certainly confusion continues to reign over the uses of the term'.[6] So much so, Gowdy once said in frustration, 'it is doubtful whether the concept of "community" refers to a useful abstraction'.[7]

After much study, however, Hillery was able to distinguish three distinctive common elements among the myriad of definitions that he had tabulated. Later Wirth, then Gowdy, confirmed Hillery's findings.

They found that, to increasing degrees of significance, a common physical location, a common social connection and a quality of common reciprocal interaction were the components most likely to constitute 'community'.[8]

Clark, picking up on the quality of conscious reciprocal interaction as the most important component in community, says in his study of *Basic Communities*: 'Community [is] essentially a sentiment which people have about themselves in relation to themselves: a sentiment expressed in action, but still basically a feeling. People have many feelings, but there are two essentials for the existence of community: a sense of significance and sense of solidarity. . . The strength of community within any given group is determined by the degree to which its members experience both a sense of solidarity and a sense of significance within it.'[9]

Toennies argues that while the quality of interaction required to produce a society involves only transient, impersonal, uni-dimensional, secondary relationships, the quality of interaction required to produce a community involves permanent, personal, multi-faceted, primary relationships.[10]

Toennies thinks that community is probably only possible for people in kinship groups. But Daley and Cobb think that while community may be easier in homogeneous groups, community may be broader, deeper, higher and wider in heterogeneous groups.[11]

Certainly that's my experience.

My concept of community involves 'a group of people who share a quality of life which reflects a commitment to common mutual concern in the context of faithful, personal, multi-faceted, relationships'. In his book on community, psychologist Scott Peck says:

> If we are going to use the word [community] mean-
> ingfully we must restrict it to a group of individuals
> who have learned to communicate honestly with each
> other, whose relationships go deeper than their masks
> of composure and who have developed some significant
> commitment to 'rejoice together, mourn together','de-
> light in each other, make others' conditions our own'.[12]

After researching five different intentional communities in depth, sociologist Luther Smith writes in his report:

The primary indicator of communal well-being is that members feel their. . . fellowship approximates the qualities of a caring family. Hardship and failures. . . will be the occasion for creative solutions and increased resolve. They do not break the spirit of a community. . . But loss of mutual respect and steadfast caring strikes a deathblow at the very heart of a community.

The prevailing sense of family is not always easy for these communities to determine. The division of labour which pleases some members is the very issue which oppresses others. . . Members can have opposing reactions to the same communal realities.

Communities. . . thrive when able to create a fellowship not dependent upon conformity, but which encourages members to remain enthusiastically involved even when they disagree with decisions. While decision-making may not always reflect a member's [understanding], it must indicate that the member's ideas have been. . . respected.

Life in community is never all good or bad — it is life, with the full range of joys and frustrations. . . Community, however, tends to accentuate conflicts that might ordinarily be overlooked in the locality. The interrelatedness of communal life causes a decision about one matter to have an impact on most other realities of communal life.

Communities must therefore address intense feeling about the quality of. . . life together without fragmenting their fellowship. This is accomplished when members accept deep struggles as necessary and healthy.

Community is only possible when a sufficient number of members persevere through the turmoil that is part of sustaining community. They must believe that community is worth the struggle and that continuing in relationship is more promising than leaving. This is not merely persisting because one believes that a community's escutcheon of happiness is near.

It is giving oneself to a fellowship because community is the means through which [their] vocation is fulfilled.[13]

My concept of community includes the following:

* it is a safe space
* there is acceptance of people as part of a group
* there is respect for the unity and diversity of people in the group
* there is responsibility for the welfare of each person in that group
* every person participates in the decisions of the group
* there is support for processes that do justice to the most disadvantaged — not only those inside the group, but also those outside the group.

☐ *First*, community is a safe place

Community is a safe space. It is not a place where there is no fear, but it is a place where there is no *reason* for fear — because, as Henri Nouwen says, it is a place where hostility is confronted and transformed into hospitality:

We can say that during the last years, strangers have become more and more subject to hostility than to hospitality.

In fact, we have protected our apartments with dogs and double locks, our buildings with vigilant doormen, our roads with anti-hitchhike signs, our subways with security guards, our airports with safety officials, our cities with armed police and our country with an omnipresent military.

Although we might want to show sympathy for the
poor, the lonely. . . and the rejected, our feelings toward
a stranger knocking on our door and asking for food
and shelter is ambivalent at the least.

[But] fear and hostility are not limited to encounters
with [strangers]. In a world so pervaded with competition, even those who are very close to each other, such
as classmates, teammates. . . colleagues at work, can
become infected by fear and hostility when they experience each other as a threat to their. . . safety.

Many places that were created to bring people closer
together and help them form a peaceful community have
degenerated into [psychological, if not physical] battle-
fields.

Students in classrooms, teachers in faculty meetings,
staff members in hospitals and co-workers in projects
often find themselves paralysed by mutual hostility, unable to realise their purposes because of fear, suspicion
and even blatant aggression. Sometimes institutions ex-
plicitly created to offer free time and free space to develop
the most precious human potentials have become so
dominated by hostile defensiveness that some of the best
ideas and some of the most valuable feelings remain
unexpressed. . .

We are called to move [from hostility to] hospitality.
The German word for 'hospitality' is *Gastfreundschaft*,
which means friendship for the guest. The Dutch word
for 'hospitality', *gastvrijheid*, means the freedom of the
guest. It shows hospitality wants to offer friendship
without binding the guest, freedom without leaving [the
guest] alone.

Hospitality, therefore, means primarily the creation
of a free space where the stranger can enter and become
a friend instead of an enemy.

Hospitality is not to change people, but to offer them
space where change can take place. It is not to bring
men and women over to our side, but to offer freedom

not disturbed by dividing lines. It is not to lead our neighbour into a corner where there are no alternatives left, but to open a wide spectrum of options for choice and commitment. It is not an educated intimidation with good books, good stories and good work, but the liberation of fearful hearts. . .

The paradox of hospitality is that it wants to create emptiness — not a fearful emptiness, but a friendly emptiness, where strangers can enter and discover themselves as created free — free to sing their own songs, speak their own languages, dance their own dances; free also to leave and follow their own vocations.

Hospitality is not a subtle invitation to adopt the lifestyle of the host, but the gift of a chance for the guest to find [their] own.[14]

Hostility destroys community. Hospitality restores community. For community is nothing, if not the creation of free, friendly, safe space.

☐ *Second*, community means acceptance of people as part of a group

If people are forgotten, rejected, or ignored, they don't feel part of a group. It is only if people are actually remembered, acknowledged and recognised as people that they feel part of a group. According to Jean Vanier, community is all about the constant practice of unconditional acceptance over and above the erratic byplay of petty sympathies and antipathies:

The two great dangers of community are friends and enemies. People very quickly get together with those who are like themselves; we all like to be with someone who pleases us, who shares our ideas — our ways of looking at life. . . Human friendships can very quickly become a club of mediocrities, enclosed in mutual flattery. . .

Friendship is then no longer a spur to grow, to go further, to be of greater service to our brothers and sisters. . . Friendship then becomes a barrier between ourselves and others. . .

There are always people with whom we don't agree, who block us, who contradict us. We seem incapable of expressing ourselves, or even of living peacefully, when we are with them. Others ask too much of us; we cannot respond to their incessant demands and we have to push them away.

These are the 'enemies'. They endanger us and, even if we dare not admit it, we hate them. Certainly, this is not deliberate. But even so, we just wish these people didn't exist!

These. . . affinities and aversions between different personalities are natural. They come from an emotional immaturity and from many elements from our childhood over which we have no control. It would be foolish to deny them.

But if we let ourselves be guided by our emotional reactions, cliques will form. . . It will no longer be a community, a place of communion, but a collection of people more or less. . . cut off one from another.

When you go into some communities, you can quickly sense tensions. . . People don't look each other in the face. They pass each other in the corridors like ships in the night.

A community is only a community when most of the members have consciously decided to break these barriers and come out of their 'friendship(s)' to (reach) out. . . to their 'enemies'.[15]

Both affinities and aversions create cliques. Only acceptance creates community.

☐ *Third*, **community means respect for the unity and diversity of people in a group**

If there is no respect for unity, there is no group. But if there is no respect for diversity, there is no place for various people in a given group. According to Scott Peck, community is all about the constant practice of dedicated inclusivity over against dismissive exclusivity:

> Community is, and must be, inclusive. The great enemy of community is exclusivity. Groups that exclude others because they are poor or doubters . . . or sinners or of some different race or nationality are not communities: they are cliques — actually defensive bastions against community.
>
> Inclusiveness is not an absolute. Long-term communities must invariably struggle over the degree to which they are going to be inclusive. Even short-term communities must sometimes make that difficult decision.
>
> But for most groups, it is easier to exclude than include. Clubs and corporations give little thought to being inclusive unless the law compels them to do so.
>
> True communities, on the other hand, if they want to remain such, are always reaching to extend themselves. The burden of proof falls upon exclusivity. Communities do not ask: 'How can we justify taking this person in?' Instead the question is: 'Is it at all justifiable to keep this person out?' In relation to other groupings, communities are always relatively inclusive. . .
>
> The inclusiveness of any community extends along all its parameters. There is an 'allness' to community. It is not merely a matter of including different sexes, races and creeds. It is also inclusive of the full range of human emotions. Tears are as welcome as laughter, fear as well as faith. And different styles: hawks and doves, straights and gays. . . the talkative and the silent. All human differences are included.

How is this possible? How can such differences be absorbed, such different people coexist? Commitment — the willingness to coexist — is crucial. Sooner or later, somewhere along the line (and preferably sooner), the members of a group in some way must commit themselves to one another if they are to become or [continue to be] a community.

Exclusivity, the great enemy to community, appears in two forms: excluding the other and excluding yourself. If you conclude under your breath, 'Well, this group just isn't for me — they're too much this or too much that — and I'm just going to quietly pick up my marbles and go. . .', it would be as destructive to community as it would be to a marriage. . .

Community, like marriage, requires that we hang in there when the going gets a little rough. It requires a certain degree of commitment.

If we do hang in there, we usually find after a while that 'the rough places are made plain'. A friend correctly defined community as 'a group that has learned to transcend its differences'. 'Transcend' does not mean 'obliterate' or 'demolish'. It literally means 'to climb over'. The achievement of community can be compared to the reaching of a mountaintop.[16]

Exclusive unity creates conformity and exclusive diversity creates incompatibility. Only a unity and diversity that is truly inclusive creates community.

☐ *Fourth*, community means having a sense of responsibility for the welfare of each person in the group

If the group is to fulfil its function, it cannot exist as an end in itself. The group exists as a means to the end of helping people to grow as people. According to Jean Vanier, community is all about the constant practice of conscious responsibility for empowering people, enabling them to realise their potential:

> In community people care for each other and not just for the community in the abstract — as an institution or as an ideal way of life.
>
> It is *people* that matter; to care for the people that are there, just as they are. . . And it is not just caring in a passing way, but in a permanent way.
>
> So many people enter groups in order to develop a certain form of spirituality or to acquire knowledge about humanity.
>
> But that is not community. It becomes community only when people start truly caring for each other's growth.

Esther de Waal, writing about the Rule of St Benedict (guidelines for the religious living together in community), says:

> It is noticeable how the abbot and the cellerer are concerned about the [people], caring for each singly in all their uniqueness, rather than with the community *en bloc*, that ideal which seems to haunt so much contemporary ideology. The common life never becomes a piece of abstract idealisation or idealism.
>
> St Benedict would probably have appreciated Dietrich Bonhoeffer's aphorism: 'Those who love community destroy community, those who love people build community.'

Some communities — which are more sects — tend to suppress the individual in the interest of a greater unity.

They tend to stop people from thinking. . . Everyone must think alike. Unity here is based on fear

— the fear of being yourself. Community must never take precedence over people.

It is for people and for their growth. In fact, its beauty come[s] from the radiance of each person [as they grow] in their truth [and their] love. . .[17]

Individual concern creates individuality and collective concern creates collectivity. Only care for people that is really personal creates community.

☐ *Fifth*, **community means every person participating in the decisions of the group**
People do not expect to make every decision that affects them. But if they are part of a group, people expect to play a part in every decision the group makes that affects them. According to John Cobb, community is all about the constant practice of conscientious participation by every member of a group in the decisions that affect their lives:

> To have a communal character. . . does not entail intimacy among all the participants. It does entail that membership in the society contributes to self-identification (and self-development).
>
> To illustrate, for the alienated youth in large cities, those cities remain the societies of which they are members, but they do not constitute, for them, communities.
>
> A society should not be called a community unless there is extensive participation by its members in the decisions by which its life is governed. . .
>
> By [this] definition, there can be a totalitarian society but there can be no totalitarian community.
>
> Community is a matter of the extent to which [a society] participate[s] in its governance. . .[18]

Scott Peck contributes this:

We are so unfamiliar with genuine community that we have never developed an adequate vocabulary for the politics. . . When we ponder on how individual differences can be accommodated, perhaps the first mechanism we turn to (probably because it is the most childlike) is that of the strong individual leader. Differences, like those of squabbling siblings, we instinctively think can be resolved by a mummy or daddy — a benevolent dictator, or so we hope.

But community, encouraging individuality as it does, can never be totalitarian.

So we jump to a somewhat less primitive way of resolving individual differences which we call democracy. We take a vote, and the majority determines which differences prevail.

Majority rules.

Yet that process excludes the aspirations of the minority. How do we transcend differences in such a way as to include a minority?

It seems like a conundrum.

How do you go beyond democracy? In the genuine communities of which I have been a member, a thousand or more group decisions have been made and I have never yet witnessed a vote.

I do not mean to imply that we. . . should discard democratic machinery any more than we should abolish organisation. But I do mean to imply that a community, in transcending individual differences, routinely goes beyond even democracy.

In the vocabulary of this transcendence we thus far have only one word: 'consensus'.

Decisions in genuine community are arrived at through consensus, in a process that is not unlike a community of jurors for whom consensual decision-making is mandated.[19]

Autocracy creates a satisfied minority at odds with a dissatisfied majority. Democracy creates a satisfied majority at odds with a dissatisfied minority. Only consensus can create community.

☐ *Sixth*, community means support for processes that do justice to the most disadvantaged

This means not only the disadvantaged inside the group, but also those outside the group. People do not expect all their needs to be met. But they do expect a group that is ostensibly concerned for people to do all they can to meet unmet needs.

According to Amatai Etzioni, community is all about the constant practice of consistent support for processes that do justice to the most disadvantaged, whether they are part of the group or not:

> A communitarian position on social justice (for all groups) includes the following elements:
> *First, people have a moral responsibility to help themselves as best as they can.*
> At first, it may seem heartless to ask, say, disabled people, older people who have lost their jobs and minority young people who have suffered discrimination to participate actively in improving their lot.
> There is a valid sense that we owe them, that they are entitled to our help. But the laying of a claim to participate actively in advancing their lives on those who are disadvantaged in one form or another. . . [is] based on the concept of human dignity. It is respectful of human dignity to encourage people to control their fate the best they can. . .
> For some, taking responsibility for themselves may

mean. . . learning to feed themselves following a stroke. For still others, it may mean admitting illiteracy and learning how to read. For others, it could mean continuing to look for a job following several rejections.

But people should not be exempt from responsibility for themselves. . .

The second line of responsibility lies with those closest to the person, including kin, friends, neighbours and other community members.

They are next in line because they know best what the genuine needs are. . . and are able to tailor the help to what is required.

When the government provides meals on wheels, everybody either eats the same meals or must choose from a limited menu. But when neighbours take turns bringing food to a needy person, they can take into account personal tastes. When a friend or neighbour provides counsel, it is likely to be based on more personalised knowledge.

One reason many homeless people prefer the streets over government-run shelters is that they tend to be cavernous hangers with a strict regimen, in which everyone has to be in bed by a certain time, lights are turned down on cue and so on.

When neighbours take in a new immigrant they tailor their assistance to the specific person. Moreover, in close relations with one's community, reciprocity is most sustainable. Not the cold-blooded calculations that economists presume drive human exchanges, but the open-ended mutual support among neighbours. . .

For the same reason, as a rule, every community ought to be expected to do the best it can to look after its own. . . Society, as a community of communities, should encourage the expectation that attending to welfare is the responsibility of the local community.

We follow this rule already when there is a fire. The local fire company is the first one to be called in; only if it cannot handle the blaze are companies from other communities mobilised. Likewise, whether the problem is mounting garbage. . . drug abuse, or any of the well-known host of social problems that beset us, the [primary] social responsibility lies with those who share a community.

Last but not least, societies, which are nothing but communities of communities, must help those communities whose ability to help their members is severely limited. Charity ought to begin at home, but not end at home. Indeed, one of the gravest dangers in rebuilding communities is that they will tend to become insular and indifferent to the fate of [others]. Each community must be expected to reach out to members of other communities that are less well endowed and hence less well able to deal with their own problems.

The ways are almost endless, from sending food [to] sending volunteers when a neighbouring community is overwhelmed [and] housing refugees. . .

Social justice is an inter-community issue, not only an intra-community matter.[20]

As the beloved Bengali social justice activist and academic, Sugata Dasgupta, once said:

We do not want the rise
    of the few,
    not even of the many,
    nor for that matter the rise
    of the greatest number.
We are not satisfied
    with the greatest good
    of the greatest number.
We can be satisfied only
    with the good of one and all,
    of the high and the low,
    of the strong and the weak;
only then will we be satisfied.[21]

4

Communities kicking up their heels:

'Everybody gets a chance to dance!'

THE COMMUNITY WE ARE TALKING ABOUT is an ideal, but it is not just an ideal. It's not merely a figment of our imagination. The community we are talking about is very much a reality.

✠ THE DISCOVERY OF COMMUNITY:
'A community I never thought existed'

We can discover the reality of community in a variety of ways. We may grow up in community traditionally. Or we may grow into community accidentally or incidentally. Or we may grow community intentionally.

❏ Traditional community

Community may be something we have grown up with all our lives, yet we may never have recognised it as such.

In the middle of my neighbourhood is Musgrave Park. It has been a meeting place for the murries of the Kurilpa tribe for as long as anyone can remember. So Aboriginal people have always had a strong presence in South Brisbane.

However, I have a friend who grew up in South Brisbane who swears she was never aware of the presence of Aboriginal people. She was brought up to relate to whites, not blacks, so she didn't even notice them, until one day she met an Aborigine who impressed her as a person — and, through her, was introduced to a traditional community she had actually grown up with, but never knew anything about.

Around Musgrave Park is the largest range of cheap rental accommodation in Queensland. Successive waves of migrants from Europe and Asia have settled in South Brisbane. When they migrated to Australia from Greece, my wife's family sponsored the settlement of as many relatives as they could. So Highgate Hill is populated with Rihiotes.

Many of the next generation didn't appreciate the significance of the traditional community they grew up in and couldn't wait to get out of the neighbourhood.

But now they are getting older, they are beginning to appreciate what the older generation have going for them — like the friendships which not only endure the years, but make the years endurable.

So they come back to the old neighbourhood in the hope of being able to experience the traditions of the communities that made them strong — like the ritual cup of coffee that my father-in-law still has every morning at the break of day with friends he used to herd goats with on a hillside over seventy years ago.

For some of us who have grown up with traditional communities, discovering community may be a matter of waking up to ourselves.

☐ Accidental community

Community may be something that we have grown
into gradually. Yet, because it's happened slowly in the
ordinary course of our everyday lives, we've not realised
it.

My wife Ange and I chose to live in our neighbourhood to be near her family. Her mother and father live
down the road and her sister lives round the corner. She
has one cousin that lives at one end of the street and
another cousin that lives at the other end. When we
chose where to live, we were able to choose our neighbourhood, but we weren't able to choose our
neighbours. They came with the territory. It was a bit
like taking pot luck at an office party.

However, over time, we got to know Len and Marie
pretty well. We didn't stop at sharing a fence. We
started to share over the fence, borrowing tools, lending
condiments and swapping juicy bits of local knowledge.
So it wasn't long before we became good friends.

My brother Phil and his wife Karen moved into their
house without knowing a soul in their street. But they
hadn't been there long before their neighbour, Al, invited them over for a drink. From then on they were
in one another's houses all the time. Al adopted Phil
and Karen as his own kids. He would do anything he
could for them. Nothing was too much. Phil and
Karen adopted Al as an honorary grandad to their kids.
Adrian, their son, brought Al a lot of joy. And, when
they named Alina, their daughter, after him, Al was on
top of the world. They had become family.

For some of us who have grown into community

gradually through accidents in the ordinary course of our lives, discovering community may be a matter of becoming more aware of our situation.

❒ Incidental community

Community may be something we have grown into dramatically. And, because it's happened so quickly, changing the ordinary course of our lives overnight, we are acutely conscious of it.

Twenty years ago, Brisbane suffered its worst natural disaster. The Australia Day Floods of 1974 claimed fourteen lives, washed away fifty-six houses and damaged another eight-and-a-half thousand in the deluge.

David Fagan, a Brisbane resident, remembers it well:

> Such disasters always produce their heroes. In Brisbane, two men are often cited as the heroes of the 1974 flood. Leo Hartas skippered the launch that caught runaway barges before they could run into the oil tanker, *Robert Miller*, which had broken its moorings in the city reach of the river. Mathew Carrell was the first mate of the Cape Morton lighthouse tender who dangled a metre above the floodwaters to free his ship's anchor from a thirty-five thousand volt submarine power line.
>
> But such heroics are only a part of a bigger picture. . . Hundreds of. . . volunteers quietly saved the day in 1974.
>
> Most of the flood victims were on the receiving end of a huge community effort.

Carmel Benham was one of those 'flood victims'. She recalls the day her house went under water. She says she was on the receiving end of a huge effort 'from a community I never thought existed'.

Carmel particularly remembers the help the Benhams received from the Browns. Now the Browns had moved into the neighbourhood only two days before the floods. They didn't know anyone. And no-one knew them. But on the day the floods hit town, the Browns were quick to join their neighbours in putting up their hands to help.

The Browns were hurriedly directed to the Benham's house down the road. There they found Grandad Benham, Mum and Dad Benham and seven little Benham kids, including Carmel, standing around, staring at their submerged abode, trying to come to terms with the loss of all their worldly goods.

The Browns introduced themselves to the Benhams and asked them if there was anything they could do. The most immediate need was for some clean clothes and some alternative accommodation. Once that was taken care of, they turned their attention towards other things — like scrubbing the house from top to bottom over the next two weeks as the water subsided to make it habitable again.

Carmel never forgot that fortnight. She always remembered it as an extraordinary time.

For some of us like Carmel, who have grown into community dramatically through incidents that have changed the ordinary course of our lives, there is an acute consciousness of the significance of community. But the sense of community we discover that comes with a crisis usually goes with the crisis, unless that incidental overnight community becomes an intentional everyday community.

❏ Intentional community

Community is something we will only really know if we grow it ourselves.

Twenty years after the Australia Day floods, Carmel Benham bumped into the Browns once again. They had both, coincidentally, just moved into the South Brisbane area within two weeks of one another. Upon meeting one another once again for the first time in almost twenty years, there was a lot of catching up to do. So they arranged to get together over a cup of tea for a chat.

As they spoke, they not only recalled the disaster that had brought them together, but also relived the togetherness that the disaster had brought into their lives. And, the more they spoke about it, the more they realised how much they wanted it to continue.

So they decided to get reacquainted. They began by starting to visit one another frequently: getting to know one another again; not just talking about the old days, but taking each new day a day at a time. Listening deeply to one another. Hearing one another's stories about the struggles that they faced in their daily life. Mourning the losses and celebrating the gains. Together.

As their sense of community developed with one another, they decided to not only continue the relationships themselves, but also extend those relationships to others who, like themselves, might be searching for a safe space in the city.

So they made it a practice to welcome vulnerable people round the place into their group, including a lot of very fragile men and women in great mental and emotional turmoil.

Because of their efforts, there are probably up to a hundred people in our neighbourhood who once felt like they literally had nowhere to go, who now feel a lot more at home in South Brisbane.

Whether or not we grow up in community traditionally, or grow into community accidentally or incidentally, a continuing sense of community depends on developing a sense of community intentionally.

✠ THE DEVELOPMENT OF COMMUNITY:
'Growing a mutually supportive network of relationships'

The experience of community that we need to develop is the experience of being a part of 'a readily available, mutually supportive network of relationships'.[1]

George Lovell, who has been involved as a community development worker in encouraging community emerging in the city for years tells us:

> Community gives out the constant interaction of people as they live, work, worship and play together, meeting in the street, in clubs, churches, pubs and each other's homes. In short, people build up or break down a sense of community in the places where they are.
>
> A healthy community is one which offers all its members, regardless of class, colour or creed, significance, status and a sense of belonging and which provides incentives and opportunities for them to care for one another. Such a community does not necessarily evolve naturally. Some of the forces which mitigate against it come from patterns of urban living in which people lose

the relationship with each other which they once had in small towns. These people feel most acutely the effects of. . . mobility. They need help to build the sort of communities they want.[2]

Regardless of how underdeveloped a locality may be, each locality has a range of embryonic networks of relationships inherent in it which we can work with to encourage a sense of community in the city.

This range of embryonic networks of relationships include: personal networks of family and friends, neighbour networks of acquaintances, solidarity networks of peers, voluntary networks of helpers, and patronage networks of sponsors.

We can always call on the contacts which such a range of embryonic networks of relationships provide in order to get the community together with a reasonable chance of moderate success, because community studies show most people prefer to turn for help in solving almost any non-health problem to non-formal community groups rather than formal institutional organisations.

If anyone has any doubts about this at all, they should consider the potential Kris Saunders and Teresa Scott discovered hidden in a most unlikely place.

✠ DEVELOPING COMMUNITY IN THE CITY: 'The potential is there, waiting for something to happen'

A couple of years ago, Kris and Teresa went to Kingston, a suburb on the outskirts of Brisbane. It is a sprawling settlement merging into the sprawling settlements around it. The population is young rather than old, with more than thirty per cent of the population under the age of fifteen. So there aren't many established institutions that hold the locality together.

The culture that exists in the housing commission sector, which overshadows the suburbs, could be described as a culture of poverty, represented by single parent families trying desperately to make ends meet on welfare payments that are well below the poverty line.

The ugly image that Kingston has is one of the major difficulties the folk in Kingston have to contend with in order to believe they can make anything beautiful of their lives. So Kris and Teresa did not seem to have a lot going for them in Kingston. If anything, it seemed there was very little going for them and a whole lot going against them. But they managed to make some contacts by gathering up their courage to go visiting from house to house in their neighbourhood to meet their neighbours.

Then, they called on the contacts they had made to get together to develop a community group through which they could begin to work on some common concerns, including the demoralising image that Kingston had got and which had got everybody in Kingston down.

Kris and Teresa thought the people might have not been up to it. But, to their surprise, they discovered 'how much untapped potential exists in the suburbs of our large cities in Queensland, just ready to be tapped to meet the needs of the people in our communities'.[3]

✠ DEVELOPING VARIOUS TYPES OF COMMUNITY IN THE CITY:

'There is a whole array of attempts'

The West End area of Brisbane, including West End, Hill End, Highgate Hill and South Brisbane, is located in a bend of the Brisbane River. Though it is only twenty minutes walk from the Queen Street Mall in the Brisbane CBD, there is very little through traffic. So our area has been able to develop a unique urban village identity, over against the background of the general suburban sprawl.

West End has a pretty stable population of about fifteen thousand people. Even though there are lots of transients, there is a very large percentage of older long-term residents, so the traditions in the neighbourhood are very well established.

In the middle of West End is Musgrave Park. In times gone by, the river flats were known for their abundant food, so the original Aboriginal inhabitants used the park as a ritual meeting place for tribal celebrations.

The arrival of successive waves of migrants from Mediterranean Europe, Latin America and Indochina at the South Brisbane Railway Station and the availability of the greatest stock of cheap rental accommodation in Queensland meant that West End became a thriving cosmopolitan centre.

Once you step onto Boundary Street that runs through the heart of West End, you can feel the casual communitarian atmosphere which characterises the area. It's in the anarchic crowds wandering up and down the road; and it's in the animated conversation breaking out of the coffee shops and bursting onto the sidewalks.

However, you don't have to look far to realise all is not well in West End. Up to seventy-five per cent of the people live below the poverty line. Over fifty per cent of the people live in rented accommodation, the price of which is continually escalating beyond their means to pay. We have the highest rate of robbery, the second highest rate of car theft, the third highest rate of break and enters, the fourth highest rate of sexual offences and the highest rate of violent crime in the state, including murder, attempted murder, conspiracy to murder and manslaughter.

At the moment, there are a whole array of attempts to develop true community in our locality. People are experimenting with the following types of community which I shall now look at in some detail:

* temporary community — real, but occasional community
* therapeutic community — continual, but categorical community
* transitional community — general, but volatile community
* testamental community — desirable, but ideological community
* integral community — not actually, but potentially, whole community

✠ DEVELOPING TEMPORARY COMMUNITY:
'A short time together of wonderful intimacy'
Tony Kmita, one of my next door neighbours, loves camping as a way of introducing people from the locality

to community. His favourite camping expedition involves taking a whole bunch of city slickers on a wild weekend fishing trip to Moreton Island, just off the coast of Brisbane, in the middle of shark-infested Moreton Bay.

Digby Hannah, who runs a campsite outside Melbourne and who has got to be the most dedicated inveterate camper I know, says:

> 'Camping' is a term which means many things. For some, it refers to certain unfortunate and unavoidable occurrences to be endured as part of growing up. Amongst other things it invokes. . . separations, leaking tents, flyblown wash up bowls, forced marches with heavy packs, sunburn, sandflies, stiff boots and blisters. For others, [it] refers to cherished peak times of growth . . .times of sensing a closeness with nature, with the Creator, and a small group of people — having for a short period of time enjoyed a common life and known wonderful intimacy. . . Thus the term 'temporary community' has been used to better describe this real but ephemeral experience in which their souls touch and their spirits soar.

According to Digby, who is always taking with him camping people who are 'abused', 'disabled' or 'disadvantaged', 'temporary community provides the opportunity to. . . create a micro society in which there is equality, dignity, respect and unity of spirit within a diversity of people. The harmony [may] be well short of perfect and. . . all too temporary. [But] it can nevertheless linger as a kind of foretaste. . . of the kind of society. . . we would like to create. . .'

Here is a description by Digby of such a camping experience:

Already it is the fourth day. Sixty people have come together to create community for a week in a large rambling building which resembles a monastery. . . These people are sharing living quarters, dining together and daily organising themselves around a flexible communal program.

They have celebrated together with song, dance and story. They have revelled in the sights, sounds and sensations of the outdoors during the day and at night they have communed beside the coffee pot and campfire for hours about children, families, sickness, separation, sadness and hope. Unique experiences have been shared and special, lasting bonds formed between people.

In the dining hall at a table scattered with pens and assorted scraps of paper sits Fiona. She has been writing 'warm fuzzies' — affirming messages to other campers — and placing them in their already bulging fuzzy bags which are arrayed in alphabetical order on the wall behind her. Fiona has a loud laugh, a warm smile and an approachable personality. A child care worker, who first came fifteen years ago. . . Fiona is now married with four children, and returns regularly as a volunteer.

Opposite Fiona sits Sharon, an understandably weary mother who, from the birth of her youngest, has had sole charge of three young children and a lively teenager. Sharon and Fiona, who first met on a camp several years ago, are midway through one of their regular conversations about the frustrations and pleasures of living with children. They enjoy each other's sense of humour and Sharon draws strength from Fiona's buoyancy and optimism.

Sharon's adolescent daughter, Amber, has been rebellious of late, refusing to tell her mother where she is and when she will be home. Sharon has not been sleeping, is afraid she is losing her grip on life and fears for her children. For her, the time at camp is like an oasis. Her children are all happy and occupied.

Even Amber, who has been given some responsibilities supervising craft activities, has been a model of perfect behaviour. Camp always gives Sharon a strange though pleasant feeling — she is with her precious children, able to share their pleasure and yet, in a way, be separate from them. She is free from the incessant demands to meet needs, to constantly arbitrate disputes and to chide recalcitrant and rumbustious children.

At home, she never feels off duty. Here, she finds herself able to disengage from some of the negative and destructive ways in which she has become accustomed to dealing with her children. Here, they are absorbed and happy and she is free to enjoy them in a fresh way. At the present moment, her youngest is in the playground, two are out surfing with volunteers and Amber is with a small group making puppets upstairs. Sharon values highly her chats with Fiona as so rarely does she have the opportunity to indulge in adult conversation of any sort.

Outside in the alcove having a smoke is Julia. In a wheelchair beside her and sharing this dubious habit is twenty-four-year-old Wayne. Julia and Wayne have more than nicotine in common. Both have spent years of their lives in institutions and both agree that to escape their accustomed environment is a rare treat. Wayne normally lives in residence with dozens of other cerebral palsy sufferers. During the week, he is employed with other people with disabilities in a sheltered workshop. For Wayne, coming away here means feeling 'normal' and, for a change, having some 'normal' friends.

Soon, Julia will push Wayne away for one of their regular half-hour walks to the local shop; Julia, too, is familiar with the label 'abnormal'. She suffers from a congenital condition which exhibits a collection of physical and intellectual disabilities. Her two teenage children, Russell and Brent, display similar symptoms. The reality is that these two children have been raised 'in care' because their mother has not been equipped to provide for them. As she has lived in the country and they in the city, the family has rarely been together. They do, however, spend a week together every twelve months. . .

This is a time to which they all look forward, a time when they are together, when they are safe and in the company of friends. Russell and Brent have memories of collecting shells with their mother and making the shell boxes which still sit proudly on bedside tables at their family group home. They remember canoe trips and camping expeditions shared together as a family with friends like Arthur.

Right now Arthur, along with his able assistant, Russell, [is] in the kitchen preparing a batch of their famous coleslaw for the evening meal. Arthur is twenty-eight years old, currently out of work and living on his own. He is tertiary-trained, but has for years found it difficult to gain employment. He has a variety of skills which are put to great use on his regular visits. . .

Arthur met Russell and Brent. . . many years ago. As he resides quite close to the boy's family group home, Arthur has become a good friend, taking them to [football] matches whenever their respective teams have been playing. On a free weekend, he has occasionally taken them to visit their mother. While Russell works contentedly in the kitchen, his brother Brent is equally happy in the playground helping Kerryn supervise the toddlers. Brent is running awkwardly with a ball with several toddlers in hot pursuit while Kerryn retrieves a runaway from half up the slide.

Kerryn, a seventeen-year-old girl, first participated eighteen months ago as one of several homeless teenagers in the company of their social worker. Kerryn enjoyed the experience and expressed her keen desire to return as a volunteer. At the time, volunteers were plentiful and her attendance was not strongly encouraged, but she was told that if she could arrange her own transport from such a great distance, she would be welcome. Kerryn arrived with a bright smile on the first day.

Already she has proven herself to be a most reliable helper, especially with young children. One of her favourites is two-year-old Dillon. Having rescued him from the slide, she distracts him with tickles and cuddles. Dillon is the youngest of three children who are in the care of their father, Ray, who has taken advantage of being child-free and retreated with Craig and his borrowed fishing rods. . .

The friendship between Ray and Craig is one of several unlikely liaisons which have already begun to emerge from this temporary community. A young unemployed lad complete with standard tattoos, earrings and a single dreadlock, Craig has become firm friends with Ray, a fairly conservative man many years his senior.

Ray is a single father with a psychiatric history who has the full responsibility of providing domestically for his children. Ray has been able to manage this challenge effectively because, in addition to his commonwealth pension and occasional visits from a social worker, he receives regular help from the local church who are always there for him in times of stress or crisis.

Part of their strategy for relieving Ray of some of the extra stress of parenting during school holiday times has been to arrange for him and his family to spend a week at [camp] every six months or so. Members from the church have assisted Ray's family with transport and funding. Craig has got on well with Ray's children. At the conclusion of this time away the friendship between Craig, Ray and his family will no doubt remain.

There are many other interesting people who comprise this temporary community. They include a teenager who, having attended a previous adventure camp, returned as a volunteer; a seventeen-year-old intellectually disabled boy who after coming for twelve years as a camper is now making a significant contribution as a volunteer, a mother with four children who was almost too shy to survive the first day but who stayed to make many new friends; a welfare worker who has returned to camp with husband and children after six years; and a young and talented couple attending as volunteers just weeks prior to their marriage.

All in all, there are sixty very diverse people from disparate backgrounds with widely diverging interests. . . welded together in temporary community .

Underlying the positive interactions between individuals within the group has been the collective understanding that God has made each member different but all precious, equally benefiting from his grace. Some of these deeper values have been celebrated each morning in story, drama and song.

These times have been simple and participatory, but important as an attempt to articulate something of the faith which allows us to give and receive forgiveness, renew hope and to start afresh. Many of the members of this small community have experienced the humiliation. . . of second-class citizen status. They are familiar with the stigmas associated with being unsuccessful at school, in foster care, unemployed, homeless, with [a physical] disability, a psychiatric disorder, or being a single parent.

Within this temporary community, however, there has been an attempt to treat each person with dignity. Each individual has a contribution to make to the collective good. Each person displays qualities. . . Each deserves due recognition. At the conclusion of the week, each person's particular gifts will be officially recognised and celebrated in an award-giving ceremony.

The experiences of this week are indeed special, but

not unique. They are typical of the. . . camaraderie of temporary community.

The sense of bonding between individuals will long outlive this present brief encounter of six days. For certain members of the group, the attachment they have draws upon a long mutual history. More than three-quarters of them have been to this place before and many were well acquainted with each other before camp commenced. There is a strong sense of being 'at home' and a sense of place for many because it is familiar territory. They are no strangers to these old but stately brick buildings, with their tranquil surroundings. Many times before they have breathed deeply the fresh, salty air and gazed across the bay where the pelicans come and go with the tides. Often they have watched their children disappearing, bucket in hand, to search for treasures, collect flotsom and chase crabs.

It's no wonder that those who have experienced temporary community have every intention of allowing the ripples which have arisen during their short time together to continue into the future.[4]

✠ DEVELOPING THERAPEUTIC COMMUNITY:

'Sharing the painful stages of growth'

Quite a few of my mates are involved in a group called 'Grow'. Grow is a self-help, peer-support group which seeks to enable people to struggle more effectively to-gether with issues that tend to cause mental and emotional trauma in our society.

Grow began in Sydney in 1957, when a group of psychiatric survivors decided to use a twelve step pro-gram as a method for their own rehabilitation. As they say:

1. We admitted we were inadequate or maladjusted to life.
2. We cooperated with help.
3. We surrendered to the healing power of God.
4. We made a personal inventory and accepted ourselves.
5. We made a moral inventory and cleaned out our hearts.
6. We endured until cured.
7. We took care and control of our bodies.
8. We learned to think by reason rather than feelings. . .
9. We trained our wills to govern our feelings.
10. We took our responsible and caring place in society.
11. We grew daily closer to maturity.
12. We carried the *Grow* message to others in need.[5]

Since they started, more than five hundred *Grow* groups have been set up round Australia, helping people who have had breakdowns put the pieces of their lives back together again — and develop, maintain and sustain a healthy way of life by showing them how to avoid unnecessary pitfalls in future.

Grow is both anonymous and inclusive; it is open to all people, regardless of colour, class or creed, who respect the group and would like to participate in the group in order to enhance the mental and emotional health of our society.

My mates in *Grow* believe individual problems require individual solutions, collective problems require collective solutions — and a 'sick society' like ours desperately needs therapeutic community, as the following extracts from *Grow* point out:

> Beyond the whole humanity of the person and their close relationships, the developing adult cannot but be concerned with the wholeness of their human community. For, to the extent that they do not participate in the building of a community of persons, the progressively depersonalised social body which they go along with will tend to undermine and deform their personal life and their choicest relationships. There can be nothing static or neutral in the life of society any more than in the life of an individual.
>
> In other words, there can be no such thing as *free and whole persons* outside of *free and wholesome relationships*; nor can there be either of these profoundly healthy human realities, for any length of time, outside of a vigorously growing *free and whole community*, however small to begin with.
>
> The libertarians, who have been aggressively hell-bent on building a society based on freedom without wholeness, are as hostile to authentic human life and growth as the totalitarians who have been just as insanely committed to building society on wholeness without freedom.
>
> Both of those one-sided social theories have been, especially during this last century, complementary opposite formulas for destroying integrity of character in persons and civilisation in society.
>
> Friendship has always been the constructive bond linking integrity of character in persons and civilisation in society. Authentic freedom and wholeness can only be achieved *together*.[6]

It starts with you and me caring about each other, doing things with each other and sharing the striving of our hearts, giving each other constructive leadership. The

more deeply we are affected by the loving acceptance
and support we experienced from our earliest attendance
at the group, the more unshakably we believe in the
importance of sharing with others and nurturing them
through the painful early stages of their growth with
the group. . .

Outreach is the indispensable starting point with each
new person who comes for help, no matter how slightly
troubled or how severely disfigured by suffering he or
she is. This elementary meeting of human beings con-
tains implicitly the offer of, and invitation to, friendship.
We don't limit our outreach only to those who easily
appeal to us and with whom we feel an affinity. The
more truly we love our fellow human beings, the more
likely we are to be affected by a sense of their immense
worth when we see them most scarred by their background environment or experience. So much the more
generously, then, will we be led to reach out to them
and to bring to light the treasure buried and obscured
within them. For we all have a treasure within us, and
we're more able to realise it when we ourselves are on
the receiving end of a genuine manifestation of love.
Once touched to life by love that we have experienced,
our vision enlarges to include many whom we would
never have related to before and, potentially, all suffering
people. . .

The sicker the person is the more we must be
prepared to reach out to them, to get them moving with
us again at the point where they stopped growing —
to believe in them all the more when they no longer
believe in themselves.

In treasuring our friends, we reveal their best selves
to themselves:

summoning them forth,
    bidding them to live,
        inviting them to grow. . .

This, in my opinion, is what real love is all about. For 'love is the consistent active concern for the whole welfare of another human being as equally important to one's own'.

How many of us can say with feeling that we've been 'loved back to health'?

That is not to deny that we've had to do a great deal of work on our thinking and our actions as well. But how many, once tormented and shattered, do you know who will tell you that they were motivated to struggle and grow only because some one significant person or the group dared to be generous with their love, their time and patience in between the weekly meetings? To the extent that we have grown to a certain maturity through the experience of friendship ourselves, and the example of other friendships round about us, we are able to give of ourselves with like generosity to help so many other lost ones who still have to find themselves.

The seeking and finding of ourselves only comes about through a sharing with another person who is prepared to cherish us as another self. For we are all other selves to each other.

I like to recall often a beautiful thought I heard years ago, attributed to Rabbi Brasch. Commenting on the commandment 'Love thy neighbour as thyself', he explained that in the original Hebrew the precise meaning was: 'Love thy neighbour for s/he is thy self'.

In the group, we find our personalities constantly undergoing change. The moving principle in this change is growth into adult relationships — by dependability, helpfulness, appreciation and compassion — and then into fully shared living or friendship. This is not only friendships within one's own sex, but real and precious friendships across the sexes. This is one of the features of our life together that so often provokes comment, 'How easily you people express your feelings for one another. And how relaxed men and women are in relating to one another'.

The fact is that in the community we have come to believe in the real possibility and the inestimable value of these friendships, which can minister to each other's vital needs — to be somebody, to be at home and to be going somewhere. Recently, I was present at a meeting in which one lonely person spontaneously invited another lonely person to play tennis one weekend. As a result of the group's enthusiastic support, that person now has the opportunity to play with four men and women every second Saturday of the month.

Our regular live-in community weekends are another happy occasion for growing into one another's lives and enjoying, in some cases for the very first time, the delicious experience of feeling at home.

Usually, we have a guest speaker to address us on a particular topic. It could be, for example a subject such as 'Managing Close Personal Relationships', 'Sexual Maturity' or 'Guilt', to mention only a few. The speaker only introduces the subject, highlighting key perspectives and any special areas of doubt or disagreement.

The aim of the discussion is threefold: to make us think, bring out our thoughts and come to a better understanding of life and ourselves. The point is, we find we do all this so much better by doing it together. On the subject discussed, we deliberately aim to summarise and keep, from what has been said, what we call the highest common factor of agreement.

As such, it becomes potential material for the program. . .

In this way, the program can go on expanding, being refined and being renewed, which is the condition of its staying alive and continuing to meet people's needs. Saturday night at these weekends is always popular. . . The emphasis here is on using our talents by playing games, dancing, singing around a piano, guitar or nothing at all when there's no instrument, getting to know one another better in [a] relaxed atmosphere. . .

Sharing — shared living, shared growth in maturity — is the feature that characterises a real community. Growth in community is a gradual experience. However, once we are on a growth curve, we know we can outgrow mediocre expectations. . .

Mary came to the community after years of struggle in rearing two children on her own. She was then a bitter woman, a mainlining drug addict with a long way to go. . .

She made no secret of the drastic disorders she was battling with or what she had to do to change. Within two or three years, she quit shooting up and from then on never looked back. She became a living example of God's healing work amongst us and a personal link with many people. . .

When I first met Mary, I found her very strong personality difficult to cope with, for I was also very sick then. But, strange to say, Mary and I soon forged bonds of easy affection and became firm friends. From those earliest years, we grew out of maladjustment together. . .

She was often like a stiff dose of shock treatment to me. I remember when, to my tormented mind, *everyone was watching me*, talking about me, hating me. However, Mary broke through to me bluntly: 'Gawd, just who do you think you are that other people would want to be talking about you all the time!'

I needed this devastatingly strong message. From then on, I stopped saying those things — and eventually stopped thinking them.

Community can bring the best out of us all.'[7]

May the spirit of friendship
        make us free and whole persons,
    and gentle builders
        of a free and whole community.[8]

✠ DEVELOPING TRANSITIONAL COMMUNITY:
'Regathering the broken fragments of reality'

The alarm bursts in on my sleep, shaking me awake. I stagger out of bed, grab my clothes, dress on the way to the door and stumble downstairs. I jump in the car and drive through the dark to Bristol Street.

Every Wednesday morning, just as the dawn is breaking, I meet with my friends at Bristol Street. Usually, Carmel greets me as I come in, giving me one of those big hugs for which she is famous and which make everyone feel at home in an instant. Gradually, the rest of the household stirs, people emerging from four or five bedrooms to gather in the lounge room together. Everyone is rugged up in blankets, bringing their bedding with them. So the lounge room becomes like a bedroom and the meeting seems more like a slumber party — which makes it all kind of cosy, I guess.

Each week, different members of the household take it in turns to lead a series of devotions, to give the household a sense of direction. Today, Annie reads a passage from *Seize the Day*, a book of meditations by Charles Ringma, based on the reflections of faithful Dietrich Bonhoeffer, the German pastor who sacrificed his life in his struggle with the Nazis.

After prayers, we move into the dining room, gathering around a large dining table, which is soon lavished with bowls of fruit, boxes of cereals and bottles of milk. We begin with a cup of tea and then, over breakfast, get down to the business of reviewing how things are going for this wonderful bunch of young people who have chosen to live in the vortex of the chaos that constitutes our locality in order to learn how to be and how to do community.

Today, two students who have been using the household as a base for their placements over the last six months are assessing the value of working out of Bristol Street. Leonie says the structure of the community provides a safe space for people in transition to explore their faith, express their values and experiment with an alternative lifestyle. Jason says the situation of the community provides a fantastic place for people in transition who want to work part-time on improving their welfare knowledge and part-time on applying their welfare skills, meeting the needs of the people in distress who drop by the house day and night.

Even as we talk, a man who has been staying overnight gets up and wanders through, bleery-eyed, to the bathroom. It reminds us that we need to talk about another guest, a woman who has been staying at the house for the last two weeks. She has just got out of prison and is going through a tough time adapting to normal life again, even with all the help of people in the household.

There's a lot to talk about. But we know we don't have a lot of time. At first light, the first visitors of the day will no doubt be on the doorstep.

We talk our way through a maze of issues. As we race through them, time rushes by. I glance at my watch. I have to go. I say goodbye. But when I leave, I take with me the memory of this wonderful bunch of people who are blossoming at Bristol Street. And during the day, I take every chance I can to recall the things they shared with me. . .

One participant, Noritta Diop, has said this:

I remember right from the start, on the first day of my placement, they really made me feel welcome. I felt a deep sense of belonging the minute I set foot on the front steps. Here, I met Carmel who went and made me a cup of tea and told me to make myself at home.

One of the things that really stood out to me was the running of the household. People are given the opportunity to be themselves and are able to express themselves in their own way. There is mutual respect between the people who live at Bristol Street.

People are actually concerned with the wellbeing of one another. For example, one of the members of the household is a vegetarian. Therefore, those whose turn it is to cook always try to take her into consideration. The cook will prepare a special vegetarian dish, especially for her. Another member is a reformed alcoholic. So the others are careful not to bring any alcoholic beverages onto the premises and visitors are asked not to do so either. One of the girls informed me that whenever she goes out to a party with this particular person, she won't drink any alcohol while she is with her.

The Bristol Street gang also treat others with the same type of respect — especially the large number of people with psychiatric disabilities who visit the place. Members of the Bristol Street household will often spend hours just sitting and talking to these people, listening to their stories. They make cups of tea for them, serve them lunch and even take them out on social outings, a picnic, a barbecue or a movie of their choice.

Now if this isn't respect for the wellbeing of your neighbour, then what is it? Must be a new phenomenon sweeping through the neighbourhood.[9]

Another participant, Jason McLeod, said this:

Bristol Street has been about drawing the fragmented realities of my life together. It has given me the chance to sincerely explore who I am, a chance to explore what it means for me, Jason McLeod, to live.

As I have tried to do this, to live out the values I believe in, I have realised, often painfully, my glaring inconsistencies. But there are no pain-free options. . .

Essentially, it is a chance to be real.

For me, the central purpose. . . is to work for justice. . . It is a revolution that shapes how we live our life, everything we do, in terms of the way we relate to the disadvantaged. It means replacing my agenda with the agenda of others so people can meet their needs in the context of mutual respect. It begins by confronting the causes inside us, our own greed and prejudice, then moves to confronting causes outside us, oppression and exploitation.

This double mandate translates into a commitment to 'simplicity', 'solidarity', and 'servanthood'.

Simplicity: When it all boils down to it, Bristol Street [is] not real flash. In fact [it is] pretty wimpy, unpretentious and ordinary.

It attempts to break the self-destructive addictions of the modern world, including individualism, materialism, consumerism, classism and all forms of capitalism.

In Bristol Street, the ordinary is valued. The ordinary involves everyday things like morning devotions, shared chores, community meals and house nights. This sort of stuff is seen as a genuine way to spend time together and build friendships in the neighbourhood.

People, like the refugees we work with, are central in this lifestyle. That is its strength.

Solidarity: A part of living with others is embracing their struggle. It is standing alongside and trying to understand.

Amongst the Salvadorens I have worked with, this means eating tomales and papusas (which I love) and drinking thick black coffee (which I hate). It means struggling to understand where they come from, hearing brutal accounts of the war — about the death squads and the five mutilated, severed heads dumped on the doorstep of my friend's house.

Servanthood: Servanthood is about doing what people ask us to. It is not only replacing one agenda with another, but making the time and having the flexibility to act on it.

I can remember looking for a house on behalf of a newly arrived family, a solo mum and her three kids, who had spent the last thirteen years in a closed refugee camp in Honduras. They wanted a three bedroomed house, with an electric stove in the kitchen and plenty of room to move about in the backyard. So we spent a couple of afternoons scouring the neighbourhood, as far as Greenslopes and Coorparoo, looking for a suitable house.

When we finally found one, they decided they didn't want one. They opted for an apartment with a gas stove and without a backyard instead. It wasn't what we'd expected. At one point of time, we'd got quite exasperated. But they were happy — and we were happy about that.

My journey in community is one of growing intimacy. Expressing myself and deepening my respect. Not growing stronger alone on my own, but strengthening the inseparable bonds that entwine us.[10]

✠ DEVELOPING TESTAMENTAL COMMUNITY: *'Resisting the powerful illusions of society'*

Not far from Bristol Street, situated on Boundary Street, the main street of West End, is Dorothy Day House, the home of the well-known Catholic Worker community in our locality:

Sixty years ago, on 1 May 1933, Dorothy Day, a young journalist, suffragette, ex-communist and new convert to Catholicism, sold the first *Catholic Worker* newspaper at a May Day rally.

Her partner in this grand adventure was Peter Maurin. Born into a French peasant family that had lived on the same piece of land for 600 years, Peter had been a teacher with the De La Salle brothers and had made his way to New York, hoping to spread some of his simple ideas gleaned from years of study of such diverse sources as the Gospels, Marx, Lenin, Bakunin and Kropotkin — philosophers from all parts of the political spectrum, the history of the church and the history [of the world].

Forty-nine years later, Ciaron O'Reilly, Angela Jones, John Tracey and Vic Hanson began an experiment in communal living in West End, Brisbane. Sean O'Reilly joined shortly after and Jim Dowling moved in at the end of the year.

At the beginning of the next year, the few of us remaining decided to call our community the Brisbane Catholic Worker, becoming the first community in Australia to use that name.

Embracing the anarchist philosophy of the Catholic Worker movement, we set out to try to be a Christian community — not just to work for a new society, but to be a new society.

We set out not just to serve the poor, but to live with the poor and, indeed, to try to become poor by turning our backs on the seductions of our materialist society and striving for a life of voluntary poverty.

We set out not to improve our capitalist society, but to live as a sharing society, holding all things in common and working cooperatively (making soap, bread, sprouts, candles, growing vegies and fruit trees) to meet our basic needs.

We set out not just to appeal to governments to

change the violence of our society, but to non-violently resist these structures to the point of arrest and imprisonment.

We attempted to do this with a spirit of prayer. . .

In all of these areas we have failed often. We have failed to offer effective resistance, we have failed to offer effective nurturing for one another, we have failed to disengage from our securities, we have failed to be a community of prayer. Yet, always aware that faithfulness is more important than success, we continue in faith to struggle, experiment and challenge one another in being community.

I have come to see our first goal to be a prophetic witness to these things, to point out 'the pearl of great price' we have discovered in a world of illusion.

The following are some glimpses of. . . that pearl:

Hospitality: *We have never intended to offer a soup kitchen or beds for large numbers, but we have always had more than one 'Christ room' for people needing support. Hundreds of guests have passed through our community.*

Some have stayed a lot longer than many community members, such as Eddie (four years and still here) who takes great delight in teaching our two-year-old Murri words, or Arnold who for three or four years was our nutritional expert and spiritual guide in the Orthodox tradition.

Two of our former guests have suicided in local prisons and a third one in a psychiatric hospital. The former two were both known to be suicidal and little or nothing was done to prevent the deaths.

The majority of women who have found themselves needing accommodation with us were victims of sexual assault as children — and many of the men also.

We constantly marvel at the ability of some people to survive their past and present suffering.

Cooperation: *Capitalism has come to value people by their monetary worth — what they can produce or what* *they can induce others to produce. The suffering of the poor under this system grows daily, both locally and globally.*

The cry of the *Catholic Worker* in response has been 'Sack the bosses!'

We have attempted largely successfully to work co-operatively to meet our basic needs by producing vegetable oil soap and wholemeal bread (and, at various times, candles, greeting cards and more). These industries, operated from home, have provided the bulk of our income:

To a similar end, in 1984 we opened Justice Products to encourage the consumption of justly produced goods, especially goods produced by coops, and boycott the products of exploitation.

Poverty: *Common work and common purse go very well together in community. It becomes unnecessary to decide who produced how much or to pay wages.*

A commitment to voluntary poverty makes it easier to boycott the seductions of transnational corporations, or even live happily without electricity for six months.

I am not saying there has never been a conflict over defining the limits of 'voluntary poverty', but this issue has not become as large a problem as other issues have.

For a little time, we used an allowance system where each community member was given $10 a week to spend luxuries (movies, cappucinos or whatever).

We have found it to be a better system to keep our money in one place, people taking what they need, and leaving open for discussion any doubtful spending.

If we find we have more money than we need we give it away. In the last ten years, we have only once had to borrow money to pay the rent.

Resistance: Perhaps what we have been most well known for is what we have termed 'resistance'.

We have endeavoured to live lives of non-cooperation with the institutionalised violence of war, poverty, racism, sexism and abortion.

Politically, we have been involved in many issues, including free speech, justice for Aboriginal people, affordable housing and environmental concerns. The impact of our resistance is often the hardest to gauge of all the things we do. Our message is often conveniently, if not deliberately, misunderstood.

An example: In 1983, we carried our banner reading 'Defend Life: Stop Abortion and Nuclear Weapons', first in a Right to Life rally and then in a peace rally. When we tried to leaflet the crowd at the Right to Life rally, we were loudly denounced by one man, 'Don't take their leaflets — they're communists!'

At the peace rally, after attempts were made to hide our banner and tear up leaflets, a friend took to the stage to defend our right of free speech, but the microphone was wrested from his hands by a woman who shouted, 'They just want to stop people f—ing!'

Recently, Anthony, Joanne and Ciaron have all been involved in 'plowshares' actions (personally dismantling weapons of war).

On the first of January 1991, Ciaron, Moana Cole and two others hammered and poured blood on a B52 at a US Air Force base. All four suffered the ordeal of thirteen months in US prisons. Eight months later, Anthony hammered and poured blood on a B52 in Darwin. His original sentence of three months was reduced to ten days.

Land: *Long before the failed 'green revolution' of the 1950s/6Os, Peter Maurin used the same term to describe his vision of Christians living simply on the land, as an alternative to the alienation of modern industrial societies.*

We are presently looking at starting a *Catholic Worker* farm at Dayboro, forty-five minutes' drive from Brisbane. Here, we hope to have permanent presence, as well as a place of retreat for city members and guests.

This only provides small snippets of our history. I have written very little of the personal struggles of the people who have passed through the *Catholic Worker*, perhaps the most important part of the story. Nor have I mentioned the influence of the unique wider community of West End where we live — a strange mix of religious, political and ethnic groups, which has helped shape our lives.[11]

✠ DEVELOPING INTEGRAL COMMUNITY:
'Reweaving the unravelled threads of community'

Some experiments in community, while not actually incorporating everyone in a locality, have the potential to do so.

A lot of the potential that exists in my suburb has already been tapped by a succession of community workers, both paid and unpaid, who have used the potential of the people in West End to turn our locality into an inner city urban village.

West End is, as I have said, located in a bend in the Brisbane River, with very little through traffic. It is a meeting place for people at the centre of the suburb and is within walking distance for just about everybody in the neighbourhood.

It has a fairly stable population with a larger percentage of older residents, so that even though there are a lot of visitors coming and going, the traditions of the area are well established. The traditions in the area are not so much the Anglo Saxon or Anglo Celtic Aussie traditions, with an emphasis on the individual rather than the collective. The traditions in the area are more Aboriginal and migrant traditions, particularly Greek and Italian, and more recently Indo-Chinese, with an emphasis on family — not just the nuclear family, but the extended family and, of course, the community.

Even though there is a lot of diversity in the locality, there is also a lot of unity in the diversity because, by and large, people have developed an attitude of tolerance, if not acceptance and respect, in order to survive in the inner city.

However, even in our locality with the degree of tolerance that it has developed, there is still a lot to be done if we are going to get beyond a passive attitude of tolerance and bring about an active movement of acceptance and respect for one another which can create true community in our locality.

I believe we should be satisfied with nothing less than developing integral community in our locality which 'offers to all its members, regardless of class, colour or creed, significance status and a sense of belonging, and an incentive to care for one another'.[12]

In order to help develop such community in our locality, my wife Ange and I and a few friends started what we call, for the want of another name, the 'Waiters' Union'.

The 'Waiters' Union' constitutes some thirty or so households out of the six thousand or so in West End. We do not see ourselves apart from the locality. We see ourselves as a part of the locality. In fact, we see ourselves as a network of residents working towards community that is integral to our locality.

We call ourselves the 'Waiters' Union' because we want to be 'waiters' in our area. We don't want to set any agendas or set up any organisations. We just want to hang around and help out. We particularly want to help to develop a sense of hospitality in the area so that all people, especially people who are usually displaced, can really feel at home in our area.

We are not a high profile group. We are a low profile group, as 'waiters' no doubt should be. In fact, a lot of people in our area whom we know may know us well as people, but not even know about the group we are part of — which is fine by us, because the group exists to promote relationships, not to promote the group. It is our friendships, not our profile, that matter.

We try to be self-effacing — not up front, but in the background, as 'waiters' indeed should be. However, we are not secretive at all. We welcome enquiries and answer questions as freely and as fully as we can. We are inclusive, not exclusive. We invite everyone who relates to us and what we are trying to do to join with us to whatever degree they want.

We seek to promote respect for the aspirations of the original inhabitants of the neighbourhood, the Aborigines, for whom Musgrave Park, at the centre of the neighbourhood, is sacred ground.

We seek to support refugees by sponsoring their settlement and setting up groups with them to enable them to work through the anguish they go through in resettlement.

We seek to help migrants by learning their languages and teaching them more of our own.

And last, but not least, even though they are so often considered last and treated as the least important people in our locality, we seek to relate to mentally and emotionally disturbed folk in our community as friends.

None of what we are doing seems all that great. We know that. However, we constantly encourage one another to remember that what is really great is not doing big things but little things, with a lot of love over the long haul of our lives.

It's through doing what we do that we are trying to develop integral community in the locality 'which offers to all its members, regardless of class, colour or creed, significance, status and a sense of belonging, and an incentive to care for one another'.[13]

If your attempt to develop community is anything like ours, no doubt you will have already discovered that, in the process of community development, you can go through some very difficult phases indeed.

Not every group will go through these phases in exactly the same way we do. Your group may skip one or two, or go forward a couple of steps and then go back a step, before making any progress. But I think the following phases are typical of the experience of most community groups.[14]

The first phase of community development is false community. This occurs when people are happy to reach out to one another, as long as they keep one another at arm's length; when people pretend to be pleasant, but suppress their displeasure; when everyone enjoys getting together as long as no-one acts disgracefully. And the dream of community remains a dream.

This phase lasts for as long as people in the group can prevent conflicts from erupting. Once those conflicts erupt, the group moves to the next phase. . .

The second phase of community development is chaos. This occurs when people are no longer polite and everyone who acted like an angel begins to act like a devil; when people no longer pretend, discussions turn into disputes and arguments turn into fights. And the dream of community becomes a nightmare. This phase lasts as long as people can cope with the conflict that has erupted.

Once a group decides it can't cope with the conflict any longer, it can either try to deal with the conflict through institutional measures, such as regulations, or it can try to deal with the conflict by communal means, such as reconciliation.

If the group decides to opt for institutional measures and imposes law and order on the situation to deal with the conflict, the people will move back as a group to the previous phase of false, but comfortable, community.

If the group decides to opt for communal means and explores love and understanding of the situation to deal with the conflict, the people can move on as a group to the next phase. . .

The third phase in community development is compassion. This occurs when people no longer live their lives apart, but live side by side, sharing the limitations and the contradictions of their lives; when people no longer keep one another at a distance, but embrace one another, sharing the disappointment and despair of not being able to make their dreams of community come true.

This phase lasts as long as people can cope with the discomfort associated with affirming those with whom we have unresolved conflict without resolving the conflict. Once a group decides it can't cope with the discomfort any longer, it will either resume the conflict or resolve the conflict.

If the group decides to resume the conflict, people will either quit the group, or quickly move the group back into false, but comfortable community before everybody else quits.

If the group decides to resolve the conflict, it can move onto the next phase. . .

The fourth phase in community development is true community. In this phase, people relate to one another as they would like others to relate to them — not as angels one day and devils the next, but as beautiful, yet fallible human beings; as those who need one another and need to continually resolve their conflicts with one another in order to meet one another's needs — and to enable one another to make their dreams of community come true.

Now, in the light of this perspective, it's not surprising that most groups that start out by trying to develop community end up with false community rather than true community. Very few groups are willing to endure the chaos and embrace the compassion which produces real community.

But if we are to create true community groups rather than false community groups, then we need to encourage one another to endure chaos and embrace compassion, for there is no other way that I know of that we can make our dreams for community come true.

One day, we discovered that there were about twenty hostels in our area, with up to twenty residents in each and every hostel amounting to some 400 people in all.

However, over a few months, we observed that these people had next to no contact at all with the locality in which they were located. Less than fifteen per cent of them had any connections with anyone outside their hostel, apart from their case worker, who was paid to relate to them regularly. They had few people to visit them — and even fewer places for them to visit. They were, it seemed, almost as isolated in our area as they would have been in an asylum.

We had visions of breaking down some of these barriers of isolation and building come bridges of friendship. We envisaged developing a community with an extended family with our forgotten brothers and sisters throughout the neighbourhood.

We began by visiting the people in the hostels. And we actually developed a sense of community with them quite quickly. We didn't realise it was a false sense of community until they began to pay us visits in our houses in return for our visits to their hostels. And some of us began to panic about how to handle the situation.

In the chaos that ensued, people in the group went through the whole gamut of emotions, from anger through to guilt, until compassion suffused the chaos and the group got its empathic act together again. Then we began again, inviting people to our parties, going out with one another on picnics and having regular community meals together.

Now it would be nice to be able to say that these events are always expressions of a true sense of community that we have realised. Sometimes they are. But sometimes they are not. At some of these events, we move back and forth between a false sense of community and a true sense of community and people experience everything from the chaos to the compassion in between when we get together.

I can remember one time there was a big fight. The meal had started out happily enough. But soon a dispute erupted. People actually came to blows. It was a disaster. But people stayed with us through the disaster. They didn't disassociate themselves from it. They tried to deal with it. They didn't lay down the law. They just got involved themselves. There was a little screaming and a lot of swearing. But there were no more blows. Gradually, everybody worked it out together. The antagonists eventually embraced and the group ordered another round of coffee to celebrate the resolution of the conflict and the very real sense of community that we all felt.

In my experience, it is possible for us to move from false community to true community. But in order to do so, we need to make sure that when things get tough, we do not try to organise our way out of it, but simply try to hang in there while we work our way through it together, in spite of all the difficulties involved. That, to me, is what real community is all about.

I can remember a time we had a dance. Everybody was into it — everybody, that is, except for one man who, everyone knew, had real difficulty in relating to women appropriately. He often acted quite unacceptably. And it was as if, as a punishment, he was deliberately being left out of the festivities.

The reaction was understandable. But, in true community, no-one ought to be left out. So as soon as a woman, called Wendy, noticed what was happening, she went over to 'William' and invited him to dance.

Now, it is important to note that she did not do this naively. When Wendy asked 'William' to dance, she did so in a manner that communicated, loud and clear, that she'd like to dance with him, but she wouldn't take any nonsense from him. And he agreed.

So everybody got to dance, including Wendy and 'William'. To me, true community is about everybody getting a chance to dance.

Part C: The challenge

5

The challenge of community in a bureaucratic world:

'I refuse to be intimidated by reality any more'

WE DREAM OF DEVELOPING A GREAT SOCIETY of small communities, but the world in which we are trying to make our dreams come true is a world dominated by huge government and non-government bureaucracies.

✣ THE REALITY OF BUREAUCRACY:
'The bureaucracy above you hampers your every move'

We are all compelled to work in a political milieu which is manipulated by massive corporations of enormous power that reward compliance, punish protest and open and close options for everything from jobs to grants, according to their own agendas, without any regard for love or justice.

So it's not very surprising that many of us who set out to strive for change end up in complete resignation.

Some become discouraged because the institution they work for has totally frustrated their efforts to bring about any change for the good of the community.

Others become discouraged because some institution

113

that they had nothing to do with, but which had everything to do with the community they were working with, totally frustrated their efforts to bring about any change that was deemed contrary to the agenda of the institution concerned.

Alan Twelvetrees probably speaks for a lot of us when he says:

> [It's] an impossible job. The bureaucracy above you appears intent on hampering your every move. . . Many who have been working for a few years find they are exhausted on account of dealing with the same kind of problem again and again. You are continually trying to retrieve something from the mess created by the lack of human policies![1]

In a society in which our lives are dominated by so many institutions, there often seems to be no scope for dreaming about community and no hope of making our dreams about community come true.

✠ THE IRONY OF BUREAUCRACY:
'Our institutions can deliver a service, but not care'

The irony is that many of the institutions which now inhibit much of our work for community are structures that were ostensibly created to enable us to do our work for community better.

One state government's green paper on a proposed piece of 'community welfare legislation' speaks specifically of developing 'mutual support and understanding, collective responsibility and interdependence, and harmonious and cooperative participation'.[2]

Whether government or non-government bureaucracies, institutions were expected to provide a 'service to the community' that would otherwise 'not be forthcoming from the community'.

Many regarded institutions as the only way we could care for the community. 'Institutions were a way. . . to redeem an uncaring community.'[3]

Government and non-government bureaucracies were established with the expectation that these institutions would not only provide the services, but also provide the care that the community required. Gradually, people came to realise that there was no way that institutions could care for the community. 'Our institutions. . . can deliver a service, [but] cannot deliver care.'[4]

However, while a few came to realise that one could no more program an institution to care than one could program an institution to laugh or cry, many did not. Many still persisted in trying to program their institutions to care. And, being unable to care for us, they took care of us by taking control of our lives for us.

The intentions may have been good, but the unintended consequences have been regarded by many as quite evil. 'Evil' may be defined as 'the exercise of political power that imposes one's will upon others, by overt or covert coercion, without due regard for love or justice'.[5]

And there is little doubt in my mind that a lot of so-called 'community organisations', which impose the will of their respective bureaucracies upon us 'for our good' without due regard for the deleterious effects they have on our lives, could be classified as 'evil'.

✠ THE TRAGEDY OF BUREAUCRACY:
'We are able to equate the institution with evil'

It was not very long ago that I was discussing this issue with a chap named Michael Kendrick, who has been at the centre of an international movement for the reform of welfare institutions for many years. 'In our generation,' comments Kendrick, 'we are able to equate the institution with some kind of evil.'[6]

'Now a few people may recall,' he recalls, 'that institutions were, in their day, a passionate, righteous cause.'[7] 'We thought,' he recollects, 'that if we had these attractive programs, things were going to get better.'[8]

'The sadness is,' he says, 'that I made a promise, as did all of us, that this would be a better world with our new attractive services. People's lives were committed to these services and changed by them. But of course services are full of their own kinds of limitations. . .' He pauses. 'So we broke our promises.'[9]

'What I have lived through,' he concludes, 'is the creation of a whole new generation of evils that were not even on the landscape a few decades ago!'[10]

'For instance,' he says in closing, 'services have become technologised and bureaucratised and agencies that start out good lose their way. People that go in hoping to serve other people find themselves serving the powers that be.'[11]

Kendrick's judgment is categorical. His lament is long. His language is strong. But there are many of us who would, no doubt, join Kendrick in singing the bureaucratic blues, because we share the sense of tragedy of which he speaks.

✠ FROM PSYCHIATRIC SERVICES TO CONCENTRATION CAMPS:
'We were prisoners with no rights and no dignity'

My wife Ange and I have got to know a lot of vulnerable groups of people in our neighbourhood. Among the most vulnerable we know are people who are mentally and emotionally disturbed. These people struggle to maintain their sanity in the midst of maddening circumstances.

No matter how many times they try to put the pieces of their shattered experiences back together again, they seem to do so without the prospect of much success. So, in spite of everything they try to do to the contrary, they are compelled to live with an inescapable sense of total and utter failure. Fortunately, there are many individuals in the community who care for our tormented friends and who provide crucial services which help them survive at critical times in their lives. But unfortunately, many of the institutions in the locality which are supposed to care for them often dehumanise them through the kind of help that they provide.

I have noticed that my friends are very quickly categorised. Their identities are readily reduced to labels. And they take on the roles of 'schizophrenics' that they have been given as models for themselves.

I have also noticed that my friends are very quickly

stigmatised. Psychiatrically disabled people are considered quite contemptible in a capitalist society. Because they are 'handicapped', they are of 'no use' as producers and, because they are 'pensioners', they are of 'no value' as consumers. So in a society that measures worth in terms of production and consumption, they are often treated as totally worthless.

Many of my friends have been segregated — put into hospitals, prisons and hostels. In these institutions, separate from the rest of the community, their lives have generally been regimented, medicated and regulated in a manner that would not be tolerated in the rest of the community. But it would seem that these 'abnormal' people do not have the same rights as 'normal' people have to fight for their rights. Any complaints can be easily attributed to 'paranoia' and any protests can be readily treated as 'psychosis'.

The government and non-government bureaucracies, which relate in such a dehumanising manner towards some of the most vulnerable human beings in our community, might be deemed 'a necessary evil'. But just how intolerable such a so-called 'necessary evil' can become is indicated by the testimony of Trish Vanderwal and is demonstrated in the case of Ward 10B and Chelmsford Private Hospital.

Trish Vanderwal tells us:

> We lived in fear. We cringed. We cowered. We were prisoners with no rights and no dignity. We were the despised and rejected, subject to beatings and bullying.
> Were we POWs in some horrific concentration camp during the war? No. We were mental health patients

in psychiatric hospitals where the caring component had been eroded away, leaving the way clear for abuse and neglect. I witnessed terrible things in hospital. Due to the nature of our illness, our credibility was low. Staff always managed to write up their notes so that bruises and injuries were accounted for.

Some patients were refused visitors until their bruises were no longer obvious, though who would have believed a mental health patient anyway? Intimidation became the norm. If a patient became too assertive, they would be deemed 'psychotic' and hustled off to a single room, injected with heavy tranquillisers and locked in. Under the 'bully gang', we all kept silent to survive.[12]

Ward 10B is the psychiatric ward of the Townsville General Hospital. It was the subject of a recent Royal Commission of Inquiry which amounted to a five-hundred page indictment of 'bureaucratic indifference' in the face of 'grossly negligent', 'unethical' and 'unsafe' treatment.

According to Commissioner Bill Carter QC, during a period of thirteen years from 1975 to 1988, hundreds of patients, including three of my friends, were arbitrarily restrained, inappropriately medicated and physically assaulted, resulting in what were described euphemistically as 'numerous suspicious patient deaths'.[13]

On 20 December 1990, Matron Julie Smith reported that at Chelmsford Private Hospital, regard for the rights of patients was 'a sick joke'. Patients were, she said, not consulted at all about their treatment. If they challenged the kind of treatment they got, she said they were dealt with by being given an overdose of drugs that put them into 'deep sleep' and 'kept them quiet'.

According to Dr Sydney Smith, this hospital treated the patients in such 'an extraordinarily careless and callous manner' that, as a result, twenty-six people were killed and twenty-two others killed themselves. 'It was like a concentration camp.'[14]

✠ THE APPARENT INVULNERABILITY OF INSTITUTIONS:
'The psychic power emanated by organisations overpowers people'

While I do not believe all institutions are evil, I believe that there is a tendency for all institutions, even those intended for good, to become evil. There are a number of factors which seem to contribute to this almost invariable tendency for institutions, especially those intended for good, to become evil:

❐ *First*, the spirit of an institution disempowers

Charles Elliott cites the significance of the 'spirit' of an institution in determining its dominant and dominating character in the community.

Elliott says the 'spirit' of an institution is the 'psychic power emanated by organisations' which, more often than not is 'bent on overpowering others'.[15] He says that an institution 'can hardly help being repressive. . . for that is its essence'.[16] According to Elliott, the 'spirit' of an institution invariably tends to overpower people rather than empower people. I would argue in that sense that even a 'good' institution can be 'evil'.

In our work with our vulnerable friends in the

community, many times we have had cause to consult with the government and non-government bureaucracies which control important aspects of their lives. I can remember only a couple of instances when those bureaucracies did not seek somehow to try to extend the control they had over our friends and over our involvement with them as well.

In our consultation with these bureaucracies, we would usually start out exploring the possibility of cooperation with regard to a particular person and end up trying to stop them from coopting us, along with the person concerned, into some program or other they were going to organise.

In my experience, institutions almost invariably act as if they have a divine right to rule the community. It is expected that, in most encounters, the community will give way and allow the institutions to take over. It's overpowering, rather than empowering, but that's the 'spirit' in which most consultations take place.

☐ *Second*, the structure of an institution disempowers

Robert Chambers cites the significance of the 'structure' of an institution in determining its dominant and dominating character in the community.

Chambers says that most bureaucracies 'have a centre -periphery orientation'[17]: 'Their structure [is] often authoritarian, hierarchical and punitive. From the centre come the commands. From the periphery comes a flow of information which placates. Senior officers do not learn from their subordinates and subordinates do not learn from their clients. [People] are cajoled and given orders. Promotion comes through compliance; deviant initiatives are rewarded by punishment. Appearances of achievement are applauded. Real problems of implementation are repressed.'[18]

According to Chambers, the 'structure' of an institution invariably tends to warp perceptions, corrupt processes, manipulate programs and exploit people. I could argue in that sense that no matter how 'good' the aims of the institution may be, the means that the institution employs may be 'evil'.

I can remember talking to some representatives of a welfare organisation in our area about a series of activities we had planned with some of the people in the community they were involved with. I did so, not only to inform them, but also to invite them to participate if they so desired. They suggested that the activities we had planned should be done under their auspices. After all, they said, their structure was the appropriate structure through which to do what we wanted to do.

When we rejected the suggestion that our activities should be done under their auspices, they got most upset. Then, when we had the temerity to suggest that their structure may have been appropriate for service delivery, but was not appropriate to enable people to develop a sense of responsibility for themselves, they became almost apoplectic with rage at our impudence. They threatened to do their best to discredit us. And they did.

In my experience, institutions almost invariably act as if they are the centre of the universe and anyone not involved with them is rather peripheral to their world.

They act as if the only way anyone could be involved meaningfully in the community is through the agency of 'their structure'.

They can only relate to people in terms of their organisations. They can only react to people in terms of their regulations. Should anyone have the tenacity to resist the imposition of such warped perceptions and corrupted processes, which inevitably manipulate people and exploit people, the institutions quickly move to censure their opponents and impose sanctions against them in order to protect the place of their 'structure' in the community.

◻ *Third*, the tradition of the institution disempowers

George Foster cites the significance of the 'tradition' of an institution as a major factor in determining its dominant and dominating character in the community.

Foster says: 'A bureaucracy of substantial size is simply another kind of social grouping with the same features [like traditions]. . . found in a tribe or a village.'[19] He says: 'Bureaucrats, like all other human beings, jealously guard their traditional positions and perquisites, willingly surrendering vested interests only in exchange for something good or better.'[20] 'In bureaucracies,' he says, 'this leads to organisational inflexibility.'[21]

According to Foster, the 'tradition' of an institution invariably tends to render it inflexible and, I would argue that in that sense, no matter how 'good' the institution is, because it is inflexible it is inevitable that it will do 'evil'.

Recently, a friend of mine contacted a welfare organisation to discuss the problem of a person she was working with. She wanted to know some of the options she could explore in helping the person she was concerned with through a crisis. However, the social worker she consulted was committed to a tradition which refused to consider any other option in a case such as this apart from intervention. My friend was given no other option than to report the person to the police.

When my friend protested, saying that perhaps other options like counselling might be more appropriate, the case was literally taken out of her hands and the social worker reported the case to the police herself. In the process, my friend was dismissed, the person she was working with was distressed and the friendship that they had been developing, by working through the crisis together, was destroyed.

In my experience, institutions almost invariably act as if they have a monopoly on virtue and anyone involved with them would approve of their work. They act as if the only way that anyone could be involved meaningfully in the community is in the light of 'their traditions'. They cannot relate to people outside the purview of their experience. They can only treat people in view of their expertise.

The inflexibility of such a 'tradition' means the institution will inevitably hurt the people in the community it purports to help.

◻ *Fourth*, the culture of an institution disempowers

Scott Peck cites the significance of the 'culture' of an institution in determining its dominant and dominating character in the community.

Peck says that bureaucracies 'tend to behave in the same way as. . . individuals, except at a level that is more. . . immature than one might expect'.[22] One reason for this immaturity is what he refers to as 'the fragmentation of a conscience' in a group. 'Whenever the roles of individuals within a group become specialised it becomes. . . possible. . . for the individual to pass the moral buck to some other part of the group. In this way, not only does the individual forsake his conscience, but the conscience of the group becomes so fragmented [in a bureaucracy]. . . as to be nonexistent'.[23] According to Peck, the 'culture' of an institution invariably tends to render it non-reflective and, I would argue, because it is non-reflective, the institution will continue to do any 'evil' it does unchecked, regardless of how many 'good' people might be associated with the particular group.

A few months ago, a friend of mine wanted to confront a particular group, of which he was a part, about the whole way it was operating in the community. The group was meant to be providing support for disadvantaged people but, he said, the whole way it went about providing that help was so patronising that it only served to marginalise disadvantaged people more.

However, my friend found it difficult to find people in the group who cared to discuss the issue. It was not, he said, as if they were uncaring. They had great concern for the part they played in the group. But they all believed that the part the whole group played in the community was not their concern. Everyone said it should be the concern of someone or other. But no-one, he said, would accept the responsibility of that concern themselves.

So the issue, about the whole way the group was operating in the community, was dismissed due to lack of interest. And the people in the group got back to business as usual. The group has continued to do its charitable service and, in so doing, has continued to do a terrible disservice, marginalising disadvantaged people, unchecked, till this very day.

In my experience, few people ever seriously reflect on the activities of the groups they are associated with. The institutions try to get their own way and the community tends to let them get away with it. That's just the way things are. It's the 'culture' which institutions tend to encourage and to which the community tends to acquiesce, even though it means institutions can continue to do the people in the community it purports to serve a terrible disservice.

A repressive spirit, augmented by an oppressive structure, aided by an implacable tradition and abetted by an apathetic culture are all major factors which combine to produce an invariable tendency for institutions, even those intended for 'good', to become 'evil'.

✠ THE ACTUAL VULNERABILITY OF INSTITUTIONS:
'Every institution is dependent upon people for its power'

Because of the tendency for institutions to become the dominant and dominating realities in our lives, there is a tendency for us to believe that they are not only invariable, but also invulnerable.

Many of us tend to believe that the institutions in our communities represent 'relatively fixed quantums, discrete unit quantities of energy which may be undesirable, but are nevertheless independent and durable, if not totally indestructible, self-organising, self-regulating, self-reinforcing and self-propagating forces'.[24]

Now if that were true, the institutions in our communities could only be controlled by either the voluntary restraint of the management of these institutions or by involuntary constraint of the management of these institutions imposed by other institutions.

Obviously, it is in the interest of the institutions in our communities to persuade us that they represent the powers that be. It is in their vested interest to convince us that the only power people can get to moderate the power of the institutions is by joining the management of one institution or another for, in so doing, people who may join one institution or another, even with a reformist agenda, will inevitably amplify the power of the institutions over the community.

But the institutions in our community are better understood as a 'relatively flexible gestalt', not a 'relatively fixed quantum' — 'a corporate pattern of organisation', rather than 'a separate unit of energy'. Contrary to what many of us have been led to believe, institutions are actually quite 'vulnerable', not totally 'invulnerable' — because each and every institution is essentially dependent upon, rather than ultimately independent of, the people for its power.[25]

As Gene Sharp explains, each and every institution in the community, without exception, depends on the support of the people for its power. The control that any institution exercises over a community depends on the degree to which the people accept its authority, assist with its activities, share their knowledge and skills and resources with its agencies and subordinate themselves to its sanctions.[26]

If people obey the dictates of the institutions, either because of a sense of obligation, or an ongoing habit due to identification with the group, or fear of acting independently of the group, then institutions can exercise amazing control over communities.[27]

But if people do not obey the dictates of institutions, then the institutions cannot exercise any control over the communities in which they are located.[28]

Sharp says: 'Obedience, though usual, is not inevitable. It always varies in degree with the individual concerned and with the social and political situation. Obedience is never universally practiced by the whole population. Many people disobey. Some people do so frequently. Under some certain conditions, subjects may be willing to put up with disruption of their lives rather than continue to obey policies they can no longer tolerate.'[29] 'Changes which result in the withdrawal of obedience can create extreme difficulties for the system.'[30]

In stating his case, Sharp refers to the famous lectures of John Austin, in which he said: 'If the bulk of the community were fully determined to destroy it (i.e. the system) and to. . . endure the evils through which they must pass (to serve) their object, the might of the government itself. . . could scarcely suffice to preserve it or even retard its subversion.'[31]

Now, if that were true, the institutions could be controlled by the very people they try to control, including some of the most vulnerable groups of people in our community.

Obviously, it is not in the interest of the institutions to let people know about the power they have, not only to tame them, but also to transform them. Nevertheless the news is out, the rumours are circulating and ordinary men and women are here, there and everywhere, beginning to try to do something about subverting the institutions that hitherto have been the dominant and dominating realities in our lives.

☐ Individuals are discovering that they have the power to contribute to the spirit of an institution

Charles Elliott, who stresses the significance of the spirit of an institution in determining its character, suggests that people have a crucial role to play in contributing to the spirit of an institution.

Elliott says the spirit or the psychic power of an institution is a product, not only of the institution, but also of the individuals who comprise the institution. It is, he says, 'made up of individuals acting upon each other influencing and being influenced by the institution'.[32]

Therefore, Elliott says, individuals can affect the consciousness of institutions through the choices they make. 'All individuals and [institutions] find themselves confronted with the process of discovering who they are as they exercise life choices. As they make choices, they both discover who they are and they demonstrate who they are.'[33]

I can remember the day Kay Thompson came to work in the office of 'Help Incorporated', a welfare organisation I was working with at the time. Kay was a single individual, just one among many staff, but she affected the consciousness of the whole office, if not the whole organisation, by the way she chose to live her life at the office.

Kay was competent in her job, but she was not preoccupied with her work at the expense of relationships. She made the department seem like an apartment, a place of hospitality, where people felt at home with one another, as well as with their work.

Kay was very caring towards everyone she encountered, from the executive director through to the casual assistant — and anyone who would happen to drop by for a visit. She was compassionate without being pretentious, lacing her kindness with lashes of laughter. She often wept with those that wept, but as often as not left them with a smile. She made life at the office fun for everyone.

I would dearly like to introduce Kay to anyone who has doubts about the power an individual has to contribute to the 'spirit' of community in an institution.

❏ Individuals are discovering that they have the power to challenge the structure of an institution

Robert Chambers, who stresses the significance of the structure of an institution in determining its character, suggests that people have a crucial role to play in challenging the structure of an institution.

Chambers says the structure of an institution is 'neither universal nor inevitable'.[34] Certainly, it is easier to challenge 'small non-government agencies than to challenge large government organisations'. But, Chambers says, 'it comes back to personal choice. . . there is always something that can be done'.[35]

'Some may feel there is nothing they can do. But in every country there are courageous people — political and religious leaders, academics, scientists, civil servants and others — who have stuck by their principles and whose lives are a strong example of what can be done.'[36]

Chris Brown is a shining example to me of what can be done in circumstances in which most of us would have considered nothing could have been done at all. Chris does not come across as very heroic. He is a rather shy, self-effacing character. He's not what anyone would think of as an activist. In fact, in many ways he'd be what many of us would think of as a typical academic. But Chris actually has the quiet courage of a fifth column reformer.

Ever since I can remember, when he has not been working at the University of Queensland, Chris has devoted himself to the reform of 'Queensland Care', a large non-government organisation we have been associated with. For twelve years, Chris constantly raised the issue of quality care at the board on which he served.

But, as often as not, his comments were met with complete contempt. For twelve years, Chris withstood the withering gaze of the chairman, who would brook no dissent from any members of the board, as Chris stood time and time again to raise the issue of the need for a more open, more responsive and more compassionate approach to the people the organisation purported to serve through its various institutions.

But it was all to no avail. The organisation became, if anything, even more bureaucratic. And, in due course, the services of Chris Brown as a consultant were terminated. At that juncture, I think Chris was entitled to think he had done everything he could and that there was nothing more he could do.

But Chris told me he would not give up without giving it another go. He believed there was still something he could do — maybe not at the level of the direction of the institutions, but at the level of the delivery of the services. So Chris got involved in actually modelling the kind of quality care he had been advocating in one of the residential units associated with the organisation.

Much to my surprise, the board which had categorically rejected what he had said, enthusiastically embraced what he did and Chris was invited by the board to translate his experiment into policy for the organisation. So Chris is in the process of setting up an alternative program within the organisation, which will establish the more open, more responsive and more compassionate structure which he envisaged.

Chris Brown gives me the courage to imagine that an individual has the power to challenge the status quo and advocate more of a community structure in an institution.

❑ Individuals are discovering that they have the power to change the tradition of an institution

George Foster, who stresses the significance of the traditions of an institution in determining its character, suggests that people have a crucial role to play in changing the traditions of an institution.

Foster says: 'When a [group] is faced with a suggestion of change, there exists a balance of forces. On one side of the scales are those forces which are against change — conservatism and the like; and on the other side are the forces for change — dissatisfaction with existing conditions. . . and so on. Successful community development consists largely of choosing those projects where the balance is almost even and then trying to lighten the forces against change or to increase the factors making for change'.[37]

Trevor Boucher is a man who has committed himself to changing a very large government organisation. From the time he became the Australian Tax Commissioner five or six years ago, he made it his mission to turn the ethos of the tax office inside out and upside down.

He wanted to turn the tradition of service in the office inside out so it would develop a reputation for service outside the office and the general public would perceive the tax office as a helper rather than an exploiter. He also wanted to turn the tradition of collection from the little people rather than the big corporations upside down so that the ordinary taxpayer could begin to feel that they were being treated fairly by a tax office which was ensuring everybody paid their fair share.

Boucher was faced with the seemingly impossible task of trying to turn around an office of over 18 000 employees, many of whom had worked in the department for twenty to thirty years with a long tradition of well established work practices in place.

But Boucher had a number of things going for him. The average employee of the office was, as a member of the public, committed to more client service and a more equitable system. Moreover, most of the staff were excited about the possibility of developing an image of themselves as respectable public servants who could own their work, rather than disreputable social pariahs who had to keep their work secret.

Boucher began by going to work on the counter in the Sydney tax office for two weeks. He wanted to interface with the public in order to understand the public perceptions of his office and his office's problems in serving the public. He then employed management consultants to enable people within his office to develop their consciousness of client service and resolve the problems which they encountered in delivering it adequately across the counter.

Boucher then started to audit the top hundred companies in Australia. He demanded that they pay their fair share of tax. Some, like Ariadne, got a bill for $150 million. And slowly the Australian public started to believe the tax office was becoming fair dinkum about an equitable system of tax for all.

The tax office developed the tax pack to enable ordinary people to do their own tax assessment for themselves. This was an expression of trust by the tax office in the ordinary taxpayer to do the right thing if they were given the information they required to fill out their own tax forms themselves.

The tax office has consequently started to develop a reputation for being more friendly. And the staff at the tax office are reportedly more ready to tell people at a party who they work for and more readily greeted with a smile rather than a scowl when they do so.

Trevor Boucher gives me a reason to believe an individual has the power to change the status quo and actualise more of a community tradition in an institution.

☐ Individuals are discovering that they have the power to call the culture of an institution to account

Scott Peck, who stresses the significance of the culture of an institution in determining its character, suggests people have a crucial role in conscientising the culture in which the institution exists.

Peck says that institutions may well be evil in the sense that they 'exercise political power that is the imposition of one's will upon others; either overt or covert coercion. . .', but if an institution seeks to impose its will upon others and goes gunning for someone 'the triggers are pulled by individuals'.[38]

Peck says that institutionalised evil can be effectively dealt with by individual goodness. He says: 'Orders are given, [taken] and executed by individuals. In the last analysis, every single act is ultimately the result of individual choice.'[39]

Peck says: 'There are dozens of ways to deal with evil. . . All of them are facets of the truth that the only ultimate way to conquer evil is to let it be smothered within a willing, living human being. When it is absorbed there like. . . a spear into one's heart, it loses its power and goes no further.'[40]

Barry Hart is a good example of someone who was determined to make sure that the evil he was subjected to would go no further, no matter how difficult it was for him as an individual to confront the institution that constituted his reign of terror. Barry was one of the psychiatric patients in the 'house of horrors' at Chelmsford Private Hospital.

Barry, like all the other patients at the hospital, suffered terribly at the hands of the staff. He realised, he says, 'that there was no way the staff would dob in their mates', so he resolved to 'stand up to them' himself.

Barry didn't have a chance to do much while in hospital, but when he got out of the hospital he organised a campaign to rally the conscience of the community to confront not only the institution, but also the whole infrastructure which supported it.

To start with, Barry didn't have much success. It was all too easy for the staff to attribute criticism to the paranoia of a patient. But Barry felt the issue was too important for him to fail. So he carried on year after year, trying to convince the authorities the seriousness of the situation was more than a mere figment of his imagination.

In the end, Barry did succeed. Eventually, he was able to convince the authorities that his criticism was not based on fantasy, but fact — and it was the staff, not the patients, who were crazy. A Royal Commission last year finally vindicated Barry Hart and the patients' association and condemned Dr Harry Bailey and his staff associates.

Barry Hart gives us all an example of how an individual, even a pretty vulnerable one, can have the power to rally the conscience of a community so effectively as to call an institution, even an apparently invulnerable one, to account.

6

The change towards community in a bureaucratic world:

'I have cast in my lot with those who reconstitute the world'

MANY OF US FEEL SYMPATHY with Jane Wagner, who says:

> I refuse to be intimidated by
>   reality any more.
> After all, what is reality anyway?
>   Nothin' but. . .
> a primitive method of crowd control
>   that got out of hand.
> In my view, it's absurdity
>   dressed up
>   in a three-piece business suit.
> I made some studies,
>   and reality is the leading cause
>   of stress amongst those in touch with it.
> I can take it in small doses,
>   but as a lifestyle
>   I found it too confining.
> It expected me to be
>   there for it all the time,
> and with all I have to do —
>   I had to let something go.[1]

We want to take a stand with Adrienne Rich who says: 'I have to cast in my lot with those who, age after age, perversely, with no extraordinary power, reconstitute the world.'[2]

But Lyle Schaller, in his book *The Change Agent*, warns us that 'anyone seriously interested in planned social change should be well advised to recognise two facts of life. First, despite the claims of many, relatively little is known about how to achieve predictable change. Second, much of what is known will not work'.[3]

✠ AGENTS OF CHANGE:
'It is wise to determine what is worth struggling for'

Michael Kendrick, who himself struggled for change, only to realise that much of what he achieved was exactly the opposite of what he was striving for, tells us: 'It is very wise. . . to determine what might be worth struggling for and what might not be worth the trouble.'[4]

Daniel P. Monyham, a prominent advocate of change in our generation says: 'We constantly underestimate difficulties, over-promise results and avoid any evidence of incompatibility and conflict, thus repeatedly creating the conditions of failure out of a desperate desire for success.'[5]

The way to bring about change most effectively is to establish friendships with people in the group you want to encourage to change. Then, in the context of those friendships, we need to negotiate an agreement about change, demonstrate that the change envisaged is viable, feasible and safe, and work with the group to make the change together.[6]

Along the way, we need to anticipate the responses of a group, recognise the initial reaction is usually negative, realise that we need to deal with the negative reactions positively, help people to deal with issues constructively, develop empathy, depersonalise dissent, encourage total participation in discussions and both personal and corporate investment in decisions, and create a context of trust in which people will be secure enough to take risks.[7]

As T.R. Batten, a community development worker in the UK says, the agent of change is more important than the program for change in effectively advocating change. He says the agent 'is even more important than the program. . . [because] it is his attitude to the people and his skill in working with them that mainly makes for success or failure'.[8]

✠ CHANGE STRATEGIES:
'Both first order and second order change are of value'

There are two types of change that we can try to bring about in order to start a movement towards community in a society dominated by institutions.

A change of the first order is a vertical strategy which enables groups to do what they are doing better. In an institutionalised society, a first order change means enabling the institutions in society to do what they are already doing with regard to the community, better.

A first order change involves helping groups develop more community-orientated institutional services.

A change of the second order is a lateral strategy which enables groups to do better by setting aside what they are already doing and trying to do something else. In an institutionalised society, a second order change means enabling various communities, individually and collectively, to stop projecting the responsibilities for their welfare onto institutions and to start accepting the responsibility for their welfare themselves.

A second order change involves helping groups develop more non-institutional, community-orientated processes.

The work of Wolf Wolfensberger and Jean Vanier are classic examples of attempts to bring about first and second order changes in relation to people with disabilities.

☐ First order change

Wolfensberger sought to develop more community-orientated institutional services for disabled people by trying to 'normalise' the institutions with which disabled people in the community are associated. He sought to do this by encouraging the 'utilisation of means which are as culturally normative as possible, in order to establish and maintain personal. . . characteristics which are as culturally normative as possible'.[9]

Wolfensberger advocated a number of means by which the institutions, and the disabled people who are dependent upon their services, could become more 'normal'. He advised reducing the size of the institutions, so they could be located in the community less obtrusively. He suggested separating the domicile from the other functions, so the residents would have to move around the locality in order to meet their needs, like everyone else in the community.

He recommended providing specialised attention for specialised needs to allow for general heterogeneity without universal regulation, so the people living in these institutions did not have to contend with any more restrictions than anyone else in the community. He envisaged total integration of the institutions with the community, so that the people supported by these services could 'intermingle with typical citizens in typical activities'.

The advantages and disadvantages associated with opting for a vertical strategy of first order change are evident in Wolfensberger's work.

On the one hand, Wolfensberger has had a significant impact in providing better community-orientated institutional services for disabled people. He has developed an ethos of accountability in human services. He has developed the knowledge and skills necessary for assessing the quality of those human services. And he has developed those institutional services for disabled people in the community and in relation to the community.[10]

But on the other hand, the impact that Wolfensberger has had may have made matters worse for many of the very people he has been trying to help. The institutions have used his views to rationalise not only the reduction in the size. It has also meant a reduction in the range of services provided for disabled people, and also the relocation of disabled people into the community without the necessary structural supports they require to adjust to the community or the community requires to adjust to them.[11]

☐ Second order change

Vanier sought to develop more non-institutional, community-orientated processes with disabled people by moving in with a couple of mentally and emotionally handicapped people himself and by encouraging other people in his locality to share their lives with others. (This is in recognition of the fact that we are all handicapped to one degree or other and we are all in need of help at one time or other.)

Since Vanier founded the first community in France in 1964, L'Arche communities with handicapped people have been created in fourteen countries around the world, from Haiti to India. Vanier says: 'Nobody is more surprised than myself by the growth of L'Arche.'[12]

But the life that Vanier leads and the care his assistants share with the mentally and emotionally handicapped people they live with has become an inspiring example of the kind of authentic community that everybody, not only those labelled 'disabled', needs. Vanier says:

> For the handicapped people who have felt abandoned, there is only one reality that will bring them back to life: an authentic, tender and faithful relationship. They must discover that they are loved. . . Only then will they discover they are worthwhile. And to love is not

to do something for someone; it is to be with them. It is to rejoice in their presence; it is to give them confidence in the value of their being. It is to listen to them and to their needs and desires. It is to help them find their confidence in themselves and in their capacity to please, to do, to serve and to be useful.

This healing process can take a very long time when someone has been deeply hurt, when the wounds of rejection have been violent. [But] each one of our L'Arche communities has experienced men and women who are chaotic, broken and spiritually dead, evolving — after years in a big institution — into men and women of peace and light.

These are not mere words. We have seen the dead rise. It has happened before our own eyes. In our [own] homes.[13]

The disadvantages and advantages associated with opting for a lateral strategy of second order change are evident in Vanier's work.

On the one hand, the non-institutional, community-orientated processes Vanier has developed demand an enormous amount of effort in order to provide a small range of options compared to the large number of places required, and so defy any of the established measures of efficiency in standard time and motion studies.[14]

On the other hand, the groups Vanier has developed with disabled people create an authentic sense of community which can, as he says, bring those that society has given up on as dead, back to life again, as fully human and fully alive.[15]

Those of us who want to work for change need to work not only *vertically* for first order change, developing more community-orientated institutional services, but also *laterally*, for second order change, developing more non-institutional community-orientated processes.

✠ TAKING ON THE SYSTEM:

'Just pick an institution, join it and change it'

Robert Greenleaf, considered by many to be one of the sages of our generation, says that 'the overshadowing challenge of our times' is to develop what he refers to as 'servant institutions'.[16] He defines a 'servant institution' as a 'gathering of people who have accepted a common purpose and a common discipline to guide the pursuit of that purpose to the end; that each person involved reaches higher fulfilment as a person through serving and being served by the common venture than would be achieved alone or in a less committed relationship'.[17]

Greenleaf suggests that what we all ought to do is just 'pick an institution', 'join it' and 'change it'.[18]

However, if we are to do as Greenleaf suggests, there are a number of indicators we should take into account in picking an institution. An institution which is more likely to become the kind of servant institution Greenleaf envisages will be characterised by:

1. an orientation towards the present, rather than the past;
2. an awareness of problems;
3. an acceptance of the importance of problem solving;
4. an appreciation of change;
5. a perception of change as positive rather than negative;

6. an assessment of the pace of change;
7. an evaluation of the pace of change in terms of its purpose and its discipline;
8. concern for people rather than programs;
9. a commitment to nurture rather than to maintenance;
10. a consideration of accountability rather than accounts;
11. an understanding of the whole rather than the parts;
12. a utilisation of a wide range of knowledge and skills.

But it is simply not possible for all of us to be able to pick institutions which show these characteristics. We may not be able to join a new innovative organisation we think we may have a chance to change. We may have to join an old established organisation that we think there is no chance to change at all.

Alan Twelvetrees says: 'It is probably more difficult to reorientate an existing group to take up [new] objectives than to work with a new group to that end.' But, he insists, 'the objective. . . should be to ensure that the organisation in which we work offers a better service to the community'.[19]

✠ COPING WITH THE SYSTEM:
'Conform as much as you can, compromise as little as you can'

If we find ourselves in an organisation which is unlikely to change, we need to know how to survive in a closed system, while working towards opening the system to change.

There are three steps which I always take in order to ensure my survival in the closed systems that I operate in. In my experience, taking these steps does not guarantee survival, but they give those who take them a better chance of surviving than those who don't.

The *first step* I take is to do my best to conform to the requirements of the institution as much as I can, while reserving the right to refuse to conform to any requirements which are contrary to my conscience.

Because I refuse to conform to anything contrary to my conscience, I am ultimately a threat to the institutions that I work in. But because I am willing to do everything I can to conform, the institutions that I work in do not immediately perceive me as a threat or treat me as a threat. This gives me time to work towards a change.

The *second step* I take is to seek a sponsor in the institution who sympathises with me and who is willing to give me a bit of space. It doesn't have to be a lot of space. Even a little space can make a lot of difference. It gives me room to breathe in an environment that would otherwise be quite suffocating.

The *third step* I take is to try to develop a support group inside the institution of people who share my concern about the closed nature of the system and who are willing to work together in a manner that is more open than the system. Such a group gives me room to move in an environment that would otherwise be quite stifling.

✠ OPENING UP THE SYSTEM:

'Ask questions that make institutions answerable'

If we get the time we need and both the room to breathe and the room to move, then we have got a chance to work towards opening up the closed system.

'How do we create openness to change in an organisation that acts as a closed system?' we might enquire.

'By asking questions,' Schaller replies. We can work towards opening up a closed system by asking questions which the organisation needs to answer and to which the organisation needs to be answerable, but which it cannot deal with as a closed system. The questions we need to ask in order to open up a closed system in which we operate are ones that challenge the very assumptions upon which a closed system operates.

Schaller says that it is not enough to question the people who operate the system. 'Whether the reason is described as organisational inertia, or simply the nature of organisations, it is increasingly difficult for a change in personnel or even in the people themselves to influence the performance of the organisation.'[20]

Schaller says we need to question the assumptions the system itself operates on. 'Unless there is a change in the value system of the organisation, frequently there are very severe limitations on what can be accomplished by changes in people.'[21]

Apparently, there is 'no slick formula' for doing it. There is only the difficult, painstaking task of confronting the system with questions about 'the consequences of their own existence' which they can only answer if they become more answerable to the community in which they are located.[22]

These are the sorts of questions we need to ask:

1. We need to question the right that a system assumes to rule.
2. We need to question the concentration of power assumed in the system.
3. We need to question the tyranny of precedent assumed in the system.
4. We need to question the monopoly of virtue assumed in the system.
5. We need to make sure that each and every system knows that they are answerable for the way that they act — not merely to themselves, but to everyone affected by their activities, particularly those affected adversely by their activities.
6. We need to call 'to account those who maintain oppressive structures, reminding them of the need to judge those structures (not from inside, but outside the system) from the standpoint of those who are oppressed, rather than from those who benefit (from the oppression)'.[23]

It is in the answering of such questions and in the answerability that such questioning requires that a closed system is opened up to the community and to the kind of changes the community demands.

✠ **TRANSFORMING THE SYSTEM:**
   'The potential in a free space and a fluid phase in institutions'
Opening up a closed system to the community and the

kind of changes the community demands is crucial. But it is just the beginning. If we are going to go on with the job, then we must discern where the system is most open and when it is most open and try to bring about the change in the system we need to there and then.

A *place* where the system is most open to change is what I call a 'free space'; a *time* when the system is most open to change is what I call a 'fluid phase'.

In my experience, 'free spaces' and 'fluid phases' are not so much to be defined as to be discerned. We can sense the 'free spaces' and the 'fluid phases' which can present us with a chance to act creatively for change within a system.

If we do not use these openings to bring about change as they present themselves, the system may close up again, unchanged. But if we utilise these openings and the opportunities they present, then, even in an otherwise closed system, we can bring about significant change.

☐ The free space

Many people think that if free space is not to be found at the bottom, then it must be found at the top of a system. So when they think of trying to bring about change, they think of trying to get from the bottom to the top of the system in order to get the free space they need to bring about change.

However, whether you are at the bottom or at the top of a system, if you are stuck in the middle of a system there is not much room to move.

We can get the most room to move, not by moving from the bottom to the top, but by moving from the middle to the edge of a system.

I feel that more free space is to be found on the sidelines of a system than virtually anywhere else. So when I think about trying to bring about change, I think about trying to move to the side of a system, either just inside or just outside it — on the sidelines, as it were.

In my opinion, this is the most appropriate place for us to begin to advocate change. We should always use the sidelines of an institution as an appropriate place to advocate the kind of change in the main game that the community demands.

Whether the main game is a problem that needs to be solved, a position paper that needs to be presented or a pilot project that needs to be developed, we can use our position on the sidelines to encourage people to not only reconsider, but also reconstruct the role of the institution in the community.

On the sideline, we can take the demands of the community and make them the terms of reference for bringing about changes in the institution which may seem inconsequential, but may be actually far more significant for the future of the institution than the institution realises.

I attend a local church. It happens to be conducted in one of the oldest buildings in one of the oldest denominations in Brisbane. So it's not surprising that St Andrew's is a very staid and conservative established religious institution.

A few of my friends have had a go at changing St Andrew's by joining the parish council and trying to influence the direction of the church through the formal decision-making mechanisms, but they found themselves blocked at every turn — by precedent here, by protocol there. They became so disheartened that they finally threw their hands up in despair and left the church, saying it was impossible to change St Andrew's.

Nevertheless, Ange and I continued to attend St Andrew's. We got to know the minister and his wife, John and Diana Arnold. We found out they had been in Pakistan at the same time we had been in India. We not only shared a passion for the subcontinent, but also shared a lot of the same perspectives about the importance of inclusivity that the subcontinent teaches all the people who stay there.

We got to know many of the members as well. We found out that some of them, like Norma Spice, were already intensely involved with the neighbourhood; and others, like Tim and Sue Herbert, were just itching for a chance to get involved with their neighbours. In consultation with the people in the church, ably brokered by Jeremy Liyanage, Ange and I and another couple, Chris and Ruth Todd, decided to explore the possibilities of experimenting with some community involvement — not formally, as part of the formal church program, but informally, as an informal community response.

So, though our experiment was associated with the church, it wasn't being processed through the church. And, as a consequence, it wasn't controlled by the church. This left us free to operate without any interference. We were far enough from the church not to be threatened or to be a threat, but close enough to the church to be a potential catalyst for change.

We began visiting people in our area: talking to them; listening to them tell us something of their modest aspirations — like getting out of the hostel every now and again and having a nice meal with some friends. And, as a result of these discussions, we decided to start what we called a 'community meal'.

Right from the start, the community meal was a shared meal. In fact, some people call the 'community meal' the 'share meal'. The term indicated the idea that the meal was not a 'welfare' event, where others provide for us, but a 'friendship' event, where we provide for one another.

Those who had a lot were encouraged to bring a lot. Those who had a little were encouraged to bring a little. But everybody was encouraged to bring something along for the meal.

Some people used to bring casseroles in crockpots. Others would bring a few tea bags or a small milk carton. Still others would check out the rubbish bins on the way and bring whatever treasures they could find. When there was just a few of us we used to meet in someone's house but, as time went on, word got out, the numbers of people who dropped in for dinner grew and we had to move into a community centre.

Over the next two or three years some fifty to a hundred people used to gather regularly, every fortnight on a Friday night, at the House of Freedom.

It was a party to which everyone was welcome, no matter how badly dressed or badly distressed. And, as such, it became a party for everyone in the area who was left off everyone else's party list, including some of the most fragile and some of the most freaked-out characters in the inner city.

The people who came appreciated the community meal so much that they'd plan for the next one as soon as the last one was over. Older women would get a new rinse, on 'special' at the local hairdressing salon. Older men would get a new suit for a 'song' from the local op shop. Young punks would sport their fashionable but savagely misnamed safety pins, poked through the flesh on various parts of their anatomy.

When we got together, we probably looked like a sideshow, but we always looked upon one another as friends. We shared not only the latest hot neighbourhood gossip, but also some of the deepest parts of our selves, along with the best kept secrets of our lives.

And, no doubt because of this undeniable beauty, when an Australian Broadcasting Corporation television crew were doing a documentary on St Andrew's, the church suggested a segment on the community meal.

It demonstrated the inclusivity John and Diana Arnold were committed to, the involvement Norma Spice had proven and Tim and Sue Herbert, among others in the parish, had started to display.

When the documentary featured the community meal as part of the church program, it represented the moment our informal experiment was formally adopted by St Andrew's. A little while later, we asked if we could move the community meal onto the church premises. Our request was granted. And, some would say, since that day St Andrew's has never been quite the same!

❏ A fluid phase

Many people think that there is no point working for change on the periphery of a system. But my point is that there is probably no other place we can work, except on the periphery, until there is a crisis in the system and, suddenly, our peripheral concerns can become the central concerns of the system.

I feel like there is free space on the periphery of the system and we should stay there and use it to accomplish as much change as we can, until such a time as there is a fluid phase, precipitated by a crisis. We can then take some of those changes we have accomplished on the periphery and place them at the centre.

To me, it doesn't matter so much whether the crisis comes sooner or later. What matters is that we recognise it when the moment comes and use it to manoeuvre our movement for change from out on the edge into the middle of the turmoil.

In my opinion, it is the most appropriate time for us to advocate change. We should always use a crisis in an institution to advocate the kind of change the community demands. Whether the crisis be a conflict in the group, a criticism of the organisation or a succession in leadership, we can use it to encourage people to transform the role of the institution in the community, from the dominant and dominating role it has played in the past into the servant role which we envisage it may play in the future.

I continued to attend St Andrew's for quite a few years before I saw any significant change. Then one day the minister, John Arnold, came to see me about a crisis he was facing in the church.

Apparently, he was scheduled to go away on sabbatical, but there was no priest to replace him. He'd discussed it with the parish council. They had an idea as to who might help with the morning service, but didn't have a clue as to whom they might ask to help with the evening service. So John enquired whether Jeremy and I would take over the evening service in his absence.

Both of us immediately saw it as an opportunity to bring some of the changes we had been involved with, on the periphery, into the very centre of the church. So we said to John that we would be willing to take on the job as long as we could turn the service into a church event that the people coming to the community meal would feel comfortable with.

He said he was more than happy with that, as he was concerned that the church not only provide a space for people to have a meal, but a place for people to be at home.

So with John's approval, in John's absence, we began to transform the service from a fairly rigid form that very few people in the community could relate to into a much more relaxed format that made many people from the community feel really at home.

We particularly tried to change the service so it could be more meaningful to some of the people with physical, intellectual and psychiatric disabilities that we knew. We made it more personal and more relational, inviting participation and tolerating interruptions. We made it more simple and more practical, raising issues and sharing responses. And we tried to make it more inspiring and more empowering by not only praying, but also partying together at church.

When John returned from his sabbatical, I'm sure he couldn't believe his eyes to begin with. Instead of six, there were over sixty people at the service, thirty per cent of whom had a serious disability, but all of whom were a hundred per cent involved in the event, singing and dancing along with everybody else.

Needless to say, had John not supported the change, it would have been difficult, if not impossible, for it to be sustained. But, in spite of his misgivings over certain matters (which he spoke to us about — and which we did our best to take into account), John gave the change his blessing and let the revolution roll on.

The significance of such a transformation in a system should not be discounted. Churches are notoriously hierarchical, patriarchal, patronising and domesticating. It is almost impossible for some people to imagine a church that is mutual, equitable, egalitarian and liberating. Yet that is exactly the miracle I encounter each week at St Andrew's.

Every Sunday night, our community gathers in the basement of the church. People amble in in dribs and drabs. And gradually a large motley crowd from around the neighbourhood forms into a large multi-layered circle of humanity.

The people that come don't leave their problems at the door. We know our problems are as welcome as we are. So we come with our distress, depression, neuroses, psychoses and schizophrenia, in the hope that together we can reaffirm our significance as people over and above our problems. We begin by lighting a candle to remind us of the radiance of hope we have that shines in the midst of our despair.

It sounds very wonderful, but is often the occasion for a furore, as different people fight for the right to light the candle. And, having settled that dispute, they often actually have so much difficulty in lighting the candle without burning themselves that they burst into a sustained bout of profanity as the service begins.

Like other churches, we enjoy singing together. But when we sing together it's like no other church I know. Some of the people that come just love to sing their favourite songs and demand that we sing them every time we meet.

Once Brad starts singing, no-one can stop him. He's a human juke box, with no off switch and an endless supply of songs. Some of the people that come can neither hear nor speak, but pick up on the vibes when we sing, running to and fro, making whatever noises they can in order to join in.

Ron got into clapping so much once that he didn't quit for the rest of the night. He clapped right through the songs, right through the sermon, right through the passing of the peace and right through the closing prayers. Everyone is encouraged to participate in the service on the assumption that everyone, regardless of disability, has a contribution to make through the service to one another's lives.

The first time Sally led the service, she sat in a back seat and spoke so quietly no-one knew what was going on. The second time Sally led the service she actually sat at the front, where everyone could see her, but no-one could hear her. The third time Sally led the service she not only sat at the front, where everyone could see her, but also she actually spoke loud enough for everyone to hear her.

I can never forget the time Kate and Jane took the service. Kate and Jane are both solo mothers who have both suffered the indignity of having both their children taken away from them by the department of family services. As a consequence, Kate and Jane have both felt quite suicidal at times. But never has the gospel been more faithfully proclaimed in that church than it was the night that Kate and Jane spoke. The good news, according to Kate and Jane, is: 'Though we may be treated like shit and be tempted to feel like shit, we're not shit!'

Through the alchemy at work at St Andrews, the locality is coming to church, the church is becoming a community and the people are finding the confidence they'd lost to be themselves and to realise more of their amazing potential.

Part D: The agenda

7

The crucial process of community development:

'To bring back life in all its completeness'

FROM TIME TO TIME WE SEE glimpses of possibilities and we hear what singer Bruce Cockburn would call 'rumours of glory'. But, as far as I know, there are no contemporary examples of perfect community societies. Nowadays, societies are only communities to a very limited degree. And our societies will only become communities to the degree we can manage to deconstruct them and reconstruct them, bit by bit, through a painstaking process of social transformation we know as 'community development'.

✠ THE CONVENTIONAL DEFINITION OF COMMUNITY DEVELOPMENT:
'Organised for the people, by the people themselves'

According to the Australian government, community development 'asks people to look towards areas which might bring improvement in lifestyle — whether that improvement be in the machinery of the government, the problems of. . . groups, or the lack of facilities in

163

urban areas. . . [It] covers an area as wide and diverse as the community itself and, fundamentally, it is involved in the problems of the people. It is a complicated process whose aim is to give people an opportunity to solve these problems. Community development depends greatly on the ability of the people to work together towards breaking down existing barriers and works best in an atmosphere of mutual. . . encouragement.'[1]

The Queensland Council of Social Services says that community development is 'a process of responsible and deliberate activity designed to encourage people in the community to come together to say what their needs and interests are and to promote these needs and interests. . . in a particular area'.[2]

The Queensland Council of Social Services says that 'community development' is imperative: 'It is our contention that state funds should not be diverted from the broad spectrum of [remedial] services, [such as] statutory child care or mental health services but, with federal aid, community development programs should be implemented.'[3]

Fred Milson explains that though the process ought to be supported by the government, community development ought to be organised for the people by the people themselves:

> It is a process where attempts are made to mobilise the total resources of the community for the protection, support and enrichment of [people] and groups [that are] part of the whole. From this single aim may spring various activities, including the spread of infor-

mation about existing provisions, the integration of social services and the inauguration of ad hoc committees and associations, acts of personal service and political action.

Wherever there is a choice, self-help will be preferred to outside help. The criterion applied to all these efforts will be how far they [realise] the possibilities of the community's self-determination. They will be judged to have succeeded or failed by the practical demonstration in all feasible areas. . . that the community should define its own needs and organise [its own] resources to satisfy them. . .[4]

Rabindrinath Tagore envisages community development as a process that involves a total multi-dimensional renewal of society in terms of community:

> to bring back life in all its completeness,
>   making people self-reliant and self-respectful,
>   acquainted with their cultural traditions
>   and competent;
> to make an efficient use of [their] resources
>   for the fullest development of
>   their physical, intellectual,
>   social and economic conditions.[5]

✠ THE PHILOSOPHICAL FOUNDATION OF COMMUNITY DEVELOPMENT: *'To know as we are known'*

Community development has a philosophical foundation. According to Henry Bugbee, 'Philosophy is *learning to leave things be.* . . By "leaving things be"', he says, 'I do not mean inaction; I mean being still in the presence of things, respecting things, letting them speak.'[6]

'When we try to pick out something by itself, we find it hitched to everything in the universe.'[7] And when we learn to 'leave things be' they speak to us of 'our unity with everything in the universe. The great truth [is] that beneath the broken surface of our lives there remains — in the words of Thomas Merton — "a hidden wholeness".'[8]

'Unity is not something we are called to create; it's something we are called to recognise.'[9]

As Parker Palmer explains:

Since the advent of atomic physics, the popular image of physical reality has been one of particles floating in an empty void. Since Darwin and Social Darwinism, the popular image of biological reality has been one of individual creatures in bloody competition over scarce resources. Though they come from different disciplines, [they are] essentially non-communal, even anti-communal.

But at the heart of science itself, these images have been challenged and changed. Community, not competition, is the metaphor that most deeply informs the work of many biologists. Among physicists, the atom is no longer seen as an independent and isolated entity but, in the words of Henry Stapp, as 'a set of relationships reaching out to other things'. So Thomas Merton's 'hidden wholeness' turns out to be more than a fantasy — the connections of community are visible at reality's very core.

We can find this communal theme not only in modern images of the nature of reality, but also in modern images of how reality is known. In the popular imagination, knowing is seen as the act of a solitary individual, a knower who uses sense and intellect to apprehend and interpret objects of knowledge 'out there'. Not only does this knower operate apart from other knowers, he or she is also set apart from the known object in order to guarantee that our knowledge will be 'objective' and pure. The popular image of how we know reality is as non-communal or anti-communal as is the popular image of the nature of reality itself.

But scholars now understand that knowing is a profoundly communal act. Nothing could possibly be known by the solitary self, since the self is inherently communal in nature. In order to know something, we depend on the consensus of the community in which we are rooted — a consensus so deep that we draw upon it unconsciously. The communal nature of knowing goes beyond the relations of the knowers; it includes a community of interaction between the knowers and the known. . . We now see that to know something is to have a living relationship with it — influencing and being influenced [by it].[10]

Given the communal nature of reality and the communal nature of the way we know reality, community development means relating to the world in a manner that is true to that reality and to the way we know that reality.

Parker Palmer goes on to say:

History suggests two primary sources for our knowledge. One is curiosity; the other is control. The one corresponds to pure, speculative knowledge, to knowledge as an end in itself. The other corresponds to applied science, to knowledge as a means to practical ends. We are inquisitive creatures, forever wanting to get inside of things and discover their hidden secrets. Our curiosity is piqued by the closed and wrapped box. We want to know its contents and, when the contents are out, we want to open them, too — down to the tiniest particle of their construction.

We are also creatures attracted by power; we want knowledge to control our environment, each other, ourselves. Since many of the boxes we have opened contained secrets that have given us more mastery over life, curiosity and control are joined as the passion behind our knowing. Curiosity sometimes kills and our desire for control has put deadly power in some very unsteady hands. We should not be surprised that knowledge launched from these sources is heading toward some terrible ends, undeflected by ethical values as basic as respect for life itself.

Curiosity is an amoral passion, a need to know that allows no guidance beyond the need itself. Control is simply another word for power, a passion notorious not only for its amorality, but for its tendency toward corruption. If curiosity and control are the primary motives for our knowing, we will generate a knowledge that eventually carries us not toward life but death.

But another kind of knowledge is available to us, one that begins in a different passion and is drawn towards other ends. This is a knowledge that originates not in curiosity or control but in compassion or love. The goal of a knowledge arising from love is the reunification and reconstruction of broken worlds. A knowledge born of compassion aims not at exploiting and manipulating creation, but at reconciling the world to itself. The mind motivated by compassion reaches out to know as the heart reaches out to love. Here, the act of knowing is an act of love, the act of entering and embracing the reality of the other, allowing the other to enter and embrace our own.

Curiosity and control create a knowledge that distances us from each other and the world, allowing us to use what we know as a plaything and to play the game by our own self-serving rules. But a knowledge that springs from love will implicate us in the web of life; it will wrap the knower and the known in compassion, in a bond of awesome responsibility as well as transforming joy; it will call us to involvement, mutuality and accountability. In such knowing, we know and are known as members of one community, and our knowing becomes a way of reweaving that community. . .[11]

Community development is all about practising the truth of this knowledge of our community with reality, applying it to the community that in reality we are developing.

Parker Palmer goes on to say:

When we examine the image hidden at the root of 'truth' it turns out to be more immediate and human than the words we use to describe this knowledge. . .

The English word 'truth' comes from a Germanic root that also gives rise to our word 'troth'. With this word, one person enters a covenant with another, a pledge to engage in a mutually accountable and transforming relationship, a relationship forged of trust in the face of unknowable risks. We find truth by pledging our troth, and knowing becomes a reunion of separated beings whose. . . bond is not of logic, but of love.

In the words of St Gregory:

Love itself is knowledge;
      the more one loves, the more one knows.'

In the words of Abraham Heschel:

It is impossible to find truth
      without being in love.

To know something or someone in truth is to enter troth with the known, to rejoin with new knowing what our minds have put asunder. To know in truth is to become betrothed, to engage the known with one's whole self, an engagement one enters with. . . goodwill.

To know in truth is to allow one's self to be known as well, to be vulnerable to the challenges and changes that any true relationship brings.

Truthful knowing weds the knower and the known. Both parties have their integrity; one cannot be collapsed into the other. But the knower and the known are implicated in one another's lives. Even in separation, the two become part of each other's fate. In truthful knowing, the knower becomes a co-participant in a community of faithful relationships with other persons, creatures and things, with whatever our knowledge makes known.[12]

The poet, Thich Nhat Hanh, struggles with the implications of practising this 'truthful knowing' of 'community with other persons, creatures and things' in his poem 'Please Call Me By My True Names':

I am the mayfly metamorphosing
    surface of the river,
and I am the bird which,
    when spring comes,
arrives in time to eat the mayfly.

I am a frog swimming happily in the
    clear water of a pond,
and I am the grass-snake who,
    approaching in silence,
feeds itself on the frog.

I am the child of Uganda,
    all skin and bones,
my legs as thin as bamboo sticks,
    and I am the arms merchant,
selling deadly weapons to Uganda.

I am the twelve-year-old girl refugee
    on a small boat,
who throws herself into the ocean after
    being raped by a sea pirate,
my heart not yet capable of seeing and loving.
I am a member of the politburo, with
    plenty of power in my hands,
and I am the man who has to pay
    his 'debt of blood' to my people
dying slowly in a forced labour camp.

My joy is like spring, so warm it makes
    flowers bloom in all walks of life.
My pain is like a river of tears,
    so full it fills all four oceans.

Please call me by my true names,
    so I can hear all my cries and laughs at once,
    so I can see that my joy and pain are one.

Please call me by my true names,
    so I can wake up,
and so the door of my heart can be left open,
    the door of compassion.[13]

Desmond Tutu, the non-violent activist archbishop, articulates the importance of practising this 'truthful knowing' for developing a 'community of faithful relationships' in a microcosm like South Africa. There, people have tended to deny the truth of our common humanity and, consequentially, tend to discount the significance of the essential interdependence and complementarity of the human family.

I, along with of hundreds, if not thousands of people who gathered to listen to him speak in King George Square, in downtown Brisbane, can well remember the words he told us that Sunday afternoon on 10 October, 1993:

> In our African language we say
>   'a person is a person through other persons'.
> I would not know how to be a human being at all
>   except I learned this from other human beings.
> We are made for a delicate network
>   of relationships, of interdependence.
> We are meant to complement each other.
> We are the 'rainbow people of God',
>   people of many kinds, of many colours,
> and it is only as we are together
>   we realise our identity, our destiny.

Having said these words, the archbishop got us all to raise our hands, wave our arms and chant 'We are the rainbow people of God.' And, as we did so, it became so. Rich and poor, black and white, old and young, women and men, believers and unbelievers alike were caught up in the consciousness of the truth of our community with one another. And, as we laughed and we cried, we prayed we might continue to make it so.

✠ THE ETHICAL FRAMEWORK OF COMMUNITY DEVELOPMENT:
'To do unto others as you would have them do unto you'

Community development has an ethical framework. According to Trevor Jordan, 'Ethics is about asking, "What is right and wrong?" and "What is good and bad?" and giving reasons for our answers.

'The terms "ethics" and "morality" can be used interchangeably. Ethical and moral behaviour would be behaviour that is arguably "right" or "good". Unethical and immoral behaviour is behaviour that is deemed "wrong" or "bad".'[14]

John Gardner states that 'no society can remain vital, or even survive, without a reasonable base of shared values. . . [And] families and communities are the ground-level generators. . . of ethical systems [which produce] and preserve. . . these values.'[15]

Amitai Etzioni, the communitarian theorist, says:

Liberal friends express concern about the use of the term 'moral'. [People] don't like to be told about morals, said one; it sounds like preaching. Another suggested that the term reminds him of the Moral Majority.

I do not mean to preach, but to share a concern. I am sorry if I remind people of the Moral Majority, because I believe that although they raised the right questions they provided the wrong answers.

However, just as we should not give up on patriotism because some politicians wrap themselves with the flag when it suits their purposes, so we should not give up on morality because some abuse it to skewer [others].[16]

Communities speak to us in moral voices. They lay claims on [us as] their members. Indeed, other than the inner self, they are the most important sustaining source of moral voices [in our society].[17]

When I discuss the value of moral voices, people tell me they are very concerned that if they lay moral claims, they will be perceived as self-righteous. If they mean by 'self-righteous' a person who comes across as without flaw, who sees himself as entitled to dictate what is right [and wrong], who lays moral claims in a sanctimonious or pompous way — there is good reason to refrain from such ways of expressing moral voices.

[But] disinclination to lay moral claims undermines moral conduct in crucial situations. During a conference on bone-marrow transplants, a psychiatrist argued that it was not proper to ask one sibling for a bone-marrow donation for another sibling, despite the fact that making such a donation does not entail any particular risk. His reason was that the sibling who refused might feel guilty, especially if, as a result, the brother or sister died.

A communitarian would argue that siblings should be asked in no uncertain terms to come to the rescue. If they refuse, they *should* feel guilty.[18]

No society can function well unless most of its members behave most of the time because they voluntarily heed their moral commitments.[19]

Although it may be true that markets work best if everybody goes out and tries to maximise his or her own self-interest (though this is by no means a well-proven proposition), communities most assuredly do not. They need people who care for one another and for shared spaces and causes. Here, clearly, it is better to give than to take, and the best way to help sustain a world in which people care for one another is to do unto others as you would wish them to do unto you.[20]

✠ THE SIMPLICITY OF ETHICS:
'We learned it all in kindergarten!'

On one level, 'doing unto others as you would wish them to do unto you' is a very simple matter.

As Robert Fulghum says, 'We learned it all in kindergarten!':

Most of what I really need to know
  about how to live,

and what to do,
and how to be,
I learned in kindergarten.
Wisdom was not at the top
of the university mountain,
but there in the sandpit.
These are the things I learned:
Share everything.
Play fair.
Don't hit people.
Put things back where
you found them.
Clean up your own mess.
Don't take things
that aren't yours.
Say you're sorry
when you hurt somebody.
Wash your hands
before you eat.
Live a balanced life.
Learn awhile. . .
and draw
and sing
and dance
and play
and work
awhile
every day.
Take a nap in the afternoon.
When you go out into the world,
watch for the traffic,
hold hands and stick together.
Be aware of wonder.
Remember the little seed
in the plastic cup.
The roots go down
and the plant goes up.

And nobody really knows why,
    but we are all like that.
Goldfish die.
    So do we.
Everything you need to know
    is in there somewhere.
The golden rule
    and basic sanitation.
Ecology and politics
    and sane living.
Think of what a better world
    it would be if we all
    had bickies and milk
    about three o'clock
    every afternoon and
then lay down for a nap.
        Or
if we had a basic policy
    in our nation
always to put things back
    where we found them
        and
cleaned up our own messes.
And it is still true,
no matter how old you are,
when you go out into the world,
it is best to hold hands and stick together.[21]

✠ THE COMPLEXITY OF ETHICS:
'Not with my daughter you don't!'

On one level, 'doing unto others as you would wish them to do unto you' can be a very simple matter. But on another level, it can be a very complex matter, as Dale Hardman shows in his article, 'Not with my daughter you don't!':

It was a balmy spring afternoon in the Blintz County workhouse. The interviewing room was only half separated from the cell corridors. The inmate looked out the dirt-specked window for some time, then returned his gaze to the social worker. 'Twelve more days. I could do twelve days on a bed of spikes. You're the reason I got fifty-five days knocked off my six months. I wouldn't a got out unless you went to bat for me.'

Oscar De Curia only nodded, but inwardly he beamed because expressions of gratitude were infrequent among workhouse clients. 'I would like,' he said, 'to get some idea of your plans when you get out. Most guys need some help getting into a job or school or. . .'

'Nah. I work for my old man putting up siding. I always got a job waiting.'

'Good. What about school?'

'Can't work and go to school, too.'

'Some guys do.' De Curia bit his lip; he knew as soon as he said it. There he was, imposing his middle-class norms on a lower-class client.

'I quit when I was fifteen. Nine years ago — too late to go back now.'

De Curia had an impulse to suggest some vocational ed. courses, but instead he just nodded and said, 'Okay then, what about your social life?'

'That's all I been thinking about since I got my commutation.'

De Curia brightened a bit. At least here he didn't have to worry about imposing his own norms. Here he could relax, be more natural, more human.

'Chicks,' said the inmate. He leaned back and clasped his fingers behind his thick black curly hair. 'Chicks is my specialty. Take the average guy in here — for him sex is just quick service stuff: roll in the hay, be on your way. No art to it. No class.'

'You're most artistic, then.'

'That's it. I'm an artist. Most guys in here wouldn't

know the difference.'

'But you do. How would you go about it that's any different from anybody else?'

'Well see, same as me — they've been locked up for six months to a year. Anything would look good to them and they'll try to make up for the whole year in the first ten minutes they're out. First broad they see. But not me. Like the soup commercial says: 'To make the best you gotta begin with the best. Then prepare it tenderly. . . carefully. . . slowly. . .' So I begin with the best. Nothing but fresh meat for me — very fresh. A virgin.'

'I see. Well, since there's not a lot of those around. . .'

'Well, ya gotta know where to look. For one thing, you gotta start young — maybe fourteen or fifteen — so you find where they hang out.'

'Hmm.' De Curia opened his mouth to point out that a sex act with an adolescent would constitute a new violation, but he again bit his tongue and admonished himself that he must not be a moralist. And certainly this client was canny enough to know the law on this point.

'They hung out a lot around Whiffly Dip, especially on weekends. Skating rinks and bowling alleys is good hunting grounds. Always full of teeny chicks.'

'Hmm.' In truth, De Curia felt a bit more uncomfortable with each self-revelation of his client. But he knew that disapproval on his part would only serve to turn off his client's verbal spigot — and certainly the man needed to talk after four months in lock-up.

'There was one little chick I met at the Rollerama just before I got busted. A virgin, I'll bet my shirt. About fourteen. Real good skater.'

'Hmm.' De Curia resolved to be non-directive if it killed him, but his discomfort continued to rise.

'I only saw her two, three times before I got sent up. Skated with her each time. I know she likes me.

I think she's the one I'll start with.'

'I see.' De Curia shifted uneasily as his tension mounted.

'Like I say, begin with the best. And she's the best. Long slender legs. Willowy. Little round bazoobs like ripe peaches. Long auburn hair, always in a pony-tail. Her name was Irma Jean something.'

Every man has a sort of safety plug in his boiler; it melts at a lower temperature than the boiler and serves to prevent the boiler from rupturing. And here De Curia blew his plug. Out spewed his professional role, his persona, in a great gust and blast, and he stood before his client a very angry human being.

'Hey, wait a minute! That's my daughter you're talking about, you lecherous bastard!'

☐ Oscar's conflict

It was several hours later that Oscar De Curia sat in his office, pondering his misdirected interview at the workhouse. In ten years of practice, he had held doggedly to the dictum of non-direction: the non-moralistic listener, eschewing judgments, never imposing his own norms, never playing God, never setting himself up as an ethical model for his clients' emulation. For ten years, he had adhered to these fundamental premises, drilled into his skull in classrooms, in texts and journals and in interaction with other social workers.

He was, he believed, the epitome of Powers and Witmer's delineation (1951): 'Modern casework is distinguished by the fact that its practitioners seldom give advice, cite ethical precepts or the consequence of anti-social behaviour, or urge particular courses of action.' True, he constantly had to remind himself in those pesky situations that clashed against his own middle-class value system. He had come, in fact, to feel a bit apologetic for being middle class or subscribing to its norms. He felt as though he had been called a dirty name when he had been referred to as middle class.

But now, suddenly, when these norms were violated close to home, his carefully cultivated professional posture had disintegrated and he had blown his cool, the interview, and the case. Although De Curia was not given to extensive self-contemplation, he was, in those brief and unaccustomed moments of introspection, essentially honest with himself. Perhaps these two facts were related: in introspection he usually came out loser, due to a basic trait of honesty, so he indulged in it rarely.

Oscar had experienced similar interviews in the past, listening with composure to expressions of sexual exploitation, tales of assaults on persons or property, and threats of vengeance or power or violence. He had often felt a rising discomfort and a need to protest and always, until today, he had successfully repressed such unprofessional impulses. But now, with his treasured, auburn-haired teenager as the proposed object. . .

At this juncture, a new thought crossed Oscar's synapses: suppose the name his client had dropped had not been Irma Jean; suppose instead it had been Sandra or Millie. Wasn't it conceivable that the fathers of other pony-tailed, knobby-kneed damsels might harbour feelings for them as tender as his? De Curia was struck by this thought much as Goliath encountered David's stony projectile: such a thing had never before entered his head. It jolted him in his tracks. A host of balding and paunchy middle-aged fathers arose in his mind's eye, like a legion of Banquo's ghosts, to ask: 'In how many hundred cases, have you said "Mm hmm" or "I see" and thereby given tacit acquiescence to illegal, immoral or violent acts?'. . .

Upon his return home, De Curia was unusually attentive to his daughter, but otherwise his manner was, for him, exceptionally subdued. His wife reckoned that he had either been fired or out philandering, but that in either case he would shortly tell her. . .

☐ Generalising the problem

During the ensuing week, Oscar De Curia resolved that he would, at whatever cost, resolve his newly mounted conflict. One of his first acts was to request that his supervisor transfer the client who had torpedoed his cool.

As has been noted, Mr De Curia was not a profoundly thoughtful man, but an honest one. His supervisor, on the other hand, was not a profoundly honest man, but a thoughtful one, and so he asked the reason for his subordinate's request. And within the next half hour, De Curia had upended the whole wretched can of worms.

The supervisor had indeed encountered this knotty question before; he had mulled it over at considerable length and then shelved it. But Oscar would not be shelved. He was a persistent clod and he insisted on answers. And answered he was. The supervisor said: 'Mm hmm.'

'Well, it's true, ain't it?' De Curia waxed ungrammatical only when be became emotional. 'From the time we enter graduate school, we're admonished against imposing our own values on people. So I don't and look what happens! My own daughter is up for grabs!'

'Mm,' said the supervisor, thoughtfully.

'Tell me honestly, Jake' (the supervisor encouraged this bit of familiarity), 'what would you do? You must have encountered this kind of incongruity before. How did you handle it?'

Jake could not admit that he had resolved the question by shelving it. So he said, 'Hmm.' Thoughtfully, that is.

'That doesn't exactly answer my question, you know,' De Curia persisted. Jake squirmed considerably. Inwardly, at least. Outwardly, he was all empathy, as a supervisor should be. He glanced at the desk phone, hoping that perhaps a call might spare him a confrontation with his untenable position. It didn't. He glanced out his window, hoping perhaps to see a tidal wave rolling across the midwestern prairie. There was not so much as a ripple. He glanced out his door, perchance to spot a client in need of his attention. A swatch of blue and a hank of white hair caught his eye. 'Hey Dave!' yelled Jake, much as a man might yell when stranded on a sandbar by high tide.

Dave had been retired from the agency for several years now, but occasionally popped in to see how things were going. These visits were usually welcome and especially so today.

'Come in, Dave, and shoot the bull a spell,' said Jake with an outward show of camaraderie and an inward sigh of relief. 'Oscar and I were just talking about lower-class norms. How they often impede therapy or progress, or whatever you wanna call it, but how we're not supposed to tamper with them.'

'So what did you tell him to do?' asked Dave.

'Huh?'

'I imagine he asked you whether he should or shouldn't impose his own value system. What did you tell him?'

I'm stabbed in the back, thought Jake. He was desperate now. 'First, I'd like to hear your opinion. You must have run into this question in your twenty-odd years here?'

'That's the biggest understatement since Genghis Khan was called unneighbourly,' said Dave. 'Not a day went by that that question didn't pop up.'

☐ Imposing some norms and supporting some norms

'Ever have a client make a pass at your daughter?' asked Oscar. 'Your thirteen-year-old daughter?'

'My friend,' said Dave, 'there is nothing in social service more frequently encountered than conflict regarding values. Every social worker I know runs into it daily and most of them, like you, never really come to grips with the realities of the problem. And every social worker I know, consciously or unconsciously, overtly or covertly, imposes [their] norms on the poor every day of [their] working life.'

'But you're different,' said Jake, with a noticeable edge to his voice.

'Only that I'm honest about it,' said Dave. 'I do it intentionally. Deliberately. In cold blood. Further, a half-dozen studies indicate that the more moralistic, value-imposing workers have better success with their clients' (Parloff, Iflund, and Goldstein, 1957; Powers and Witmer, 1951; Rosenthal, 1955).

'Did I misunderstand you when you admitted that you superimpose your own values?' said Jake.

'That's right, deliberately.'

'Then aren't you saying, in effect, that your values are better than those of the lower class?'

'Ah, now comes the stinger. I impose some middle-class values. There are quite a number of lower-class values that I prefer to middle-class ones.'

'For instance?'

'Comradeship. Closer, more intimate interpersonal relations. More egalitarian views; more emphasis on person than on status. More interpersonal, good humour. More freedom of expression. More open expression of affection' (Reissman,1962).

'Affection?'

'Yes. Take one example. When I was a kid, I worked on a string of blue-collar jobs: ranches, mines, factories, railroads, construction. It wasn't uncommon to see two guys who were buddies standing around the fire at night or around the bar or bunkhouse with an arm slung over the friend's shoulder. No-one thought anything of it. Now suppose that on some white-collar job — let's say in an insurance office — you spot two guys at the water cooler with their arms round each other. You'd nudge your neighbour and say, "Hey, Fred! Look it!" What a helluva culture when two people can't express honest affection without being considered gay.'

'Maybe there are more gays in the lower classes.'

'Fewer (Kinsey, 1948). I'll tell you another trait of the poor I'd consider keeping. When a husband and wife are at loggerheads, they are much more likely to have a good old hell-raising, whooping and hollering knock-down-drag-out battle. But in twenty minutes it's all over. You and me, when we're on the outs with the old woman, we turn on the deep freeze for about a month. We never speak or look at each other for weeks on end. Now I ask you honestly, which is better for mental health?'

'Hmm.'

'And I'll tell you another. I think there's more real honesty in the lower class.'

'Aw, come off it, Dave. Nine-tenths of our correctional clients come from the lower class.'

'I wasn't thinking of law violations specifically. However, since you've raised the point: a dozen studies of self-reported offenses show no significant class difference in crime and delinquency. Our legal machinery simply screens out more of the poor for processing (Akers, 1964; Empey and Erickson, 1968; Meyerhoff and Meyerhoff, 1964; Short and Nye, 1957; and Voss, 1966).'

'Then what do you mean by "honesty?"'

'Interpersonal honesty. If a lower-class guy doesn't like you, he will say so. Or maybe punch your nose. But we middle class will rationalise it with some kind of mealy-mouthed double-talk. I invite you, for instance, to sit in on a college promotions committee if you want to observe some fancy verbal footwork — like 'Now understand, I've got nothing personal against old Charlie. But. . . A blue-collar worker would say, much more honestly, "I can't stand the damn creep."'

'Not footwork. Tonguework,' said Jake.

'Okay, I recall one college department of about twenty-five faculty. There were some faculty cuts coming up, so two sections of the department formed a coalition and voted to abolish the third section in order to save their jobs. I have never heard of this kind of job cannibalism among blue-collar workers.'

☐ Deciding on some functional norms

'Dave, you're not being consistent,' Jake said waving his hand. 'A minute ago you were the champion of good old middle-class values. Now you've changed sides. You can't play both sides at once. What do you want?'

Dave pondered this one briefly: 'First, I want [people] to be honest about when they impose norms, whether middle-class or lower-class. Second, I want them to forget the infantile quibble about the norms of one class being better than those of another. I want. . .'

'How do you decide which norms you are going to support, then? You gonna play God?'

'Functionality is how. First we gotta decide on objectives, social workers and clients in dialogue together. And this holds true whether it's one caseworker and one client or a [community] project involving fifty workers and 10 000 clients. We can agree that employment is a goal, or marriage stability or family planning or whatever, but we have to thrash it out and arrive at some consensus regarding our objective. Once the objective is agreed upon, my job is clear: If a certain cultural norm is functional, if it aids in achieving the agreed-upon objective, I will support it. If it's dysfunctional, if it's thwarting our objectives, then it's gotta go — and I'll do my damndest to see that it goes. And I couldn't care less whether the norm comes from the lower, middle or upper class.'

'Meehl and McClosky (1947),' said Jake, 'consider that our job definition is to help the client achieve the

client's end. Period. That doesn't leave room for negotiation about objectives.'

'I'll be damned if I'm gonna help that sonofabitch
achieve my daughter's end,' said Oscar De Curia hotly.

'And I'll venture no worker worth [their] salt would,'
replied Dave. 'In fact, I think they'd draw the line on
about half the goals of our correctional clients. Plus a
number of others. For instance, I won't help a client
toward suicide, if that's his goal. Or to obtain heroin,
or to bust out of jail or a hospital. Or to defraud the
welfare office or desert his family or go AWOL. Or, in
my case, to obtain an abortion. This is why I said we
must first agree on objectives.'

'And if you and the client can't agree?'

'My personal guideline is this: I will never help
clients accomplish something that I consider morally
wrong, harmful to them or to me or to others. And
I won't help a client to rendezvous with any teenager,
not your daughter or anyone else's. . .'[22]

✠ THE PRINCIPLES OF ETHICS:
'Guidelines proven to have enduring, permanent value'

We can determine what Hardman calls 'functional
norms' by applying the principles of what Covey calls
'natural laws' to our practice in particular situations:

The reality of such natural laws becomes obvious to
anyone who thinks deeply [about] the cycles of social
history. These principles surface time and time again
and the degree to which people in a society live in
harmony with them moves them toward either survival
and stability or disintegration and destruction.

The principles I am referring to are not esoteric,
mysterious or 'religious' ideas. There is not one principle that is unique to any specific religion, including

my own. These principles are a part of most every major religion, as well as enduring social and ethical systems.

They seem to exist in all human beings, regardless of conditioning and loyalty to them, even though they might be submerged by such conditions or numbed by [incidents of] disloyalty to them.

Principles are not practices. A practice that works in one circumstance will not necessarily work in another, as parents who have tried to raise a second child exactly like they did the first can readily attest.

While practices are situationally specific, principles are fundamental truths that have universal application. They apply to marriages, to families, to private and public organisations of every kind. When these truths are internalised into habits, they empower people to create a wide variety of practices to deal with different situations.

These principles are essentially unarguable because they are self-evident. [They] are guidelines for human conduct that are proven to have enduring, permanent value. One way to quickly grasp the self-evident nature of principles is to simply consider the absurdity of attempting to live an effective life based on their opposites. . .

For example, the principle of fairness, out of which our whole concept of equity, [equality] and justice is developed. Little children seem to have an innate idea of fairness, even apart from opposite conditioning experiences. I doubt that anyone would seriously consider unfairness to be a solid foundation for lasting happiness and success.[23]

There are no short cuts. There are no quick fixes. Unless we practice these principles consistently, we cannot expect to develop community.

✠ THE PRACTICE OF ETHICS:
'The ability to guide ourselves'

The bottom line is that we need to take what we have learnt as kids and learn how to put these moral guidelines into practice as adults, so that we can get on with the job of trying to build a better world — without making matters worse in the process. Etzioni says:

A typical course on moral reasoning starts with something called 'values clarification'. In a typical lesson, students are asked to list what is dear to them — money, reputation, power — and then to rank these pursuits in terms of which they hold most important.

They fail — and are thus considered in need of moral tutoring — only if they have difficulty in deciding what is up and what is down in their scale of interests. They are further helped to clarify their preferences through exercises such as the 'lifeboat drill'. In this exercise, students are told to imagine that they are in a lifeboat with a group of people that includes a scientist, an artist, a teacher and a general (the list can vary). The boat is overloaded and they must decide whom they would cast overboard first, second, third and so on.

In this way, the students' values are revealed. For instance, do they rank art higher than arms? (Usually, the teachers are cast off first and the kids themselves last.)

As long as the pupils are clear on their preferred tossing order and hence by implication their values, their moral education is considered properly advanced. Under moral reasoning *per se*, nobody is supposed to discuss the question whether they should have cast [anyone] overboard or ask why there aren't enough lifeboats to begin with.

Such values clarification and development of moral reasoning may be helpful if and when they are provided to people who already have evolved moral commitments. They can help such people sort out how specifically to express and apply their generalised sense that they ought to do what is right and to order various moral values when these do not readily dovetail with one another. But for youngsters whose moral commitments are underdeveloped, such classes tend to become idle debating clubs.

In moral reasoning, teachers are typically expected to be passive discussion facilitators rather than active proponents of values. The students' success in these exercises is based not so much on the depth and scope of their moral sensibilities, but on how well they spin an argument.

What is missing between the development of moral reasoning [and the development of] character formation (the ability to guide oneself) is the internalisation of (i.e. making part of oneself) commitments to a set of substantive values. . .[24]

Recently, as part of a reform process started in my state as a result of the findings of the famous Fitzgerald enquiry into police corruption in Queensland, I have been tutoring a course on applied ethics for law enforcement officers.

In this course, there is a concern to restore the missing element in moral education — that is, 'the internalisation of commitments to a set of substantive values' through the lecturers' constant advocacy of personal integrity and social justice, and the students' continual assessment of case studies and current incidents.

However, though it is easy to teach about community ethics and learn about community ethics in the classroom, it is difficult, if not impossible, to actually teach community ethics and learn community ethics anywhere but in the community itself.

As Confucius said quite a few centuries ago:

> *I hear and I forget;*
> *I see and I remember;*
> *I do and I understand.*

So my friends and I invite students from the colleges where we teach to come to our neighbourhood for two to three weeks at a time to 'do' some community ethics — by trying to live in community, ethically, with us and with the disadvantaged people in our locality with whom we share our lives. Last month, we had twelve students, some from university and some from seminary, come to live with us. Having done this, twice a year, for the past eight years, probably close to 200 students have gone through what we call our 'community orientation courses'.

We introduce them to Auntie Jean, an Aboriginal elder, who not only tells them the story of her people and their painful dispossession, but also takes them with her to meet her people, some in a maximum security prison, languishing in their cells, and others in a human rights organisation, fighting for their release.

We introduce them to Father Kefle, an Eretrian priest, who shows them the scars of thirty years of civil war, and they visit refugees who have been torn away from their families, tortured by the very people who were supposed to protect them, forced to flee for their lives, and who are now struggling to rebuild a life for themselves as strangers in a strange land.

Some of the students have never actually met an Aborigine or a refugee face to face before, let alone heard their story or seen their struggle for themselves.

These encounters confront the students with essentially ethical questions that we all have to answer one way or another:

* How do we, as members of a 'white' society, deal with our 'black' history?
* How do we, as members of the human family, respond to the desperate plea from our brothers and sisters, not just to address the superficial symptoms, but the underlying causes of their lasting pain?
* And what are we going to do about it?

These are questions to us which call for answers from us — not only theoretical answers, but also practical answers. Answering these questions is a moral imperative that we can accept or reject, but which we cannot ignore.

One of the students on the last course who accepted the imperative for him to answer these questions as honestly as he could, was a policeman — we'll call Brad — who had been on the beat for many years. Brad said that, like a lot of police who only ever related in their job to people as sources of information about 'criminals', or as potential or actual 'criminals' themselves, he had become quite cynical about the public.

But, when he took the opportunity to get out of uniform and to meet people face to face, as fellow human beings, he began to change.

The first stage of change was in terms of *perspective*. What we see depends on where we stand. And standing alongside the very people he had often been expected to take a stand against helped Brad see a totally different side to the struggle for justice on the streets than the one he'd seen before. As Harrison Wildung says: 'The critical interpretations of the most [marginalised people] correct the blind spots in our own experience.'[25]

The second stage of change was in terms of *responsibility*. What we hear depends on who we listen to. And listening to people who continue to be dispossessed talk about the people that he usually listened to helped Brad hear a totally different side to the story of the history of our society than the one he'd heard before. It was, for Brad, a case of hearing that 'the very things I would like least done to me are the things that I do to others every day'.[26]

The third stage of change was in terms of *pain*. How we feel depends on what we do. And recognising that what he was doing as a police officer was often part of the problem rather than part of the solution helped Brad feel the impact of the issues in a way that he'd never felt them before. As Lebacqs says: 'The shock of recognition that one is the oppressed and the shock of recognition that one is the oppressor — both are accompanied by pain.'[27]

The fourth stage of change was in terms of *responsiveness*. We have two options for managing the pain that comes from recognising the gap between who we are and who we are meant to be. One option is rationalisation — changing the ideal of who we are meant to be so it is closer to the reality of who we already are. The other option is action — changing the reality of who we are so we are closer to the ideal of who we are meant to be. Choosing action rather than rationalisation helped Brad respond to the issues in a way that he'd thought about, but he'd never thought he'd ever really do anything about.

'Doing unto others as you would wish them to do unto you,' began quite unceremoniously, but quite significantly, for Brad, by stopping when an Aboriginal person caught his attention in the street, listening to him when he wanted to talk and looking out for him when he asked for a packet of smokes, like he would have done for any of his mates.

Of this stage, the educational activist, Paulo Friere says:

> At that point, I join the action by having the courage to commit myself, or end up with a sense of guilt because I am not doing what I know I should.
>
> I seek compensation in almsgiving, hoping that way to buy some peace. But peace cannot be purchased. It is not for sale. Peace has to be lived.
>
> I cannot live my peace without commitment to [people], my commitment to [people] cannot exist without [a commitment to] their liberation, and their liberation cannot exist without the final transformation of the structures that are dehumanising them.[28]

This was the stage of *realisation* Brad was at when he completed our 'community orientation course'.

I spoke to him about how encouraged I was about the stages of change he had gone through so far. But I cautioned him, saying that it would all be in vain unless he continued to take the change a stage further.

The fifth stage of change is in terms of *practice*. Aristotle said: 'We are what we do repeatedly. Excellence, then, is not an act, but a habit.'[29]

To choose to do good is good. But to choose to do good is not good enough if we choose to do good intermittently. To choose to do good is only good enough if we choose to do good habitually.

Amiel said: 'Moral truth can be conceived in thought. [We] can have feelings about it. [We] can will to live it. But moral truth may have been penetrated and possessed in all these ways, and escape us still. . . Only those truths that have entered into. . . our being itself, . . .unconscious as well as conscious, are really our life.'[30]

And only a really good life is a really good basis for building a better world.

8

The personal dimension of community development:

'Who of you will join me?'

LEO TOLSTOY LAMENTED, 'EVERYBODY THINKS of changing humanity and nobody thinks of changing himself.' Unfortunately for Leo Tolstoy's family, that statement included Leo Tolstoy himself.[1] He died with his wife outside the house, looking in through the window but forbidden from entering. In death, there was no mercy.

Fortunately for us, however, his disciple heeded Tolstoy's exhortation rather than Tolstoy's example, so when he started his movement for change, Mahatma Gandhi started by changing himself. This unremarkable process of personal change in one man's life was to have such a remarkable impact of international significance, that Albert Einstein said, 'Generations to come, it may be, will scarce believe that such a one as this ever in flesh and blood walked upon this earth.'[2]

Leo Tolstoy and Mahatma Gandhi represent the choice we have: either we can complain about the way things are or we can change the way things are, starting with ourselves.

✠ THE CHOICE IS OURS:
'Between stimulus and response, we have choice'

Those of us who feel tempted to think that we have no choice need to think again in the light of Viktor Frankl's findings, as this extract from Stephen Covey makes clear:

Frankl was a determinist raised in the tradition of Freudian psychology which postulates that whatever happens to you as a child shapes your personality and basically governs your whole life. The limits of your life are set and, basically, you can't do much about it.

Frankl was also a Jew. He was imprisoned in the death camps of Nazi Germany where he experienced things that were so repugnant to our sense of decency that we shudder to even repeat them. His parents, his brother and his wife died in the camps or were sent to the gas ovens. Except for his sister, his entire family perished. Frankl himself suffered torture and innumerable indignities, never knowing from one moment to the next if his path would lead to the ovens or if he would be among the 'saved' who would shovel out the ashes of those so fated.

One day, naked and alone in a small room, he began to become aware of what he later called 'the last of the human freedoms' — the freedom his Nazi captors could not take away. They could control his entire environment, they could do what they wanted to his body, but Victor Frankl himself was a self-aware being who could look as an observer at his very involvement. His basic identity was intact. He could decide within himself how all of this was going to affect him. Between what happened to him, or the stimulus, and his response to it was his freedom, or power, to choose his response.

In the midst of his experiences, Frankl would project

himself into different circumstances, such as lecturing to
his students after his release from the death camps. He
would describe himself in the classroom, in his mind's
eye, and give his students the lessons he was learning
during his very torture. Through a series of such
disciplines — mental, emotional and moral, principally
by using memory and imagination — he exercised his
small, embryonic freedom until it grew larger and larger,
until he had more freedom than his Nazi captors. They
had more liberty, more options to choose from in their
environment; but he had more freedom, more internal
power to exercise his options. He became an inspiration
to those around him, even to some of the guards. He
helped others find meaning in their suffering and dignity
in their prison existence.

In the midst of the most degrading circumstances
imaginable, Frankl used the human endowment of self-
awareness to discover a fundamental principle about
[humanity]: between stimulus and response, [we] have
the freedom to choose.[3]

✠ THE CHOICE THAT IS RESPONSIBLE:
'We have the ability to respond proactively'

We all have the ability to choose. We can either be
reactive or proactive. Stephen Covey says:

> Reactive people are often affected by their physical en-
> vironment. If the weather is good, they feel good. If
> it isn't, it affects their performance.
>
> Proactive people can carry their own weather with
> them. Whether it rains or shines makes no difference
> to them. They are value driven and, if their value is
> to produce good quality work, it isn't a function of
> whether the weather is conducive to it or not.
>
> Reactive people are also affected by their social en-
> vironment, by the 'social weather'. When people treat

them well, they feel well; when people don't, they [don't function well]. Reactive people build their lives around the behaviour of others, empowering other people to control them.[4]

Proactive people feel the affects of their social environment, take the 'social weather' into account and decide how they are going to deal with the conditions. Whether people treat them well or not, they do the best they can. Proactive people build their lives around their own behaviour, developing their power over themselves so as to exercise increasing control over their responses. It is only as people become less reactive and more proactive that they can actually become more responsible. As Covey says:

> Look at the word responsibility: 'response-ability' — the ability to choose your response. Highly proactive people recognise that responsibility. They do not blame circumstances, conditions, or conditioning for their behaviour. Their behaviour is a product of their own conscious choice based on values, rather than a product of their conditions based on [unthought-through] feelings.[5]

As people become less reactive and more proactive, they not only can become more responsible for being who they are, but also can become more responsible for being who they are meant to be.

As Covey says: 'I admit this is very hard to accept, especially if we have had years and years of explaining our misery in the name of circumstance. But until a person can say deeply and honestly, "I am what I am today because of the choices I made yesterday," that person cannot say, "Choose otherwise".[6]

A good example of a proactive person who 'chooses otherwise' rather than to complain, is Mother Teresa. As Katherine Spink explains:

> In 1948, as a solitary nun, she left behind her the relative security of the Loreto school in Calcutta and stepped out into the city's streets to live as one with the poorest of the poor and to found a new congregation committed to their service.
>
> Today, Mother Teresa's mission, which began so unpretentiously in some of India's most disease-ridden slums, is a universal one. The founding of the Missionary Sisters of Charity was only the beginning of a development which was to include a similar Order for men as well as women, contemplative branches of the two congregations, spiritual links with over four hundred enclosed Orders and an association of some 800 000 co-workers scattered throughout the world.
>
> Mother Teresa herself has become the reluctant holder of a string of honours, including that most acclaimed of all accolades, the Nobel Peace Prize, which she accepted 'unworthily' but 'gratefully in the name of the poor, the hungry, the sick and the lonely'.[7]

Social critic and political commentator Malcolm Muggeridge explains the 'great break' that set Mother Teresa on the road 'less travelled', developing community with those most forsaken by society:

> It was while she was teaching at the Loreto convent school in Calcutta that the great break in Mother Teresa's life took place. . .
>
> She had occasion to go into some of the very poorest streets of Calcutta — and where are there any poorer? — and suddenly realised that she belonged there, not in

her Loreto convent with its pleasant garden, eager school-girls, congenial colleagues and rewarding work. The only impediment to her new vocation was the happiness of happy relationships it required her to relinquish. It might seem strange to regard any religious order as an unduly easeful existence, but that was how Mother Teresa saw it in contrast with the lives of the very poor in Calcutta.

She had to wait for some two years to be released from the vows she had already taken in order to be able to go back into the world, there to take even stricter vows of her own devising. Ecclesiastical authority, I should add, is something that she accepts in the same unquestioning way that peasants accept the weather. It would never occur to her either to venerate or to challenge it. So she just waited patiently.

When at last her release came, she stepped out with a few rupees in her pocket, made her way to the poorest, wretchedest quarter of the city, found lodging there, gathered together a few abandoned children — there were plenty to choose from — and began her ministry of love. This act of superb — some would say outrageous — courage and faith made a particularly strong impression on me when I heard tell of it.

As it happened, I lived in Calcutta for eighteen months or so in the middle thirties when I was working on the *Statesman* newspaper there and found the place, even with all the comforts of a European's life — the refrigeration, the servants, the morning canter round the Maidan or out at the Jodhpur Club and so on — barely tolerable. Conditions then, in any case, were by no means as bad as they are today; for one thing, the refugees had not come pouring in from. . . Pakistan. Even so, they were bad enough and I always thought of the city as one of the [hard] places of our time.

Thus to *choose*, as Mother Teresa did, to live in the slums of Calcutta amidst all the dirt and disease and misery signified a spirit so indomitable, a faith so intractable, a love so abounding, that I felt abashed. Brooding upon it, I called to mind a particular incident which had greatly affected me at the time, to the point that it sometimes came into my dreams.

I was being driven one evening in my car when my driver knocked someone over — something as easily done then as now, with the crowded pavements spilling over into the roadway. With great resourcefulness and knowing the brawls that could so easily develop when a European car was involved in a street accident, my driver jumped out, grabbed the injured man, put him on the driving seat beside him and drove away at top speed to the nearest hospital.

There, I rather self-righteously insisted on seeing that the man was properly attended to (as it turned out, he was not seriously hurt) and, being a sahib, was able to follow him into the emergency ward. It was a scene of inconceivable confusion and horror, with patients stretched out on the floor, in the corridors, everywhere. While I was waiting, a man was brought in who had just cut his throat from ear to ear. It was too much; I made off, back to my comfortable flat and a stiff whisky and soda, to expatiate through the years to come on Bengal's wretched social conditions and what a scandal it was, and how it was greatly to be hoped that the competent authorities would [do something] and so on.

I ran away and stayed away; Mother Teresa moved in and stayed. That was the difference. She, a nun, rather slightly built with a few rupees in her pocket; not particularly clever or particularly gifted in the art of persuasion. Just with love shining about her; in her heart and on her lips. As for my expatiations on Bengal's wretched social conditions — I regret to say that I doubt whether, in any divine accounting, they will equal one single quizzical half smile bestowed by Mother Teresa on a street urchin who happened to catch her eye.[8]

Now it seems to me that the only way that any of us can avoid the regret of a Malcolm Muggeridge is by accepting the responsibility of a Mother Teresa.

I know there is only one Mother Teresa. And I know that we are all better off being first-rate characters ourselves rather than second-rate copies of somebody else. But those of us who would like to take 'the road less travelled' would do well to learn as avidly as we can from the pilgrimage of Mother Teresa, if not actually emulate the person of Mother Teresa herself.

My wife, Ange, is a Greek-Australian woman working with the Waiter's Union in the city of Brisbane. She has no desire to become an Albanian-Indian nun working with the Missionaries of Charity in the slums of Calcutta but, within our own environment, she seeks to find a way to put her guru's principles into practice and be as responsible as her guru is. For her, this level of responsibility involves a sense of vocation, a set of vows and a sacrifice of ourselves for the sake of others in the community.

✠ THE VALUE OF A SENSE OF VOCATION:
'We are called'

Carl Jung says, 'To have a vocation is to be addressed by a voice! We hear the voice. We are called.'[9]

This issue of her 'call' is something I know Ange has agonised over for as long as I've known her. She feels that there are so many voices emanating from television, radio and magazines that make claims upon our lives that it is very difficult for us to switch off the cacophony, sit in peace and quiet and listen to the still, small voice deep down inside, calling us to be the very best we can be. But over the years, somehow Ange has managed to not only get in touch with her call, but stay in touch with it, in spite of her many moments of doubt, desperation and despair.

Ange shares her call in a prose poem that goes under the challenging title of: 'Who of you will join me?'

There is precious little acceptance in our society
    of the changes in our bodies,
    brought about by sacrifice,
    by the giving of life to others.
People want us to look unscathed,
    unscarred,
    without the sagging in our breasts,
    the stretchmarks on our stomach,
    the lines of strain and struggle.
People want us to look ageless,
    timeless,
    with the model body of a young girl.
    With long flowing hair,
    fair skin,
    firm upright breasts,
    tight muscled tummy,
    slim thighs and long legs.
The image of the lithe and slender
    is what men lust for.
The image of what men lust for
    is what women strive for.
Where is the place for the beauty
    derived from love
    and developed through sacrifice?
Where are the people who will celebrate
    the signs
    of someone
    who has given

themselves
to others
through touch
in tears
with love
unnumbered times?
Who of you will join me
in forsaking the images
we idolise in our society?
Who of you will join me
in turning away
from the mirror
towards the door
that leads to the needs of others?
Who of you will join me
in the risk of being worn out
of being wrinkled,
of being thrown away?
We are not fools,
who give what we cannot keep
to gain what we cannot lose![10]

Viktor Frankl says: 'Everyone has [their] own specific vocation.'[11] And it is only as each of us heed that call we hear that we will be able to create a community world.

✠ THE VALUE OF A SET OF VOWS:
    'To liberate, to redeem, to transform'
Carl Jung says that, while our call may come to us in our own words, our 'vocation acts like a law of God. It makes demands upon us. It demands our best and, at times, even better than our best. To liberate, to redeem, to transform.'[12]

So it's not surprising that, though she hasn't joined an order, Ange has translated her sense of vocation into a set of vows. Taking a set of vows may seem a bit extreme. And I guess it probably is. But every time I've raised the matter with Ange, she smiles and replies, 'I'm simply trying to be moderate. But sometimes to be moderate you've got to be extreme!'

The first vow Ange has taken is a vow of *solidarity*. This has involved choosing to be open rather than closed to the suffering of those around us. It means choosing to see the tears, hear the cries and open ourselves up to, rather than closing ourselves off from, the agony of our neighbours.

The second vow Ange has taken is a vow of *simplicity*. This has involved living, in spite of our comparative wealth, as close as we can to the poverty line in our country. It has meant not only that we have experienced something of the struggle of the poor, but also that we have been able to share the extra time and money we've got with the poor themselves.

The third vow Ange has taken is a vow of *service*. It has involved living a life of quiet help and loud protest with many of the marginalised groups, both rich and poor, that find themselves on the periphery of our locality. It has meant not setting any agendas, but just being available to do anything we can to support them in their struggle for greater opportunity in our society.

Stephen Covey says: 'The key to the ability to change is a changeless sense of who we are, what we value and what we are on about. . .'[13] It is only as we commit ourselves to our vows that we will be able to create a community world.

✠ THE VALUE OF SACRIFICING OURSELVES FOR THE SAKE OF OTHERS:

'Without this surrender, community is impossible'

Carl Jung says: 'Any genuine personality will sacrifice self for vocation.'[14]

But for that process to be life-affirming rather than life-negating, as paradoxical as it may seem, self-sacrifice always needs to take place in the context of self care and self-control.

❑ The need for self care

At the centre of the creative use of self is self care. W. Bryan says:

> I am struck repeatedly by the degree to which people who are committed to 'good work', to making this world 'better' to live in, do not include themselves as valid environmental concerns. If you are saving the world and killing yourself [even if only by self-neglect], you will not be effective in your work. The people who you are trying to convince will not believe you. You can't abuse yourself and advocate that society not abuse the environment.[15]

Katrina Shields explains the process of exercising self care:

> It means, in the most simple sense, to attend to basic requirements — nourishing food, quality sleep, pleasant exercise and fresh air. However, taking care of ourselves extends well beyond this. Dealing with projects, people and challenges on a daily basis (especially if it is done under pressure, with uncertainty and few external rewards), slowly drains our inner reserves.

One way to 'top up' again is to nurture ourselves, perhaps by little treats and pleasures, deep relaxation exercises or meditation.[16]

Ange practices self care by maintaining a yearly, weekly and daily routine, with a range of interests that are balanced and a rhythm of involvement that is sustainable. Each year, Ange sets aside a month for relaxation and reassessment. We generally go away to stay at a friend's house in the countryside just out of the city. Ange takes the time to sit, drink tea, do embroidery and soak up the sunshine. During this time, she considers her options and sorts out her plans.

Each week, she sets a day aside for recreation and reflection. We generally stay at home, but make sure we have a bit of space for ourselves by taking the telephone off the hook. Ange takes the time to potter round the garden — planting seeds, pulling weeds and tending our ever-growing inner city rainforest. During this time, she measures her progress and monitors her priorities.

Each day Ange starts with meditating on something like *Something Beautiful for God.* Then, in the morning, she does some paid community work. In the middle of the day, like all sensible Mediterraneans, she takes a short siesta. Then in the afternoon she does some unpaid community work. She finishes each day winding down on our back verandah to the music of Wendy Mathews and Van Morrison with a variety of family and friends who may drop by for a while.

Now we all know what renews one person may not renew another, but we all need to find a way to constantly sustain ourselves if we want to continually use ourselves to create a community world.

☐ The need for self-control
At the circumference of the creative use of self is self-control. Elsewhere I have written:

> The essential problem in any situation of injustice
>   is that one human being
>   is exercising control
>   over another human being
>   and exploiting the relationship of dominance.
> The solution to the problem is not
>   simply to reverse roles
>   in the hope that,
>   once the roles have been reversed,
>   the manipulation will discontinue.
> The solution is
>   for people to stop trying to control one another.
>   All of us
>   to one degree or another
>   exploit the opportunity,
>   if we have control over another person's life.
> Common sense therefore dictates
>   that the solution to the problem of exploitation
>   cannot be through. . . controlling others,
>   but through. . . controlling ourselves
>   individually and collectively.[17]

Stephen Covey explores the process of increasing self-control:

> We each have a wide range of concerns (from the welfare of our family, through to the fate of the world).
> As we look at those things, it becomes apparent that there are some things over which we have no control

[and do nothing about] and other [things over which
we have some control and] can do something about.

We could identify the former as a circle of concern
and the latter as a circle of influence.

[Increasing self-control] depends on focusing our
efforts on our circle of influence and gradually expanding
those efforts to affect more and more of our circle of
concern.

We share in the spirit embodied in the prayer used
in Alcoholics Anonymous:

> Lord, give me the courage to change
>   the things I can,
>   the serenity to accept
>   the things I can't,
> and the wisdom to know the
>   difference.[18]

Ange sets as a goal and tries to practise self-control,
to refuse to control others or be controlled by them.
But as she would tell anyone who asks her, 'It ain't easy.'

She tries to deal with her desire to control others by
regularly writing a list of names of all the people whose
plans she would like to make for them, then ritually
blessing them one by one and letting them go.

She tries to deal with her tendency to be controlled
by others by constantly talking with the people who put
her under a lot of pressure about their expectations of
her and then carefully considering them, one at a time,
and deciding which ones to take on and which ones to
let go.

Like all of us from time to time, Ange is tempted to
feel that, in spite of all her efforts, the very things she
wants to do something about are beyond her control.

So she tries to increase her self-control by consciously bringing before her wide circle of influence — family, friends and work connections — her even wider circle of concern, which includes everything from the displacement of people groups all over the planet to the resettlement of migrants and refugees in our own backyard.

Along with a dozen or so others, Ange is a part of the West End Migrant and Support Group. With the West End Migrant Refugee Group, Ange takes on the world. They have sent relief workers all over the world — everywhere from Bosnia to Bangladesh, India to Cambodia. They have settled destitute refugees in Brisbane from all over the world — everywhere from El Salvador to Eritrea, Afghanistan to Vietnam. They try just about anything, from teaching the English language to people who don't know a word of it, to talking to the Australian government about people seeking assylum, to running bilingual support groups with torture trauma victims, to organising multi-ethnic employment programs with unrecognised, under-resourced personnel.

The amazing thing is not that many of these ventures have failed, but that so many of these endeavours have succeeded against all the odds.

Now, we all know what works for one person may not work for another. But we all need to find a way of managing ourselves, for the sake of others, if we really want to create a community world.

☐ The need for self-sacrifice

The creative use of self involves self-sacrifice. After years of often quite difficult experience with an intentional community, Art Gish wrote:

> It is important that we come to terms with our own selfishness. Unless we do that, our communities will be little more than reflections of the. . . society we hoped to overcome.
>
> It is not enough to reject the selfishness of the larger society. The condition of our inner selves needs to be transformed.
>
> Community is not based on the extent to which we see the community fulfilling our own needs or the extent to which the interest of the total community matches our self-interest, but rather the extent to which we give up self in order to live a new life.
>
> Without this surrender, community is impossible. Each of us brings with us our own agenda from the past, our different patterns of living.
>
> To the extent that each of us insists on our own way, community is impossible.
>
> Community is more than an association of independent individuals, for membership involves the very heart of a person's being in all its dimensions. One is not truly in community unless one is committed. Community always includes a price. It means giving up something else, being here rather than there, giving up other options.
>
> But the sacrifices are nothing in light of what is received. In fact, the higher the cost for us, the more valuable. . . community will be for us. Those who give little also receive little.
>
> The degree of success of communities is directly related to the strength of commitment in those communities.
>
> What we are talking about is a whole new world in which each individual lays down his/her life in love for each other.
>
> Renunciation of individual ego is no guarantee that a collective egoism will not take its place.

The selfishness of 'mine' and 'thine' can be exchanged for the selfishness of 'ours' and 'yours'.

So surrender, not only of each individual, but also of the total community is demanded.

Unless we are prepared to die for each other, we are not [able] to live for each other.[19]

Ange, like a lot of other people in community refugee resettlement groups, thoroughly enjoys her experience in resettling refugees. She enjoys meeting people from other places, making friends with people who wear life different ways and feels affirmed in her identity as a migrant by refugees.

But, like a lot of other people in community refugee resettlement groups, Ange finds resettling refugees often quite agonising.

She agonises over trying to relate to people well without a common language and trying to address the terror associated with fleeing their homeland in fear of their lives, and the trauma associated with arriving as strangers to make their home in a strange land.

As Peter Westoby, in his study of resettlement work, reports: the work is difficult, 'the commitment that's required is often demanding', the outcomes are uncertain and, as often as not, there's little appreciation and a lot of criticism 'behind my back, even when I've busted my guts for them'.[20]

So to continue to be involved with resettlement work requires sacrifice. Because the work is unpaid, it requires a sacrifice of money that might have been earnt to put the time in to help out. Because the work is unfunded, apart from a small grant which is not nearly

The personal dimension of community. . ./213

enough to meet the basic needs of the families, it requires a sacrifice of money that has been earnt to help offset expenses. Because the work is unlimited — any time, night or day, for weeks or months or even years — it requires a great ongoing sacrifice of the self for the sake of others. Without such sacrifice, resettlement of refugees, let alone developing community with them as people, would be impossible.

However, Ange would argue that, in spite of the blood, sweat and tears that they expend in their work, it is all very worthwhile. She would say it is worth the price they pay because they have been able to resettle heaps of people, start a support group, run a sewing cooperative and develop education and employment options, not only *for* refugees, but also *with* refugees themselves. And out of that process has emerged a profound sense of community with one another as people.

Now we all know what works for one person may not work for another. But we all need to find a way of giving ourselves, for the sake of others, if we really want to create a community world.

9

The social dimension of community development:

'Bringing people together'

SOME PEOPLE SAY, 'HUMAN BEINGS are a lot like crab-grass. Each blade of crabgrass sticks up into the air, appearing to be a plant all by itself. But when you try to pull it up, you discover that all the blades of crabgrass in a particular piece of lawn share the same roots and the same nourishment system.

As activist comedian Fran Peavey says: '[We]. . . are taught to think of ourselves as separate and distinct creatures with individual personalities and independent nourishment systems. But I think the crabgrass image is a more accurate description of our condition. Human beings may appear to be separate, but our connections are deep and we are inseparable.'[1]

Mike Riddell says:

Some people consider it demeaning to have a need. . . for anything else. They follow the illusion of autonomy. The teaching of the universe is that all things live together. Nothing is totally independent. All that has life is in relationship.

This is not a cause for resentment, but celebration.

The tree has need of the soil, the soil has need of the rain, the rain has need of the cloud, the cloud has need of the air, the air has need of the tree, and all have need of [all]. None detracts from the other and, in their harmony, they allow each other to be fully what they are.

Humans are intensely relational creatures. They need each other. They shrivel with rejection and loneliness, [but] flourish with love and affirmation.[2]

✠ THE POTENTIAL FOR CONNECTION: *'You are not alone'*

Gerard Dowling, a colleague of mine says: 'Community is created exponentially by undominated connectedness. It is more than the sum of the individuals. It includes the relationships between the individuals.'[3]

According to Fran Peavey, there is potential for connectedness with not just the few with whom we share an obvious and immediate affinity, but with all our brothers and sisters in the human family, regardless of the glaring differences and ongoing difficulties between us:

Those of us working for social change tend to view our adversaries as enemies, to consider them unreliable, suspect and generally of lower moral character. Saul Alinsky, a brilliant community organiser, explained the rationale for polarisation this way:

One acts decisively only in the conviction that all the angels are on one side and all the devils are on the other. A leader may struggle toward a decision and weigh the merits and demerits of a situation which is fifty-two per cent positive and forty-eight per cent negative but, once a decision is reached, he must assume that his cause is one hundred per cent positive and the opposition one hundred per cent negative. . .

Many liberals, during our attack on the then-school superintendent (in Chicago), were pointing out that after all he wasn't a one hundred per cent devil; he was a regular churchgoer, he was a good family man and he was generous in his contributions to charity. Can you imagine in the arena of conflict charging that [he was] a bastard, then diluting the impact of the attack with qualifying remarks?

This becomes political idiocy.

But demonising one's adversaries has great costs. It is a strategy that tacitly accepts and helps perpetuate our dangerous enemy mentality.

Instead of focusing on the fifty-two per cent 'devil' in my adversary, I choose to look at the other forty-eight per cent; to start from the premise that within each adversary I have an ally. That ally may be silent, faltering, or just hidden from my view. It may be only the person's sense of ambivalence about morally questionable parts of his or her job.

When I was working to stop the Vietnam War, I'd feel uneasy seeing people in military uniform. I remember thinking, 'How could that guy be so dumb as to have gotten into that uniform? How could he be so acquiescent, so credulous as to have fallen for the government's story on Vietnam?' I'd get furious inside when I imagined the horrible things he'd probably done in the war.

Several years after the end of the war, a small group of Vietnam veterans wanted to hold a retreat at our farm in Watsonville. I consented, although I felt ambivalent about hosting them.

That weekend, I had a chance to listen to a dozen

men and women who had served in Vietnam. Having returned home only to face ostracism for their involvement in the war, they were struggling to come to terms with their experiences.

They spoke of some of the awful things they'd done, as well as some things they were proud of. They told why they had enlisted in the army or cooperated with the draft: their love for [their country], their eagerness to serve, their wish to be brave and heroic. They felt their noble motives had been betrayed, leaving them with little confidence in their own judgment.

Now some questioned their own manhood or womanhood and even their basic humanity. They wondered whether they had been a positive force or a negative one overall. What meaning did their buddies' sacrifice have? Their anguish disarmed me and I could no longer view them as simply perpetrators of evil.

How had I come to view military people as my enemy? Did vilifying soldiers serve to get me off the hook and allow me to divorce myself from responsibility for what my country was doing in Vietnam? Did my own anger and righteousness keep me from seeing the situation in its full complexity?

When my youngest sister and her husband, a young career military man, visited me several years ago, I was again challenged to see the human being within the soldier. I learned that as a farm boy, he'd been recruited to be a sniper.

One night toward the end of their visit, we got talking about his work. Though he had also been trained as a medical corpsman, he could still be called on at any time to work as a sniper. He couldn't tell me much about this part of his career — he'd been sworn to secrecy. I'm not sure he would have wanted to tell me even if he could. But he did say that a sniper's work involved going abroad 'bumping off' a leader and disappearing into a crowd.

When you're given an order, he said, you're not supposed to think about it. You feel alone and helpless. Rather than take on the army and maybe the whole country himself, he chose not to consider the possibility that certain orders shouldn't be carried out.

I could see that feeling isolated can make it seem impossible to follow one's own moral standards and disobey an order. I leaned toward him and said: 'If you're ever ordered to do something that you know you shouldn't do, call me immediately and I'll find a way to help. I know a lot of people would support your stand. You're not alone.' He and my sister looked at each other and their eyes filled with tears.[4]

There haven't been too many divisions deeper in the psyche of our society in recent times than our conflict over that war in Vietnam. But Fran Peavey's story shows that, with care, even a pacifist and a sniper can find some common ground, in their humanity, in which they can flourish together as a family.

✠ THE CONNECTION THAT IS RESPONSIVE: 'Therein lies the hope for all humankind'

John and Denise Wood show how we can develop that kind of connectedness across the divides that arise in the context of the controversies we face in our ordinary everyday lives:

John and Denise Wood are known for their abilities to bring people together. The Woods' bespectacled faces — beaming with an energy that defies their thatches of grey hair — have become familiar to people of all walks of life across Pasadena.

As chairman of the City's Centennial Committee, John, 69, worked with all segments of the community.

As Director of the Office for Creative Connections at the All Saints Episcopal Church, Denise, 68, works full-time to improve the quality of life among Pasadena's diverse population.

With their aristocratic bearing and refined accents, the Woods seem a somewhat unlikely pair to be at home in the poverty pockets of town. But building bridges between different races, nations and political groups always has been in their blood. . .

John and Denise's vision is deeply rooted in a conviction that moral values are not human inventions, matters of personal preference or personal inclination. It is this spiritual conviction that is the source of power which underlies their activity in the city of Pasadena. Importantly, however, their conviction is seldom expressed in sectarian terms which would only divide rather than unite the diverse constituencies that they seek to mediate.

This vision has been [applied in four ways]:

First, John and Denise are *wonderful listeners*. This is true at two levels. Before embarking on a project they do their research, which is a form of listening to all parties who are touched by a particular issue.

But there is another level to their listening, which is what has enabled them to return again and again to people from whom they need assistance. A conversation with the two of them inevitably allows room for your personal hurts and concerns.

There is something very pastoral about their interest in people — or might one say very human?

Second, they *refuse to be confrontational*, even though the very nature of the political realm in which they are involved is, by definition, a struggle over power. Part of being good listeners is that they attempt to hear the concerns of persons on opposing sides of an issue and then appeal to 'the common good' in seeking a creative solution to a problem.

Political realists will find their approach naive. And where Saul Alinsky, for example, would organise a march or demonstration, the Woods would invite the opposition over to dinner. It seems like a strange way to do business unless one's vision of human nature allows for the possibility that deep in every human being is a desire to throw off the character armour that falsely protects us from fears about our own finitude.

Third, the Woods have a *bountiful expectancy* that refuses to accept despair. The net effect is that people around them seem to dig a little deeper and find the internal resources to work for common solutions. Cynicism is a word whose meaning they have never learned. They seem to hold a certain anticipation that people would rather do good than evil, if they can only be supported and nurtured in their struggle with the demons of compromise.

Fourth, John and Denise are *honest in their assessment* of people and issues, *but they avoid blaming*. Most of us criticise others because of the feelings of importance that it gives to us. The Woods seem to derive their power from another source. Their conviction and analysis of issues consequently have a ring of objectivity to them that provokes others to examine their motives before propounding personal philosophies and programs.

While not exhaustive, these four qualities of character and conviction are, I believe, the foundation on which the various projects described are built. The actual method of their work has focused on creating coalitions in which people can seek the common good in their city.

In many ways, their contribution to Pasadena has been to serve as the catalyst for bringing people together who share common concerns.

What they discovered repeatedly in Pasadena was that there is no absence of agencies or goodwill, but people from parallel groups often do not know each other, or else never get together to think more broadly about how their individual efforts might be combined to have a more strategic impact on the city.

The Woods' unique role was that they represented no interest group. They could think for the whole city. Their friendships with hundreds of people throughout the city, many of these friendships having been nurtured over leisurely dinners in their comfortable Pasadena home, enabled them to connect to each other people with common [aims] and moral commitments.

In addition, they were the moving force behind the formation of partnerships which empowered these individuals to seek higher aims than would have been possible had they pursued their own particular ambitions. They did not seek to engineer competitive agencies; instead, they sought ways to bring institutions and individuals into complementary relationships, which on many occasions involved interest groups joining together in common projects.

Denise Woods' career, and particularly her years in Pasadena, was not the result of careful planning, any more than were the achievements of her husband.

They were both very conscious that whatever they accomplished in and for Pasadena was the outcome of the organic growth of friendships developed with many people. Her latest project that opened up for her in May 1983 was the result of just such a friendship — one with Don and Lorna Miller.

Don is associate professor of social ethics at the University of Southern California's School of Religion.

When John and Don were serving on the vestry at All Saints Church, the idea emerged of the church making a major contribution to the city to mark the centennial of All Saints.

'I remember how Don came up with his idea of listening to people,' John recollects. 'The next question was how to figure out who would undertake to find out what people were thinking. Don had the idea that Denise was the one. The idea came out of the blue, but it seemed irrefutable. The next task was simply to convince Denise!'

In June of 1983, George Regas, the rector of All Saints, formalised Don Miller's idea and asked Denise Wood to take nine months to research the quality of life in Pasadena and to write a report on her findings as All Saints' centennial 'Gift to the City'. Regas made no suggestions as to how the work should be done, leaving that up to Denise.

Perhaps because Denise was a lifelong educator, she chose two avenues of approach. One was obvious — to study material already in existence relating to the city — and so she became a familiar figure in city hall.

The second was more original, for she chose to interview a wide variety of people, always one-on-one and by appointment, to ask them their perceptions of what it was like to live in Pasadena. With her tape recorder or notebook in hand, Denise tried to go with no hidden agenda of her own which she was trying to prove, but with an open mind and a desire truly to listen to what the other person wanted to say.

Those whom she interviewed often would keep her twice as long as the scheduled appointment; frequently, they urged her to go and see so-and-so. Denise took their advice and day after day continued her journey through every part of the city, talking with people of the most diverse background. . .

Every Thursday at an early hour-and-a-half breakfast in an office at the church, Denise had the privilege of meeting with three creative, unusual people who had generously agreed to become partners with her in this project — Lou Fleming, a gifted writer of editorials for the *Los Angeles Times* and formerly the head of the *Times*' Rome bureau; her friend Don Miller; and Denis O'Pray, a dynamic young cleric newly arrived on the staff of All Saints Church.

Together, this quartet reviewed what Denise had learned during the previous week and talked over what she should do next. Denise admits she was conscious that the three were busy individuals and it forced her to encapsulate what she had heard. But their intense interest in what she was reporting kept her energies from flagging and her sense of hope alive.

When George Regas first commissioned Denise on behalf of the church to start this research project, he said he expected her to summarise her work in a report. The deadline for submitting this report was coming up in February 1984. By then she had interviewed more than one hundred people and had a stack of notes and tapes. With the help of her three counsellors, Denise went urgently to work and completed the report in time to present it to a meeting of the church vestry.

As the four were finalising the report, the thought crystallised in their minds that there was an urgent need to continue Denise's work. For O'Pray, the commitment was to answer polarisation in Pasadena, but for Denise the imperative was to face the needs of its children.

Once, while Denise was driving with Miller and O'Pray down Orange Grove Avenue wondering together just what shape that continuing commitment should take, into Leon Miller's mind came the thought 'creative connections'.

'I realised,' he said later, 'that what Denise was doing was much more than listening to people. In the course of that listening, she discovered that a lot of people in the city did not know that others were thinking similar thoughts. So part of her role was as a kind of gadfly to connect people informally.'

And so it came about that Denise incorporated into the final section of her report to the church's vestry the proposal that they create 'an Office for Creative Connections' to continue the work of research, but also to draw together the many individuals and agencies she was finding who wanted to improve the quality of life of Pasadena.

When she had finished presenting her report to the vestry, they not only gave her a standing ovation, but enthusiastically approved her proposal. So the Office for Creative Connections came into being with Denise named its first director. The vestry also underwrote the budget, providing salaries for a director and a part-time assistant along with office space and services. Five years later, Denise looked back at this time and said, 'It is wonderful the way that this church sent us out freely into the community, waiting to see what would be the fruit of this effort, making no demands that the work fit a certain pattern.'

Published in book form under the title, *Experiencing Pasadena,* Denise's finalised report revealed Pasadena as 'a community in pain', as well as being the City of Roses. Poverty, hunger, homelessness, family violence, unemployment and substandard housing were powerful realities which Denise documented with anecdotes and statistics.

Through it all, Denise described what she called the 'green shoots of hope' — activities where the quality of care, leadership and commitment, much more than the dollars spent, made a crucial difference in bringing hope into people's lives.

There was a wide range of resources already active and vital to the city which Denise described, followed by two specific suggestions in the section, 'This We Must Do', where she focused on two imperatives she felt were crucial to the well-being of the city:

1. Pasadena must not be allowed to be a polarised city — one part poor and one part rich
2. The quality of life of all of Pasadena's young people must command the highest concern.

Denise concluded *Experiencing Pasadena* by making clear the ongoing commitment of the Office for Creative Connections which would have four major functions:

1. To *listen* one-on-one in order to keep aware of people's current perceptions;
2. To *connect* individuals and groups who, by better understanding each other's aspirations, could make a vital difference in the resolution of the city's problems;
3. To *speak* out on current issues related to the two imperatives outlined in the report; and
4. To *act* by bringing into being from time to time programs or enterprises to improve the quality of life of the city.

The Office for Creative Connections would operate in conjunction with many individuals and institutions who were already active and showing their concern for the quality of life of Pasadena.

Publication of this book catapulted Denise into public life, for it was widely circulated. Soon she was in demand as a speaker and her advice was sought by an increasing number of organisations and individuals.[5]

The connections she was able to make with people once she became so well-known enabled her to put influential and determined people of goodwill in touch with the needy. These ranged from the mayor of Pasadena and his staff at city hall, to a highly experienced social worker with a great deal of energy, to parents who had had children taken away from them, to a dynamic, articulate woman from the affluent end of town who had never had dealings with non-whites, to children who had suffered abuse. She was able to make connections between these people and encourage them to cooperate in important endeavours.

On the release of a new book by Denise Woods, the *Pasadena Star-News* on June 24, 1987 had this editorial labelled, 'Growing Up':

It is all too easy to despair about the world's woes over which individuals seem to have little or no control. The seemingly unending list of problems make it difficult to imagine that solutions to many of the most pressing social problems begin at home.

Denise Wood, the author of two reports on life in Pasadena, has zeroed in on as big a chunk of the overall problem as exists under one roof — children.

Armed with the cold, hard facts about modern society's most defenseless victims, Wood is confronting head-on the outmoded conventional wisdom with which society approaches so much of what is wrong in the 80s and is struggling mightily to bury the rationalisations by which so many adults choose to ignore what is undeniably a growing cancer threatening the very existence of the family.

Her primary tools for unearthing creative solutions to the underlying causes of gangs, drug abuse, teenage pregnancy, youth crime and joblessness are hard work and hope.

The messages of Wood's new book, *Growing Up In Pasadena*, are a direct offspring of the conclusions of *Experiencing Pasadena*, her first report on the quality of life in the city. Reminding parents that what happens to all children is important to everyone is an eternal verity to which too little energy and too much lip service is too often paid.

Growing Up In Pasadena is a clarion call for mobilisation in a time of bewildering fragmentation. Wood's timely exhortation for togetherness is itself part of the solution, for it reminds us all of the universal need to 'love thy neighbour'. Therein lies the hope of a brighter future for all humankind.[6]

Denise and John's response to the city of Pasadena has been a very inspiring example for Ange and I as we have considered what kind of response we ought to make to the city of Brisbane. This level of responsiveness involves *a sense of purpose, a set of goals, a series of roles* and *a sequence of protocols for relationships* with people in the community.

✠ THE NEED FOR A SENSE OF PURPOSE:
'Giving and receiving love'

I remember meeting with a group of people in our locality who felt something was wrong in their lives, but couldn't put their finger on what it was.

I said to them, 'Let's sit down quietly, try to visualise the situation for ourselves, then draw a picture of our predicament the best we can.' After they'd been drawing for a while, I said, 'Don't forget to put yourself in the picture.' They grimaced, but willingly made the necessary adjustments to the pictures they were drawing. When they had finished, we took a look at all their pictures, assuring people it wasn't a test, still less a competition, and reassuring them that what we were really interested in was not their technique, but their perspective.

I said, 'As you look at these pictures, see if there is anything that strikes you.'

'They're all stick figures!' they sang out.

'Apart from the fact they're all stick figures?'

'Everyone has drawn themselves very small,' said one.

'Everyone has drawn what we're up against very big,' said another.

'Anything else?'

There was a few moments of silence. Then someone

said hesitantly, 'Everyone has drawn themselves with heads. Maybe ears and eyes. But no mouths, no hands and no legs.'

'Anything else?'

There were a few more moments of silence. Then someone else said tentatively, 'Nearly everyone has drawn a picture of themselves by themselves. Even if there are other people in the picture, they are not connected to one another. They're all on their own.'

As we talked about the pictures, we were able to talk about the predicament they depicted in a way they hadn't been able to articulate before.

We discussed how overwhelmed we felt by the forces at work in our lives and how we felt unable to make any progress, not only because of our disabilities, but also and, perhaps more importantly, because of our inability to get our act together as a group.

After some time, I got a bunch of magazines, a pair of scissors and a pot of glue and said, 'Rather than just talk about the problem, let's see if we can work on a solution together. Cut some pictures out of these magazines and make a collage of the way you'd all like your lives to be in, say, five years' time.'

As you can imagine, it didn't take long for the group to devolve into the chaos of conflict and confusion — people fighting over who was going to use the scissors, which pictures they were going to put in and how they were going to paste them together.

At one point of time, it didn't seem like there was any hope they were going to be able to pull off the job at all. But gradually, ever so gradually, the people stopped yelling at each other, started listening to one another and began to work on the collage as a group. When it was complete, the group proudly displayed their collage.

It was of wall-to-wall people. People working. People playing. People singing. People dancing. People just being together. And I asked them some questions about it. 'Can anyone tell me what it's about?'

'Well. . . it's about us,' they said.

'What does this say about what you want?'

Everybody looked at each, a bit nonplussed about how to reply. Then an eccentric character with a serious intellectual disability, who is affectionately known for his daily rounds, friendly disposition and free advice as Doctor Rod spoke, in a loud voice as he always does, 'Evvyboddy-need-a-lot-ov-lov! Evvyboddy-need-a-lot-ov-lov!'

'Yeah!' they cried. 'That's right!'

'Yeah!' I said. 'That's right!' Everyone clapped and whistled and cheered.

'And,' I concluded, 'the way you've worked together today shows that you not only *know* what is right, but you can *do* what is right by one another. If all of us do the right thing by one another, you never know how things might turn out round here.' If we try we might be able to create a community world!

✠ THE NEED FOR A SET OF GOALS:
'Succeeding in marriage, family and community'
In order to enable people to move towards community, Ange and I believe we need to enable people in our

locality to move from dependence through independence to interdependence.

We meet with heaps of people in our locality and we talk about interdependence morning, noon and night. But often it is as if we were talking a foreign language.

Everybody's heard about 'dependence' — and they all despise it. Everybody's heard about 'independence' — and they all aspire to it. But hardly anybody's heard about 'interdependence' — even though we can't live without it.

Stephen Covey says:

> We each begin life as an infant, totally dependent on others. We are nurtured by others. Without this nurturing, we would only live for a few hours or a few days at the most.
>
> Then gradually, over the ensuing months and years, we become more and more independent — physically, mentally, emotionally and financially — until eventually we can essentially take care of ourselves.
>
> As we continue to grow, we become increasingly aware that all of nature is interdependent, that the higher reaches of our nature have to do with our relationships with others.
>
> On the maturity continuum, dependence is the paradigm of 'You' — you take care of me; you come through for me; you didn't come through; I blame you for the results.
>
> Independence is the paradigm of 'I' — I can do it; I can choose; I am responsible; I am self-reliant.
>
> Interdependence is the paradigm of 'We' — we can do it; we can cooperate; we can combine our talents and create something greater together.
>
> Dependent people need others to get what they want.

Independent people can get what they want through their own effort. Interdependent people combine their own efforts with the efforts of others to achieve their greatest success. It's easy to see that independence is much more mature than dependence. Independence is a major achievement in and of itself.

But independence is not supreme.

Nevertheless, [our society] enthrones independence. It is the avowed goal of many social movements — as though communication, teamwork and cooperation were lesser values.

Much of our current emphasis on independence is a reaction to dependence — to having others control us, use us and [abuse] us.

The concept of interdependence appears to many to smack of dependence and, therefore, we find people leaving their marriages, abandoning their children and forsaking all kinds of responsibility — all in the name of independence.

The kind of reaction that results in people 'throwing off shackles', 'asserting themselves', and 'doing their own thing' often reveals more fundamental dependencies that cannot be run away from because they are internal rather than external.

True independence of character empowers us to act rather than be acted upon. And it is an [essential] goal. But it is not the ultimate goal in effective living.

Life is, by nature, highly interdependent. To try to achieve maximum effectiveness through independence, [rather than interdependence] is like trying to play a tennis game with a golf club — the tool is not suited to the reality.

Independent people who do not have the maturity to act interdependently may be good individual producers, but they won't be good team players. They're not coming from the paradigm necessary to succeed in marriage, family, or [community].

Interdependence is a far more mature concept than independence. If I am physically interdependent, I am capable, but I also realise that you and I working together can accomplish far more than, even at my best, I could accomplish alone. If I am emotionally interdependent, I derive a great sense of worth within myself, but I also recognise the need for giving and for receiving love from others. If I am intellectually interdependent, I realise [that for] the best thinking I need other people to join with my own.

As an interdependent person, I have the opportunity to access the vast resources of others and to share myself meaningfully with other human beings.[7]

To enable people in our locality to move towards interdependence, Ange and I both concentrate on those activities in our locality that are most likely to help people move towards interdependence.

There are some matters that we consider urgent and some matters that we consider non-urgent. Urgency is all about pressure. Urgent matters require our immediate attention. Non-urgent matters do not. There are some matters that we consider important and some matters that we consider unimportant. Importance is all about purpose. Important matters require our earnest attention. Unimportant matters do not.[8]

We found that if we focus on urgent but unimportant activities, such as filling in reports and filing papers, we could get tied up in the office all the time, without getting anywhere at all, out there, in terms of the community.

If we focus on urgent and important activities, such as managing crises and mediating conflicts, we could run around putting out fires in the community, but get burnt out in the process.

If we focus on non-urgent and unimportant activities, such as daydreaming and nightclubbing, we could avoid the crises that need managing and the conflicts that need mediating and would be able to run around footloose and fancy free, without the slightest chance of suffering any burnout, only to see the community consumed by the fires we failed to put out in the process.

If we focus our efforts on non-urgent, but important activities, such as developing relationships and solving problems, there is still a lot of work to do, but the process creates a community that can cope with crises and deal with the conflicts as they come up. So we try not to indulge in non-urgent and unimportant distractions. We transact as few of the urgent but unimportant intrusions as we can. We act on as many of the urgent and important emergencies as we need to. But we focus most of our efforts on the non-urgent but important priorities that reflect and reinforce an interdependent style of operating.

We make every effort to nurture the relationships in our marriage, in our family and in our neighbourhood. Each day, Ange and I try to find time amidst the pressures of work to spend some time together early in the morning catching up with one another and the kids. Once a week, Ange and I seek to clear space to go out to lunch together on our own. And we both try to do something special with the kids on their own, like going out to see a movie, listening to a band or having a quiet cup of coffee.

Each week, I phone my mother who lives an hour away on the highway. And each week we visit Ange's mother and father who live a few minutes down the road. We clear time to meet our brothers and sisters on our side of town every week. And we meet our brothers and sisters on the other side of town every month or so.

I swap gossip and play tennis with my neighbours frequently. We regularly have meals with our next door neighbours who we've known for years. And our kids get together with all the other kids in the block, to do everything from rollerblading up and down the road, to running meetings for the community.

We encourage both the potential and the actual non-formal support networks in the area as best we can.

We are involved in the West End Waiters' Union, which as an association of residents in the Greater West End area that works towards community in the locality with more marginalised and disadvantaged neighbours.

Through the Waiters' Union, we are involved with home groups for ongoing spiritual encouragement, therapy groups for ongoing personal growth, protest groups for ongoing social change, project groups for ongoing community development and discernment groups for careful, reflective, collective decision-making with regard to crises or conflicts.

Through these groups, we are involved with a network of Aboriginal elders, migrant and refugee families and an extraordinarily creative mixture of individuals in our locality. We encourage not only non-formal support groups, but also formal helping organisations to work together in the area as best they can.

In the last few years, this has involved facilitating consultations between the Brisbane City Council and a representative community committee to consider town planning proposals and the threat of gentrification for the area, together; the organisation of the Southbank Coalition Of Churches to jointly consider, with Aboriginal leaders, an appropriate response to the threat of racism in our area; the formation of the West End Migrant and Refugee Support Group to jointly consider, with ethnic leaders, an appropriate response to the threat of deportation from out of our area; and we are involved in increasing collaboration between the Department of Social Work of the University of Queensland, the Psychiatric Services of the Queensland Department of Health, and psychiatric survivors themselves, with regard to the mental and emotional well-being of some of our more fragile friends in the area.

All this is a step towards interdependence. It is only as we move from dependence through independence to interdependence that we will be able to create a community world.

✠ THE NEED FOR A SERIES OF ROLES:
'Being amateur, radical and revolutionary activists'

In order to enable people to move towards community, Ange and I believe we need to enable people in our locality to move from dependence through independence to interdependence by playing a whole series of roles.

There are some roles that are *formal* and some roles that are *non-formal*. The formal roles are publicly recognised; the non-formal roles are not. Though one is recognised and the other is not, both are important. There are some roles that are *paid* and some roles that are *unpaid*. The paid roles are publicly remunerated; the unpaid roles are not. Though one is remunerated and the other is not, both are important.

By definition, there are no non-formal paid roles, but there are plenty of non-formal unpaid, formal unpaid and formal paid roles that play a very important part in community development.

Most community development work, like listening, talking and relating, laughing with those that laugh, weeping with those that weep and working your butt off for a friend is non-formal and unpaid. Some community development work, like liaising, mobilising and organising, training adolescents in life skills, counselling adults and children at risk and consulting with the local neighbourhood centre is formal and occasionally paid, but usually unpaid.

The bottom line is that the vast majority of community development roles that we need to play will earn us little recognition and even less remuneration.

So, in order to play these roles that we need to play, without status or cash, we need to become what I call, rather romantically, *amateur*, *radical* and *revolutionary* activists.

The *amateur activist* is a person who is a warm person. We may be a professional, but we are exactly the opposite of the stereotype of the cold professional, because our heart is on fire with a desire to help people meet their needs in any way we can.

The English word 'amateur' comes from the Latin word *'amator'* which means 'to love'. And the amateur activist comes to the aid of the community because of our commitment to love the community. Thus, we are willing to use our knowledge and skills to serve others, whether we get paid a lot, paid a little or paid nothing at all.

Ange and I have been involved in community development work now for nigh on twenty-five years working on developing therapeutic communities, temporary communities, testamental communities and integral communities in Afghanistan, Pakistan, India and Nepal, as well as Australia. And we wouldn't have it any other way. It's been a wonderful way to live — sharing our lives with others and seeing people grow as people in the process. Not the least ourselves.

But for half that time, some twelve-and-a-half years, we have had jobs that didn't pay us anywhere near what we could have earnt had we sold our knowledge and skills to the highest bidder. And for the other half of that time, another twelve-and-a-half years, we have had jobs that didn't pay us any salary at all! We have often had to get other part-time paid work, everything from being a car park attendant to being a social research assistant to pay the bills so we could continue to do the jobs that need to be done in the community that we would never expect to get paid for.

That's the way it is. If we want to do community development work, we need to be amateurs. Otherwise, we'll never do it at all.

The *radical activist* is not a person who is a single issue activist, but a person who actively makes the welfare of the people in the community the single most important issue we are concerned with. There are three types of possible role orientations that can be observed operating every day in the welfare work round our locality:

1. a *professional* orientation, which emphasises a preoccupation with expert standards
2. a *bureaucratic* orientation, which emphasises a preoccupation with departmental policies and
3. a *client* orientation, which emphasises a preoccupation with meeting the needs of the people.

It is common knowledge that most social workers tend to be more oriented towards bureaucratic concerns than professional concerns and more oriented towards professional concerns than client concerns.[9] So social workers and radical activists are not synonymous.

There are many radical activists who have done social work. But there are many social workers who would have to redo their social work if they were to become radical activists.

Ange and I both work for welfare bureaucracies as welfare professionals. And we are aware of how these commitments can skew our concerns away from the concerns of the people in the community we work with.

So we seek to 'offset' this tendency by three means: living in the locality, working for welfare bureaucracies as welfare professionals only part-time, and making a commitment to the people in the community. When it comes to the crunch, we will fight for their welfare against the welfare bureaucracies and welfare professionals that we work for!

Living in the locality we work in means we can relate to people as neighbours, not just clients or consumers. Working for welfare bureaucracies as welfare professionals part-time rather than full-time means there is less chance they will own us and more chance we will stand up to them, for the sake of others, if we have to. And making a commitment to the people in the community means that we are free to make their welfare the single most important issue we are concerned with.

When the crunch comes — and sooner or later it always does — Ange and I take a deep breath and try to figure out how we can take a stand that is assertive, not aggressive; strong, but gentle; ready to compromise as much as possible, but not at the cost of trading off the welfare of the people in the community. We don't always get it right, but that is our aim.

We've fought a lot of battles. We've won some and lost some. I've never resigned, but I've been fired a few times.

That's the way it is. If we want to do community development work, we need to be radicals. Otherwise, we'll never do it at all.

The *revolutionary activist* is not a person who builds road blocks to defend the bastions of one ideology against another, but a person who can break through barriers to fight for the disadvantaged in our community against the biases in our society which discriminate against them. This fight for the disadvantaged in our community begins with the revolutionary activist recognising the nature of the biases that dominate us and the degree to which everybody, including ourselves, is indoctrinated by them.

We need to recognise the biases that affect our choice of the *projects* we want to work on. Most people, given a choice, will tend to select nice, clean, predictable, high-profile projects first and dirty, smelly, unpredictable, low-profile projects last.[10]

We need to recognise the biases that affect our choice of *times* and *places* we want to work in. Most people, given a choice, will tend to select easy, accessible and convenient times and places first (like nine to five, Monday to Friday, in the office, in the suburbs); and difficult, inaccessible and inconvenient times and places last (like early mornings and late nights, over the weekend, during the holidays, on the streets, in the inner city, out in the wastelands, or on the city outskirts).[11]

We need to recognise the biases that affect our choice of *people* we want to work with. Most people, given the choice, will tend to select rich, fair, educated, influential people 'with potential' first; and poor, dark, illiterate, ineffectual people 'without prospects' last.[12]

These preferences are neither accidental, nor incidental. They are crucial choices that we tend to make that profoundly affect our degree of participation in the struggle to do justice to the people, times, places and projects in the community that need us most.

These preferences are reactionary. They not only *reflect* the dominant values of our society, but they also *reinforce* those values and contribute to the continuing neglect of marginalised human beings who do not count for much in the present scheme of things.

If we are to begin to do justice to our marginalised brothers and sisters, we need to reject the dominant values of society in favour of the liberating values of community. And to do so, we need to not only evaluate our preferences, but also actually reverse our preferences.

The revolution envisaged does not involve pitting the Left against the Right, but simply putting the first last and the last first. This process may be non-violent. But, in my experience, it is not without violence. The changes required are extraordinarily difficult!

In spite of the difficulties, however, Ange and I have tried to put the first last and the last first, literally, in terms of the people we work with, the times and places we work in and the projects we work on in the community.

We often find ourselves spending more time relating to people who have no friends than we do relating to our own friends, risking the relationships we have for those who don't have any. It is hard to get the balance right. We have meetings regularly with people before work, after work and on the weekends in order to make ourselves available when it's suitable for others. We meet at our place, at their place or any other place they may choose to meet, including the park.

It isn't always easy. We get interrupted all the time — even when I'm having a bath! And some of the places we go to are the pits — every slum I've been to stinks in the rain. As you'd expect, we get stressed, we get tired and we get sick. In the short term, it is hard to see any benefits but, in the long term, this approach benefits our new friends and gives us enormous satisfaction.

We consistently refuse offers to work on high-profile projects with big perks and consciously accept requests to work on low-profile projects with 'little people'. It's tough. Colleagues come and go. They come to get experience and go when they get the opportunity. Very few comrades stay. So we often feel like we're struggling for community on our own. We have often felt like chucking it in. But we've never been quite able to convince ourselves that it would be right for us to quit.

That's the way it is. If we want to do community development work, we need to be revolutionaries. Otherwise, we'll never do it at all.

It is only as we work as amateur, radical and revolutionary activists that we will be able to create a community world.

✠ THE NEED FOR A SEQUENCE OF PROTOCOLS: *'To touch the soul of another is to walk on holy ground'*

Nikos Kazantsakis pronounces: 'Happy the youth who believes it is [a] duty to remake the world and bring it more in accord with virtue, [love] and justice; more in accord with his [or her] own heart.'[13]

However, if we are 'to remake our world' and bring it more into accord 'with virtue, love and justice', into more accord 'with our own heart', those of us that are older know that, even if it is possible, it will not be as simple as we used to think it would be when we were younger.

Tony Kelly and Sandra Sewell tell us, 'Relationship is at the heart of community building.'[14] We know there is no other way to build a community world than for everybody to rebuild broken relationships with one another, painstakingly, one by one.

We must approach this task not only with great sincerity, but also with great sensitivity because, as Stephen Covey says, 'To touch the soul of another is to walk on holy ground.'[15]

Ange and I practise a sequence of protocols to help us relate to other people as reverentially as we can.

☐ The first protocol is civility to others

Civility is more than politeness. It is 'acting appropriately with people in a relationship'. It includes honesty and integrity, acceptance and respect, modesty and commitment, humility and confession.

All relationships with people depend on the practice of honesty and integrity. Honesty means 'saying what we mean' — 'conforming our word to the truth'. And integrity means 'meaning what we say' — 'conforming our troth to our word'. If we practise honesty and integrity in our dealings with people, all people without exception all the time, then the people we are relating to will have reason to trust us, because they can trust our word. Our word is our bond.

All relationships with people depend on the practice of acceptance and respect. Acceptance means 'recognising people as people just as they are'. And respect means 'regarding people just as they are'. If we practise acceptance and respect, it doesn't mean we will always agree with what people say or how people act. But it does mean we will always express our recognition of them as people and our regard for them as people, consistently, publicly and privately, whether we agree with them or not. Our trust may be conditional, but our love is unconditional.

All relationships with people depend on the practice of modesty and commitment. Modesty is the opposite of extravagance. It means 'promising people only what we are sure we can deliver'. And commitment means 'delivering whatever we promise'. If we practise modesty and commitment, people may not be excited about us, but they will be able to count on us.

All relationships with people depend on the practice of humility and confession. Humility is the opposite of arrogance. It means 'owning responsibility for any instance where we over promise and under deliver'. And confession means 'owning up and making up for any promises we break by under promising and over delivering in future'. If we practise humility and confession, we will create a context for people to count on us even when we make mistakes and, in so doing, open up the potential for developing the relationship.

Let me give you an example. Ange was in the habit of visiting some of the hostels in our area to befriend some people who didn't have many friends. On a Wednesday, she'd catch a taxi down to Boundary Street and wander round West End, dropping in on various women she'd got to know. Ange tries not to do on her own what she can do with someone else unless she has to because, by including others in what she does, she can involve them in her community work quite easily and naturally.

Well, one Wednesday she invited a few friends to join her in dropping in on these various women she'd got to know at a local hostel. When they arrived, Ange was treated like a long-lost friend. People ran out to greet her, hug her and kiss her and tell her all the latest hot gossip.

Then, when there was a hiatus in the excitement, Ange introduced the friends she had brought with her who'd been forgotten in the rush. As Ange presented them, each one was greeted with a guarded, quizzical stare that was in stark contrast to the way Ange herself had been greeted.

'You're not social workers, are you?' they were asked. The question hung in the air like an axe, ready to fall, should they fail the test.

'No. No. We're not social workers,' they said, hoping the answer would pacify the crowd, before someone lost their head.

'Then, what are you?'

'Well. . .' they said slowly, searching for an appropriate reply, 'we're like your sisters. We live up the hill and thought we'd come down with Ange today to get to know you.'

In the twinkling of an eye the scene changed completely. The visitors who'd been objects of suspicion up until then were embraced as relatives by everyone who'd always wanted a sister, but didn't have one — at least one who'd visit. So the visit was a raging success.

On the way home, Ange was listening to her friends, in the flush of success, talk about the visit. 'Did you mean what you said about your being their sisters?'

'Sure we did!' they gushed.

'Well,' Ange said to one of them, 'I know you're having a birthday party on Saturday night and that you're going to invite all your relatives. If you were really their sister, wouldn't you invite them, too?'

She thought about it for a while and, after more discussion said, 'I'd like to go back and invite them to my birthday party.' And she did.

Now that, for me, is what civility is all about.

❏ **The second protocol is compassion for others**
Compassion is more than civility. It's more than sympathy. It's more than empathy. It is actually interacting with people in such a way as to be able to transact their pain. It includes attending and reflecting, listening and speaking, grieving and forgiving, singing and dancing.

All relationships with people, where we can transact our pain, depend on the practice of attending and reflecting. Attending means 'not pretending, but concentrating, on the other'. And reflecting means 'not only understanding, but also communicating that understanding of the other to the other, in terms they can understand'. If we practise attending and reflecting, we will be able to create a space that is safe for listening and speaking.

All relationships with people, where we can transact our pain, depend on the practice of listening and speaking. Listening means 'not hearing superficially, but hearing deeply the pain of the other'. And speaking means 'not only talking about the pain of the other, but also, after talking about their pain, talking about our own pain, too, in so far as it relates to the pain of the other'. If we practise listening and speaking, we will be able to create a period that is free for grieving and forgiving.

All relationships with people, where we can transact our pain, depend on the practice of grieving and forgiving. Grieving means 'not struggling with our anguish alone, but working through the agony of the pain together'. And forgiving means 'not holding onto the rage, but letting go of the resentment and starting all over again, in spite of the pain'. If we practise grieving and forgiving, we will be able to create the possibility, believe it or not, for singing and dancing once more.

Let me give you an example. Our daughters, Evonne and Navi, make some effort to relate to people in pain.

Evonne has developed a special relationship with one local seventy-year-old we'll call Rita. I can remember my introduction to Rita. I was sitting quietly, having a coffee, when Rita came up to me out of the blue and said, 'Hey, mister. That's my place!' And, before I could say, 'Excuse me?', she pushed me off my chair.

The most dangerous place to be in West End is between Rita and biscuits after church on Sunday night. Before I knew her well, I was foolish enough to ask her to wait till everyone had eaten their first biscuit before she ate her second. What a joke! She just shoved me aside in a trice and stuffed her mouth with hands full of biscuits before the next person in the queue could get anywhere near the tin.

Needless to say, hardly anyone I know likes Rita — except, that is, for Evonne. Evonne obviously sees something in Rita that no-one else sees. And she loves her.

Each Tuesday morning before she goes to college, Evonne drops in on Rita. They put on their glad rags, put flowers in their hair and hit the upmarket coffee shop circuit round Southbank. Comfortably ensconsed in the Cafe Babylon, Evonne and Rita sip their cappucinos. And Rita scoffs her cheesecake. Now, if there's anything Rita likes more than biscuits it's cheesecake. And if, per chance, the piece of cheesecake is too small, Rita has been known to help herself to the pieces on other customers' plates.

Once they have eaten and the other customers have been pacified, they relax. Rita has an opportunity to tell her story and Evonne has the chance to join her in trying to make some sense of the existential distress she suffers. I think Evonne probably understands her friend Rita better than anybody else alive. It's not all roses. Evonne has had squabbles with Rita that have put her fights with her sister to shame. But often as they talk, they laugh and cry. And after they talk, they sing and dance. Not too many customers sing and dance in coffee shops.

But I know two who do. . .

Recently, I went for coffee with Evonne to the Cafe

Babylon. As we were shown to our seats, the shop assistant greeted Evonne warmly and then, as we took our seats, she said something I will never forget as long as I live. She said, 'It's nice to see you again, Evonne. I especially like it when you come in here with your grandmother.' I looked at Evonne as a tear rolled down my cheek and smiled.

Now that, for me, is what compassion is all about.

☐ **The third protocol is cooperation with others**
Cooperation is more than compassion. It's more than coincidence. It's more than concurrence. It is 'actually interacting with people in such a way as to be able to transact their hopes'. It includes communication and collaboration, trusting and risking, giving and receiving, and consensus, synergy and serendipity.

All relationships with people, where we can transact our hopes, depend on the practice of communication and collaboration. Communication means 'a dialogue in which all the people concerned can speak and all the people concerned can be heard'. And collaboration means 'some sort of ongoing negotiation that takes into account the hopes of all the people concerned'. If we practise communication and collaboration, it is possible to start to transact our aspirations.

All relationships with people, where we can transact our hopes, depend on the practice of trusting and risking. Trusting means 'believing there is a chance to do something about our hopes together'. Risking means 'taking the chance to do something about our hopes together when it comes up'.

We all know there are great dangers associated with trusting and risking. We should never trust anyone more than we have reason to. And we should never risk anything more than we are prepared to lose, in the short term, for a long-term gain. But the dangers associated with not trusting and not risking are even greater than the dangers associated with trusting and risking:

> To laugh is to risk appearing the fool.
> To weep is to risk appearing sentimental.
> To reach out is to risk involvement.
> To disclose feelings is to risk disclosing your true self.
> To place your dreams before the crowd is to risk their love.
> To live is to risk dying.
> To hope is to risk despair.
> To try is to risk failure.
> But the greatest hazard in life is to risk nothing.
> The one who risks nothing does nothing and has nothing — and finally is nothing.
> They may avoid sufferings and sorrow,
> But simply cannot learn, feel, change, grow or love.
> Only one who risks is free![16]

It is only as we practise trusting and risking that we are free to explore our aspirations together.

All relationships with people depend on the practice of giving and receiving. Giving means 'sharing something of our selves in order to do something about our hopes together'. And receiving means 'welcoming something of others, apart from ourselves, in order to do something about our hopes together.' We all know that it is 'better to give than to receive', but if we only ever give without ever receiving, it doesn't do anyone any good, because we never give anyone else the chance to give.

Receiving without giving constitutes exploitation. Giving without receiving constitutes manipulation. And both are experienced by people as quite dehumanising. As Jean Vanier says:

> We all belong to the universe;
>   we receive from it
>   and give to it;
> we are all parts of the whole.
>   People must learn
>   to receive from others
>   and give to others.[17]

It is only as we practise giving and receiving that we are free to explore our aspirations together as fully functioning human beings.

All relationships with people depend on the practice of consensus, which involves synergy and serendipity. Consensus means 'finding a way forward together, in spite of our conflicts, that we can all affirm what we do is in harmony with the hopes we have'. Synergy means 'we can actually find a way to make our differences work for us rather than against us'. And serendipity means 'what works out could be far greater than any of us would have been able to imagine'.

Scott Peck says that the essence of consensus is:

> A group decision (which some members may not feel is the best decision, but which they can all live with and commit themselves not to undermine), arrived at

without voting through a process whereby the issues are fully aired, all members feel they have been adequately heard, in which everyone has equal power and responsibility, and different degrees of influence by virtue of individual stubbornness or charisma are avoided so that all are satisfied with the process.

The process requires the members to be emotionally present and engaged, frank in a loving, mutually respectful manner, sensitive to each other; to be selfless, dispassionate and capable of emptying themselves, and possessing a paradoxical awareness of the preciousness of both people and time (including knowing when the solution is satisfactory and that it is time to stop and not reopen the discussion until such time as the group determines a need for revision).[18]

Stephen Covey says synergy is intrinsic to consensus:

Synergy is the essence. It catalyses, unifies and unleashes the greatest powers within people. Simply defined, it means that the whole is greater than the sum of its parts. It means that the relationship which the parts have to each other is a part in and of itself. It is not only a part, but the most catalytic, the most unifying, the most empowering and the most exciting part.

Synergy is everywhere in nature. If you plant two plants close together, the roots comingle and improve the quality of the soil so that both plants will grow better than if they were separated. The challenge is to apply the principles of creative cooperation which we learn from nature in our social interactions.

Family life provides many opportunities to observe synergy and to practise it. The very way that a man and a woman bring a child into the world is synergistic. The essence of synergy is to value differences — to respect them, to build on strengths, to compensate for weaknesses.

We obviously value the physical differences between men and women. But what about the social, mental and emotional differences? Could these differences not also be sources of creating new, exciting forms of life — creating an environment that is truly fulfilling for each person, that nurtures the self-esteem and self-worth of each, that creates opportunities for each to mature into independence and then gradually into interdependence?[19]

Stephen Covey says serendipity is latent in synergy:

You don't know exactly what's going to happen or where it is going to lead. Synergy is almost as if a group collectively agrees to [scrap] old scripts to write a new one. Could synergy not create a new script for the next generation — one that is more geared to service and is less selfish; one that is more open, and is less protective; one that is more loving and is less judgmental?[20]

With consensus, synergy and serendipity you just don't know. All I know, in my experience, is that almost anything is possible.

Let me give you an example. When our family and friends embarked on our experiment of community development, we didn't have a clue what the outcomes would be. We all just got stuck in and did the best job we could to communicate with people and collaborate with people as much as possible in areas of common concern.

One couple started a fruit and vegie co-op which people could do a bit of work for in order to get their provisions at less than half price. Another couple started a chook co-op which neighbours could get free eggs from in return for taking a turn at feeding the chickens for a week every couple of months.

Still another couple started a finance co-op which neighbours could join, to which people would contribute five dollars a month and from which people could borrow as much as they needed to pay their bills without paying any interest on their loan.

But Ange and I had one set of neighbours who wouldn't even acknowledge one another — and there was nothing we could do about it that seemed to make a blind bit of difference. The problem was, you see, that one bloke — we'll call him Barry — had some banana trees growing in his backyard which cast a shadow across his neighbour's prize vegetable patch. And the other bloke — we'll call Bill — used to mow his lawn at seven o'clock on a Sunday morning when his neighbour was trying to sleep off his hangover from a bout of serious heavy drinking the night before. As a result of this unresolved conflict, Barry and Bill hadn't talked to each other for ten years.

Each morning I'd get up, go into my backyard, see them working in their gardens side by side and say, 'G'day, Barry! G'day, Bill!'

And both of them would look up carefully so as to avoid any eye contact, say 'G'day Dave!' to me and do their best to totally ignore the bloke standing next to them at the same time. Barry and Bill wouldn't even give one another the time of day.

We talked to them about resolving the conflict many times, but neither of them would budge. Then one day, we heard the sounds of fighting — some swearing, pushing and shoving — that ended ominously with a loud thump. Then, after a few moments' pause, someone screamed, 'Bill's killed Barry!'

By the time we got there, it was all over. Bill was hanging over the fence breathlessly, staring at Barry. And Barry was laying, sprawled, in a heap on the ground. We ran to Barry to see if he was still alive. He was knocked out cold, but would live to fight another day. So we carried him upstairs and laid him on his bed to recover. When he eventually came round, I said to him, 'Listen mate, you could have been killed today, all because you don't want to shift your banana trees. . . You've got to sort it out, 'cause next time you may not be so lucky.'

Barry looked at me and smiled.

So I said, 'Be at my place tomorrow at three for a cup of tea and we'll sort it out.'

And he nodded. Then we jumped the fence and went into Bill's place. He was sitting at the kitchen table with his wife who was chastising him in no uncertain terms. When she'd finished with him, I asked if I could say something. She was glad to have someone else have a go at him. And he was glad to have someone else, anyone else but her and the fury of the anger that she'd vented, to contend with.

So I said to him, 'Bill, you could have killed someone today all because you want to mow the lawn at seven o'clock on a Sunday morning. . . You've got to sort it out, 'cause next time you could be in big trouble, they'll toss you in gaol and throw away the key.'

Bill looked at me and grimaced.

So I said, 'Be at my place tomorrow at three for a cup of tea and we'll sort it out.' And he nodded.

The next day at three, bang on time, Barry and Bill turned up. I invited them in and they sat down, looking about rather shamefacedly. As I gave them cups of tea, I caught their eye and said, 'Well, what are we going to do?' They said nothing — just shrugged their shoulders and sat there staring back at me.

'Well,' I said. 'It seems to me that we've got to try to end this dispute before it's the end of us.'

'Yeah,' they said, looking at each other for the first time in who knew how long?

'What do you think you can do about it, Barry?' I asked.

'I could cut down my banana trees after the next bunches ripen and replant them further away from the fence.'

'What do you think of that, Bill?'

'That's all I want,' said Bill.

'What do you think you can do in return, Bill?' I asked.

'I guess I could mow the lawn a bit later.'

'How much later?' I asked.

'Two hours later.'

'What do you think of that, Barry?'

'That'll do me,' said Barry.

'Well, I reckon we might be pretty close to a deal here. What do you reckon?'

'Sure thing!' they replied, looking pretty pleased with themselves.

'Then I've just got two final questions. . .'

'Shoot!' someone said, with an unfortunate turn of phrase.

'First question is, what are you going to do next time one or other of you comes home drunk?'

Barry said, 'We don't have to hang over the fence and abuse each other. We can go to bed and sleep it off. . . as long as people let us sleep it off, that is.'

'What do you think of that, Bill?'

'Fine by me.' he said.

'So you're both happy with that?' They nodded.

'Second question is, what if something comes up — what if you get into a bit of a scrap — what are you going to do then?'

Bill said, 'No worries! We'll just come over here, have a cup of tea and sort it out!'

'What do you think of that, Barry?'

'Fine by me,' he said.

And, from then on, they did exactly what they said they'd do. From then on, there were no more fights. After they bore the next bunch, the banana trees were cut down. The lawn still got mown regularly on a Sunday, but later, much later, in the day. In fact, the only sound I ever heard from then on, early on a Sunday morning, was the sound of Barry and Bill swapping handy hints with one another about their gardens as they went about their work side by side.

It is only as we extend civility, express compassion and develop cooperation that we will be able to create a community world.

10

The cultural dimension of community development:

'Can we all call our country our home?'

JANUARY 26TH WAS JUST A WEEK AWAY. I didn't have much time if I was to organise the barbecue in our street for Australia Day. As I crossed the street to talk to Spiro about having the party on the street outside his house where there is a bit of a natural cul de sac, I fantasised about the upcoming event which I hoped would bring all my neighbours — many of them first generation migrants from England, Ireland, Greece, India and the Philippines — together as Australians, one and all, on Australia Day.

At the time, it didn't seem very unrealistic. Most of us had sent our kids to the same school and used to turn up at the same school nights, where a kaleidoscope of kids from more than fifty different countries would regularly bring the house down at the finale by singing a stirring rendition of 'I Still Call Australia Home'. And none of us left without a tear in our eye.

But as soon as I ran my idea of an Australia Day barbecue by Spiro, I knew that there was no chance my dream for our community was going to come true that year.

When I asked him if we could have the barbecue in the street in front of his house, actually blocking his driveway for four or five hours, Spiro was more than happy to comply. Nothing was too much trouble for him. But when I asked him to come to the barbecue with his family himself, he shook his head slowly but surely and politely declined.

'Why won't you come, Theo?' I asked him respectfully, using the common honorific for 'uncle', as I could see the hurt in his eyes.

'I work for the council all my life and I know how Australians are once they have a few drinks.'

'How's that?' I prodded.

'If I bring my wife, she feels left out. She doesn't speak much English. If they hear her speak in Greek, they tell her, 'Speak in English!' When I say she doesn't speak much English, they tell us, "Go back to Greece!"'

'I've seen that kind of thing happen and it must feel awful. But,' I persisted, 'this will be different. We are your neighbours; you know none of us will treat you like that. And this is your street; you have the right to speak your language in your street. And my wife would be more than happy to speak to your wife in Greek.'

He just shook his head and said, 'No. You have the barbecue. You can have it in front of my house. But I won't come.'

And he didn't. We still have a long way to go before everybody really feels they can call Australia 'home' in our street.

260/The cultural dimension of community. . .

✠ COMMUNITY DEVELOPMENT MEANS
RESOLVING CULTURAL ISSUES:
'What we consider good and bad manners are important'

Community development depends on resolving the issues that revolve around issues of cultural unity and diversity. According to Ina Corrine Brown:

> Our culture is our routine of sleeping, bathing, dressing, eating and getting to work. It is our household chores and the actions we perform on the job, the way we buy goods and services, write and mail a letter, take a taxi or board a bus, make a telephone call, go to a movie, or attend church. [It] is the way we greet friends or address a stranger, the admonitions we give our children and the way they regard what we consider good and bad manners and, even to a large extent, what we consider right and wrong. . .
>
> All these and thousands of other ways of thinking, feeling, acting seem so natural that we may even wonder how else one could do it. But to other millions of people in the world every one of these acts would seem strange, awkward, incomprehensible and unnatural. These people would perform many, if not all, of the same acts, but they would be done in different ways that to them would seem natural, logical and right.[1]

Ferdinand Toennies asserts that these differences between 'us' and 'them' are so profound, it is only possible for 'us' to develop community within a culture, with people like 'us', not between cultures, with people like 'them'.

Toennies argues that while the quality of interaction required to produce a society involves only transient, impersonal, unidimensional, secondary relationships, the quality of interaction required to produce a community involves permanent, personal, multifaceted, primary relationships.

Toennies thinks that community is only possible for people who have blood, place and mind in common. Without the prerequisites of kinship, township and mateship, Toennies thinks we don't have a chance to develop community.[2]

Community, according to this perspective, is essentially *mono*-cultural.

Herman Daley and John Cobb contend that, while the differences between 'us' and 'them' are profound, it is still possible for 'us' to develop community, not only in a culture with people like 'us', but also between cultures with people like 'them'.

Daley and Cobb think that while the quality of interaction required to produce a community may be easier in homogeneous groups, those permanent, personal, multifaceted, primary relationships which characterise community may be broader, deeper, higher and wider in heterogeneous groups.[3]

Community, according to this perspective, is potentially *multi*-cultural.

✠ COMMUNITY DEVELOPMENT –
THE MONOCULTURAL OPTION:
'We must civilise the savages'

Australia, like most countries, has been resolutely monocultural in its community development until recently.

Anyone is welcome as long as:

* 'they are not robbing Australians of jobs';
* 'they do not lower the Australian standard of living (by imposing too much strain on our welfare system)';
* 'they import things (especially their food), which enriches our culture';
* 'they leave their own cultural tensions behind and do not import conflict into the Australian culture';
* 'they are largely assimilated (with some tolerance for the preservation of "quaint" ethnic customs)';
* 'they make the learning of the English language a top priority';
* 'they are prepared to embrace the Australian way of life'.[4]

This monocultural approach to community development at its best has still managed to be quite hospitable. But unfortunately, this monocultural approach to community development has, more often than not, been anything but hospitable and has, at its worst, been guilty, not only of prejudice, but also of genocide.

Indigenous people have lived in Australia for some 40 000 years. They dwelt in small extended family groups which constituted some 500 semi-nomadic hunting and gathering communities which travelled around the country according to the rhythm of seasons and ceremonies. When the first migrant arrived, there were about 300 000 Aborigines and islanders. After a hundred years of settlement, there were over three-and-a-half million migrants and barely 50 000 Aborigines and islanders left.

In places like Tasmania, the whole indigenous population was systematically wiped out, while in my own state of Queensland, indigenous people were either assimilated in an attempt 'to civilise the savages' or segregated as a way 'to smooth the dying pillow'.

The first voluntary migrants were English, then Scottish, Welsh and Irish, followed then by Europeans and Americans. This sequence of migration became a caste system that has dominated the cultural reality of the continent ever since.

Last century, during the gold rushes, many Chinese migrated to Australia, only to run up against a wall of anti-Asian hostility.

Early this century, the Australian government officially adopted what came to be known infamously as the 'White Australia Policy'. During this time, 'red and yellow, black and brown' applicants were refused entry to Australia, but more than a million 'whites' were welcomed as migrants with open arms. It is only in the latter part of this century that the White Australia Policy has been scrapped, the rights of indigenous people have been recognised and migrants have been taken in from all over the world, regardless of the culture of their origin.

Discrimination still exists. But now there is growing recognition in Australia that though there is one country, there are many cultures. So to be an Australian is to be multicultural, whether we like it or not.

This adaptation of an American article makes the point well:

There can be no question about the average Australian's desire to preserve their precious heritage at all costs. Nevertheless, some multicultural practices have already been incorporated into this ostensibly monocultural civilisation without anyone realising what was going on.

Thus, dawn finds the unsuspecting patriotic Australian male garbed in pyjamas, a garment of East Indian origin; and lying in a bed built on a pattern which originated in either Persia or Asia Minor. He is wrapped in cotton, first domesticated in India; linen, domesticated in the Near East; wool from an animal native to Asia Minor; or silk whose uses were first discovered by the Chinese. If the weather is cold enough, he may even be sleeping under an eiderdown quilt, invented in Scandinavia.

On awakening, he glances at the clock, a medieval European invention, uses one potent Latin word in abbreviated form, rises in haste and goes to the bathroom. Here, if he stops to think about it, he must feel himself in the presence of a great Australian institution; he will have heard stories of both the quality and frequency of foreign plumbing and will know that in no other country does the average person perform his ablutions in the midst of such splendour. But multicultural influences pursue him even here. Glass was invented by the ancient Egyptians, the use of glazed tiles for floors and walls in the Near East, porcelain in China, and the art of enamelling on metal by Mediterranean artisans of the Bronze Age. Even his bathtub and toilet are but slightly modified copies of Roman originals.

In his bathroom, the Australian washes with soap invented by the ancient Gauls. Next he cleans his teeth, a subversive European practice which did come to Australia until the latter part of the eighteenth century. He then shaves, a masochistic rite first developed by the priests of ancient Egypt and Sumer. The process is made less of a penance by the fact that his razor is made of steel, an iron-carbon alloy discovered either in India or Turkestan. Lastly, he dries himself on a Turkish towel.

Returning to the bedroom, he removes his clothes from a chair, invented in the Near East, and proceeds to dress. He puts on close-fitting tailored garments whose form derives from the skin clothing of the ancient nomads of the Asiatic steppes and fastens them with buttons whose prototypes appeared in Europe at the close of the Stone Age. This costume is appropriate enough for outdoor exercise in a cold, European climate, but is quite unsuited to hot Australian weather. Nevertheless, he sees his clothes as fashionably Australian.

He puts on his feet stiff coverings made from hide prepared by a process invented in ancient Egypt and cut to a pattern which can be traced back to ancient Greece, and makes sure they are properly polished, also a Greek idea.

Lastly, he ties about his neck a strip of bright-coloured cloth he bought which is a vestigial survival of the shoulder shawls worn by seventeenth century Croats. He gives himself a final appraisal in the mirror, an old Mediterranean invention, and goes to breakfast.

His food and drink are placed before him in pottery vessels, the popular name of which, 'china', is sufficient evidence of their origin. His fork is a medieval Italian invention and his spoon a copy of a Roman original.

He will usually begin the meal with coffee, an Abyssinian plant first discovered by Arabs. The Australian is quite likely to need it to dispel the after-effects of over-indulgence in fermented drinks, invented in the Near East, or distilled ones, invented by the alchemists of medieval Europe. Whereas the Arabs took their coffee straight, he will probably sweeten it with sugar, discovered in India and dilute it with cream, both the domestication of cattle and the technique of milking having originated in Asia Minor.

If our patriot is old-fashioned enough to adhere to

the traditional breakfast, his coffee will be accompanied by an orange, domesticated in the Mediterranean region. He will follow this with a bowl of cereal made from grain domesticated in the Near East and prepared by methods also invented there.

From this he will go on to bread, an Arabian invention, with plenty of butter, originally a Near-Eastern cosmetic. As a side dish he may have the egg of a bird domesticated in South-East Asia and strips of the flesh of an animal domesticated in the same region which have been salted and smoked by a process invented in northern Europe.

Breakfast over, he places upon his head a folded piece of felt, invented by the nomads of eastern Asia and, if it looks like raining takes an umbrella, invented in India.

He then sprints for his train — the train, not the sprinting, being an English invention. At the station, he pauses for a moment to buy a newspaper, paying for it with coins invented in ancient Lydia. Once on board, he settles back to inhale the fumes of a cigarette invented in Mexico or a cigar invented in Brazil.

Meanwhile, he reads the news of the day, imprinted in characters invented by the ancient Semites by a process invented in Germany upon a material invented in China. As he scans the latest editorial celebrating the greatness of our country, he will not fail to thank a Hebrew God in an Indo-European language that he is one hundred per cent Australian (from *Terra Australis*, a Latin term for the Aboriginal and Islander land in which he lives)![5]

✠ COMMUNITY DEVELOPMENT —
THE MULTICULTURAL OPTION:
'People should practise their own cultures'

Australia, only recently, has tried to be more multicultural in its community development. Like most countries, it still has a long way to go.

Most Australians are still struggling to come to terms with demographic multiculturalism — that is, the fact that the indigenous people of this country and the migrants to this country all come from a variety of cultures. Social commentator Hugh Mackay says:

> There seems little doubt that one reason for Australians' current reservations about the concept of multiculturalism is their perception that the racial balance of migration is shifting markedly towards Asian migrants and away from the traditional European sources of Australia's immigrants.
>
> The reality is that about four per cent of Australians were born in Asia. If the present trends in immigration were maintained, the proportion could rise to about seven per cent by the year 2021, according to *Australia's Population Trends and Prospects* (1990, Australian Government Printing Service).
>
> But the perception of the level of Asian migration is much higher than this, a perception which is possibly influenced by the visual evidence of large numbers of Asian tourists as well as Asian migrants themselves.
>
> It is the perception of the fast-growing Asian immigrant population that has most sorely tested Australians' willingness to embrace the idea of positively encouraging ethnic diversity. When confronted with an ethnic group which is regarded as being so obviously different from the Australian mainstream, Australians begin to wonder whether their multiculturalism can extend this far.[6]

While most Australians are still trying to come to terms with demographic multiculturalism, some Australians are trying to move on to social multiculturalism and political multiculturalism.

The advocates of social multiculturalism argue that

we should not only recognise the fact that people come to this country from a variety of cultures, but also value the fact that when they come to this country they bring their various cultures with them. The advocates of political multiculturalism argue that it is not enough for people to bring their various cultures with them. To have any impact on this country, they need to not only have a presence in this country, but also have some power in this country.

Some Australians believe the advocates of social multiculturalism and political multiculturalism are going too far. Researchers James Jupp and M. Kabala say:

> Multiculturalism in political terms means 'the acceptance of organised interests based on ethnicity as a legitimate element in the policy-making process alongside other interests'.
> [The] implementation of multiculturalism illustrates how democratic processes and the legal system in Australia can be circumvented by powerful interest groups.[7]

But some Australians believe the advocates of social multiculturalism and political multiculturalism are not going far enough. Aboriginal leader Pat Dodson says:

> If you listen to the rhetoric of multiculturalism, you hear phrases like 'Many different people fitting together to make a whole','the multicultural Australian nation'.
> The Australian nation state is always built in as the unifying concept before we start seeking diversity.
> As if the framework itself is unproblematic!
> In *Multiculturalism for All Australians*, it says: 'The council does not believe the encouragement of Australian cultures, including Aboriginal cultures, weakens the Aus-

tralian peoples' sense of identification, as long as they occur within the appropriate multicultural framework.'

Who defines 'the appropriate multicultural framework'? Not us! When the rhetoric refers to 'inclusion', we would ask 'inclusion into what?' And the unspoken answer is, 'inclusion into political and social structures which are themselves culture specific. . . and exclusive![8]

These criticisms notwithstanding, John Evans says, 'The principles of multiculturalism enunciated by the Australian Council on Population and Ethnic Affairs provide useful criteria for the change we seek.'[9]

These measures for balanced multicultural community development include ensuring *equality of opportunity and responsibility*, the *unity of social and political cohesion* and the *diversity of indigenous and migrant cultures*.[10]

✠ COMMUNITY DEVELOPMENT MEANS WORKING FOR EQUALITY OF OPPORTUNITY AND RESPONSIBILITY: *'Equity between people'*

The International Covenant on Civil and Political Rights, to which Australia and many other countries are signatories, asserts the rights of all peoples to include:

* their culture, language and religion;
* their security as people, individually and collectively;
* their liberty of expression, movement, association and assembly;
* their equal treatment, with others, under the law; and
* their equal participation, with others, in society.[11]

All of us who are committed to community should advocate these human rights and the opportunities and responsibilities that they represent.

Among the most well-known and most well-loved of all the advocates of human rights in Australia was the late Fred Hollows.

The irrepressible and irascible 'wild colonial boy of Australian surgery', as Tom Keneally once called him, set a pace that it would be very difficult for the rest of us to keep up with, but he set a lead along a path of practical, personal and social justice that we refuse to follow at our own peril. In his autobiography, Fred reflected on the path he had taken:

> Some years ago, a friend sent me a card with a snatch
> of verse, attributed to Ralph Waldo Emerson, on it.
> I put it on my office wall. It goes:
>
>> To laugh often and much.
>> To win the respect of intelligent people
>>   and the affection of children.
>> To earn the appreciation of honest critics
>>   and to endure the betrayal of false friends.
>> To appreciate beauty.
>> To find the best in others.
>> To leave the world a bit better,
>> whether by
>>   a healthy child,
>>   a garden patch,
>>   or a redeemed social condition.
>> To know even one life has breathed easier
>>   because you lived —
>>   this is to have succeeded.
>
> I regard that as a pretty good summary of what life
> is all about. Evaluating my own life in those terms,

I've had some mixed results. I've hurt some people and disappointed others, but I hope that, on balance, I've given more than I've taken. I believe that my view of what a 'redeemed social condition' is has been consistent equity between people and I've tried always to work to that end. . .

In 1968, Frank Hardy published *The Unlucky Australians*, his book on the strike by the Gurindjis at Wave Hill cattle station in the Northern Territory. I'd read his *Power Without Glory* when I was a student in New Zealand, so I was interested to hear that he was talking on the subject of the blacks' strike at the Teachers' Federation in Sussex Street. I went along and I found him a very persuasive speaker. When he asked donations at the end of the meeting I passed in a cheque for $300. They thought it was a bit iffy, never having got a donation of that size before. I told them I was an eye doctor at the Prince of Wales, wrote my name on the back and that was all right. The next week someone from the committee Frank was on rang me and asked me if I'd take a look at two Gurindji men who seemed to have eye trouble.

Donald Nangiari and Vincent Lyngian came along to the clinic. They had three working eyes between them and a lot of problems, some cataract, blocked ducts with regurgitated pus and signs of trachoma. They also had a strange hazing of the cornea, hazing in a place which is exposed when the eyelids are open and is normally clear. I'd never seen it before and I called in Roger McGuinness to take a look. In Australia, Roger had only practised in Sydney and he'd never seen an Aborigine before as a patient. (Neither had I.) Roger took a look, thought for a second and said, 'That's Labrador keratopathy.'

As soon as he said it I knew he was right. I'd read about Labrador keratopathy, but I'd never seen it and never expected to see it. It turned out that Roger had worked in London with an eye man who'd spent some time in Labrador and seen this condition. It had also been described for Africa. It's a function of the reflection of ultraviolet light from snow or sand.

I thought this was interesting — the first time the condition had been detected in Australia. My interest was still basically scientific then. I'd read a bit about the plight of the Aborigines, but I hadn't taken much of it in. I'd assumed it was a variety of the Maori story where the people had been dispossessed of their land by stealth after a treaty, or something such. I didn't know anything about the doctrine of *terra nullius*, the handy British idea that the land had been unoccupied.

But when the Gurindji committee told me they were taking Donald and Vincent back to the Northern Territory and there were some seats on the planes for a few doctors who were willing to make themselves useful, I jumped at the chance to go. Barry Pascoe, who was an endocrinologist and general physician and Ferry Grundseit, a pediatrician, were interested, so we flew up to the Gurindji camp. It took us three days to get there.

Just before we turned in, Vincent asked me what I wanted to do in the morning and I said I wanted to see all the grown men in the camp. We slept the first night under a tarpaulin, all in together — pilots, a nurse, the lot — and it was mayhem. This was the Watti Creek camp. The bloody dogs fought all night and ran over us and I'd had hardly any sleep when Vincent woke me up with a gentle shake on the shoulder.

'Fred,' he says, 'the men are ready.'

About twenty or thirty men were sitting quietly under a shelter waiting. I got my magnifiers on and went over and had a look at them. Every man who'd been a stockman for any length of time had Labrador keratopathy. It was cattle camp country and the stockmen worked long hours in the daylight. Their hats didn't protect them from this scatter of reflected light from the ground. It wasn't a blinding condition, but it impaired sight. As well, there were cataracts that were blinding them and signs of advanced trachoma. . .

The next day I saw all the women. The day after that all the children. They were free of the hazy cornea condition, because they weren't obliged to work in the sun all day, but the women had a lot of cataract and trachoma and there were signs of the juvenile forms of trachoma in most of the children.

Corneal blindness from prolonged trachoma is the end of the road. Trachoma has two stages follicular, indicated by the presence of small white or creamy objects (collections of white blood cells) found inside the conjunctiva, and cicatricial, referring to the scarring and other damage to the eyelids and eye. When trachoma reaches its vision-threatening stage, characterised by in-turned upper eyelashes and ulceration, it is a very painful condition.

It was a shock to me. I'd been working at the hospital and in my private practice and seen a parade of eye disorders, but nothing like this. I thought I'd seen every sick eye condition there was to be seen, but I was wrong. It was like something out of the medical history books — eye diseases of a kind and degree that hadn't been seen in Western society for generations! The neglect this implied, the suffering and wasted quality of human life were appalling.

I went wild, walked over to Wave Hill station and virtually commandeered the radio. I got on to Darwin and demanded that they send a doctor down to look at this situation. . .

Not long after I'd been quoted in the press as saying that the discrepancy between rural and metropolitan health care in Australia was a scandal, Ross McKenna from the French Department of the University of New South Wales began sending me notes inviting me to attend a meeting of the Redfern Aboriginal Legal Service.

I knew that the university had helped to set up a sort of shopfront legal centre for blacks in Redfern (along the lines of some of the services set up by the Black Panthers and others in the States), but legal matters bore me to tears, so I hadn't taken any particular interest. However, Ross was very persistent; his notes pursued me all over the university and the hospital and one Friday night, after a bit of a drinking session at the pub, I decided to go along and see what it was all about.

After some toing-and-froing — Redfern was unfamiliar territory to me then — I got to the meeting. I took a seat and prepared to be bored for a while. It was a small group — two or three whites, three or four Aborigines — and, to my surprise, they were talking about medical matters. There were no doctors, maybe a nurse in the group; I was the only medico present and it was impossible not to be interested in what they were saying in general and in particular.

In general, the legal service was getting swamped by people with a whole range of social and medical problems. In particular, they were talking about a case in which a sick Aborigine had died in the back of Gordon Briscoe's car. Gordon Briscoe was a field officer with the legal service. He is an Aborigine from the Centre and not many people have had a more profound influence on my life than him. At that time, he was one of the very few Aborigines in Sydney who had a car, an old Volkswagen.

Briscoe was at the meeting along with Shirley Smith, 'Mumshirl', who's done a lot for Aborigines over more than thirty years, and Gary Foley; and they asked me if I could help them set up a medical service for blacks. I said that whatever lawyers could do doctors could do and I agreed to talk to a few people.

Next Friday, there was another meeting, better attended. The Aborigines started to outline the case for a medical service and they were utterly convincing:

blacks weren't welcome in doctors' surgeries, they got pushed to the back of the line in casualty wards and public hospital clinics and so on. Paul Beaumont stood up and he said, 'You only need six things to start a medical service. Doctors (Fred and I can get the doctors); premises (Len Russells can organise that); Aboriginal receptionists and managers (Shirley Smith can find them); publicity in the pubs and shops (Ross McKenna can do that); and transport (Eddie Newman can handle that).

Everyone there saw that he was right and they got very excited. Someone said, 'When can we start?' Someone else said, 'Monday night.' I said, 'Whoa, it might take a bit longer than that.'

But, in fact, we opened just ten days later. One of the first things I did was to check out the one doctor in the area who the Aborigines had any time for. I had to make sure that our service wasn't going to bugger up something that was already in existence. I went to see this doctor who said that he paid calls on Aborigines and collected the tiny fee the government paid GPs for services to 'indigent persons'. It was next to nothing. He admitted that he didn't see blacks in his surgery because, if he did, the whites wouldn't come and the practice would go broke. He said that a medical service for blacks would be the best thing possible.

So we went ahead. We plundered the Prince of Wales Hospital for equipment — stethoscopes, thermometers, scales, all the accoutrements of a medical practice we shamelessly stole. And we learnt as we went along. I remember seeing a man early in the piece, deciding what he needed and writing out a script.

He said, 'What's this, doc?'

'Take it to a chemist and you'll get the medicine.'

He shook his head. 'No money, doc.'

We backed a truck up to the pharmacy at the hospital and loaded it half full — tens of thousands of dollars worth of pharmaceuticals.

It wasn't always a matter of clandestine raids; there were some sympathetic people around. Pretty soon we had more doctors, GPs, specialists, professors of this and that volunteering their services than we could handle. The medical service was a great success and there are more than sixty of them now Australia-wide, in the cities and in country towns, all owing something to that original model and the principles on which it was based.

One of the most important of those principles was that the Aborigines staffed and managed it to the fullest extent possible.[12]

✠ COMMUNITY DEVELOPMENT MEANS WORKING FOR UNITY AND DIVERSITY: *'The best of both worlds'*

The *assimilative* among us, who are pro-majority and anti-minority in terms of relating to other cultures, would tend to say that 'the majority culture is good and minority cultures should adjust to the majority culture'.

The *disassociative* among us, who are anti-majority and pro-minority in terms of relating to other cultures, would tend to say that 'minority cultures are good and the majority culture should adapt to minority cultures'.

The *acculturative* among us, who are both pro-majority and pro-minority in terms of relating to other cultures, would tend to say that 'both the majority culture and minority cultures are good, and we need to work out a way forward, together, which combines the best of both worlds'.

The *disconnected* among us, who are both anti-majority and anti-minority in terms of relating to other cultures, would probably say, 'To hell with everybody!'

If we are 'assimilative', we will not be able to work for true diversity in the community, because everything we do will tend towards the ethnocentric hegemony of the majority culture.

If we are 'disassociative', we will not be able to work for true unity in the community, because everything we do will tend towards the ethnocentric fragmentation of minority cultures.

If we are 'disconnected', we will not be able to work for either true unity or true diversity, because everything we do will tend to be a counter-productive projection of our egocentric preoccupations.

It is only if we are 'acculturative', committed simultaneously to the good of both majority and minority cultures and the need to work out a way forward together that combines the best of both worlds, that we can work towards true unity and true diversity between the cultures in the community.[13]

This acculturative approach is currently best demonstrated in Australia by Mandawuy Yunupingu, the leader of the rock band, Yothu Yindi.

When most of us think of this indigenous rock band from northeast Arnhem Land at the Top End of Australia, we immediately think of 'the successful fusion of didgeridoo and clapsticks with synthesizer and sampler' that put Aboriginal music, including lyrics from an Aboriginal language, on the radio all round the world.

But Mandaway Yunupingu and Yothu Yindi are concerned with a lot more than entertainment:

When the dance music remix of Yothu Yindi's 'Treaty'

finally burst into the Australian top twenty, the sound of consciences being salved was almost audible. For years, there had been veiled accusations of racism aimed at the Australian music industry, particularly commercial radio, concerning the lack of recognition given to Aboriginal musicians.

Suddenly, those accusations seemed to have less substance; a round of communal back-slapping ensued and the band's commercial success was followed by a plethora of awards for the single, its accompanying video clip and the album from which it was taken, *Tribal Voice*.

For Yothu Yindi's leader, Mandawuy Yunupingu, this recognition is just reward for years of hard work and determination. Essentially optimistic, you get the impression he always felt commercial success was just around the next corner, despite the lack of precedents. Yet Mandawuy's outlook hasn't always been so positive.

'In my time I've been without hope, ' he says. 'I was angry, I got into fights. I've turned to drinking, I've been locked up. . . But I've changed now because I know my family is really strong and powerful. Instead of being angry and turning away, I'd rather challenge and find a positive solution.'

The family Mandawuy refers to is indeed strong, both spiritually and politically.[14]

'Yeah, I got a big family. Got one mother, two sisters and a brother,' Mandawuy recalls. 'But I got a lot more brothers in a bigger sense. My father had something like twelve wives, so there's really a big family structure there.'

Mandawuy's family is a remarkable one. His mother? 'She gave me a lot of insight into life. My mother taught me honesty, taught me all those behaviours one should have in order to be proud, in order to have a good solid basis to operate from.'

His father took on the tribal responsibilities in his early forties and imbued in his children not only a strong sense of kinship, but also strong political beliefs as the leader of the first land rights protest. He was into making sure that his tribe's pattern of living was always there, that it wasn't lost. That was the sense of leadership he gave us. And then he balanced that with the view of wanting to develop his ability to live in a contemporary sense.

In 1963, Mandawuy's father, Munggarawuy Yunupingu, led the Gumatj clan in protest over the mining of bauxite on their land. They sent a bark painting outlining their concerns to the politicians in Canberra, asking that the miners leave. His father's political action made a strong impression on Mandawuy as a child. 'That was the biggest political milestone for me,' says Mandawuy. 'I saw him operate, the way he talked with men in power. . . And he talked to us, to the family, about the important things of how not to sell out, how to be strong.'

Unfortunately, their protest was unsuccessful. 'Of course, he lost that case when he took it to the High Court, but then Mabo turned it around.'

His sons did not forget their father's protest. In fact, the broken promises of past governments are the subject of Yothu Yindi's hit song, 'Treaty'.

And Mandawuy's brother, Galarrwuy Yunupingu, who also provides vocals on a track on *Tribal Voice*, today carries on his father's political work as chairman of the Darwin-based Northern Land Council, which represents more than 20 000 traditional landowners.[15]

For his part, Mandawuy decided the future of his people lay in education. He became the first Aboriginal university graduate from his region of Gove and is now the principal of the Yirrkala school, where he's pioneering a curriculum that emphasises both *Yolngu* (Aboriginal) and *Balanda* (European) learning.

This marriage of cultures is typical of the approach taken by Mandawuy and his Gumatj clan. Mandawuy is neither militant nor separatist; rather, he's a realist who believes that retaining Aboriginality does not mean rejecting the best of what other cultures have to offer. This is reflected not only in Mandawuy's approach to education and politics, but also to music and technology.

'These days we're doing more compromising in terms of cultural situations — and you've got to do it because you're dealing with the commercial aspects of the music industry. As long as our values, beliefs and principles remain intact — and I reckon we've got the strength to do that — then I think that's the way to go. We may have made some compromises, but we've retained the essence, our *Yolngu* integrity is not being threatened. In fact, we're enriching our culture.'[16]

These days, Mandawuy has his own family to look after. He and his wife have six children, all girls, aged five to thirteen. 'I like their company,' Mandawuy says proudly of his daughters. 'They are sweet girls, my girls.' Many of the things he wishes for them seem remarkably similar to the aspirations his own parents had for him. 'I would like to give them a little bit of balance in their life,' he says. 'That is what I am striving to formulate for them in a way that they will grow with strength. I want to give them every possible way that is not going to be hard for them. This is what I am trying to do — open those barriers so they grow up with the best of both worlds.'

It seems impossible to overestimate the importance of family, or kinship, within Aboriginal society. Indeed, its entire social framework is based on kinship, a kinship of opposites similar to the Eastern Yin and Yang symbols.

'Everything in the Aboriginal world is divided into two aspects of reality,' says Mandawuy. 'There is the *yindi* and *yothu*, the *yothu* and the *yindi*. They say mother earth is *yindi* and *yothu* are the people her children. That's what we follow, that's what constitutes our law. And it's how we structure our pattern of living.

'My family is the Gumatj people. Everyone is related, everyone has an identity that is kinship. For me, I am the hawk, the crocodile and the kangaroo.' These symbols tie the individual to the family and environment.

'It's about living and sharing. And it's that sharing bit that is an important part of Aboriginal existence. Sharing is part of family involvement and participation, whether it be hunting and gathering together or uniting for a special ceremony. All these things make us think about how important family is and how important tribal connections are.

'Dad gave me encouragement to keep up our law, so that it doesn't wither away by other forces,' recalls Mandawuy. 'That's probably been my basic motivation; to defend my existence and make sure that freedom is there always for my people.'

With the very basis of Aboriginal life defined in terms of a mother-child relationship, it is easy to understand how important family is within that society. It is equally easy to see its significance to Manduway, for the name he has chosen for his band, Yothu Yindi, says it all.

Indeed, the band seems to operate like a large family itself. Many of the members are related and several have been 'adopted' by the lead singer as brothers. But the impression of the band as 'family' extends even further than just closeness: they actually operate under the same kind of principles that govern their whole society.

'When you start to live with people, you start to understand one another's differences and respect for their differences and you try to live like this,' says Mandawuy. The way we have managed to structure our existence in Yothu Yindi is by applying things that are relevant, things that we believe should be part of today's society. Living with one another is one of those things. Not living with racism, not living with negative parts; they are the types of things we commonly reject. The momentum is to take what we think is the right way and change attitudes.'

One day, he hopes, those attitudes will have changed sufficiently for black and white Australia to have reached reconciliation. And he believes that the Aboriginal notion of kinship, of *yothu yindi*, is what is needed to achieve that aim.

'I'd like to formulate the *yothu yindi* kinship, that sort of pattern', he says. 'If they [the rest of the country] could relate to that, then *Bang!*, we've got a big family!'[17]

✠ COMMUNITY DEVELOPMENT MEANS GETTING OUR ACT TOGETHER AS A COMMUNITY: *'Becoming friends, even with our enemies'*

Lois O'Donoghue, chairperson of the Aboriginal and Torres Strait Islander Commission in Australia, sees our task as exercising what she calls 'wise counsel' in everything we do, in order to do everything we can to 'bring together [separate] parts of [our] family'.[18]

The Port Augusta story is a good example of precisely what Lois O'Donaghue is talking about:

Port Augusta, in South Australia's 'iron triangle', has traditionally been considered by South Australians to be an archetype of racial conflict. Much of this perception has been fuelled by prejudice about the dry and dusty town. But there has been an element of truth in these perceptions owing to divisions in the town's multiracial population (about one quarter of which is Aboriginal).

Like most places derided by those who misunderstand them, however, Port Augusta has a proud and resourceful populace. The town has in fact made significant strides toward reconciliation between black and white. . .

These steps toward reconciliation have been small and simple, based on carefully built relationships of trust between individuals and communities. Through these friendships, the community is starting to address the major justice issues which have divided Australia for decades.

Mark Cooper's first step on arrival at All Saints Church from his last posting in Queensland was, with the support of his local parishioners, to extend a hand in friendship to the Aboriginal community. He had noticed that the Aboriginal and non-Aboriginal communities in Port Augusta rarely met. The church was no better: 'I found when I came to the parish that a significant part of the Port Augusta population was Aboriginal, but that wasn't reflected in the people who felt welcome in the church,' Mark said. 'People weren't aware of how they could simply *invite* Aboriginal people. People can find that threatening [because] in Port Augusta there has been a history of tension.'

Mark's first move was to go to the local pub frequented exclusively by Aboriginal people. But, far from feeling threatened, Mark found he was welcomed by the pub's patrons, particularly once they discovered his motives, and was given access to other sections of the Aboriginal community.

He went to the local police and spoke to Aboriginal juvenile offenders and families from Port Augusta, offering himself as a support person for them; he made frequent visits to the Aboriginal 'reserve' and made himself known to local Aboriginal organisations. He put Council of Aboriginal Reconciliation literature in the church and, with assistance, arranged a study group on Aboriginal issues.

Meanwhile, across town at the Uniting Church, local Aboriginal woman Denise Champion was also considering how to break down the wall between Aboriginal and non-Aboriginal people. Denise began a program in 1992, with the help of a small group of family and friends, which could hopefully become a model for reconciliation across the country.

Based on the Uniting Church's national 'About Face' program, Denise arranged for non-Aboriginal individuals and families from Port Augusta, the Riverland and Adelaide to live with Aboriginal families in Port Augusta for a week. In the face of public perceptions that Aboriginal issues are impossibly complex, Denise's idea was disarmingly simple and effective. . .

How much prejudice could survive a week at close quarters? Not much, if any, Denise thought. With her husband Eddie and their three children, Denise has so far welcomed many families into her home. In total, about one hundred non-Aboriginal people have spent time with Aboriginal families in Port Augusta.

'One of the good things is that people are accepted into the family — you build that sort of relationship with them,' Denise said. 'You become friends. I guess that's what reconciliation is — to create friends where there had been enemies.'

It would be wrong to give the impression that this has been an easy exercise, in the light of the fact that non-Aboriginal people are presented with the tragic reality of Aboriginal history. People can become gripped with fear in the days leading up to the event.

The unravelling of this kind of misunderstanding often brings out strong emotions, particularly in the non-Aboriginal participants as they begin to feel the pain of their Aboriginal hosts. 'What we are doing is "two-way" learning,' Denise said. 'I have learned to live the white man's way very well. . . They see the history of Aboriginal people and have to learn how to deal with it.'

The 'About Face' program is disarmingly simple: Aboriginal families are given freedom to live their normal lives, to show their visitors their day-to-day experiences.

People talk to each other in the non-threatening environment of the family home. At the end of the program, in the Aboriginal custom, visitors are usually told they are part of the family now: 'Please drop in if you're passing through. If you need to get away from your day-to-day life, come and stay with us.'

Non-Aboriginal people leave the program with a challenge: 'To create links between Aboriginal and non-Aboriginal people in their own communities and to educate themselves and their communities about Aboriginal issues.'

Within the Port Augusta community, the efforts of Mark Cooper's parish have also reaped solid friendships. Simple occasions, such as reconciliation sports events which enable Aboriginal and non-Aboriginal kids to play footy together, have been the building blocks of these friendships. Last Christmas, the Port Augusta Carols by Candlelight had a reconciliation theme and attracted its biggest crowd ever.

Significantly, a group of about fifty parishioners has formed a cross-cultural exchange group to carry on this kind of work. The group's aim is to bring black and white together through social activities, sports days, camping weekends in the nearby Flinders Ranges and to organise prayer, particularly during the national Week of Prayer for Reconciliation which takes place in late May each year.

There have been some negative reactions to this process within the parish, but the overwhelming response has been positive. There are now a number of Aboriginal people coming to the church, particularly young people. And their presence has been a learning experience for the church.

'One thing that I believe is significant in relation to the Aboriginal input is that Aboriginal people help us to focus on family,' Mark said. 'They really challenge us on our ideas of the wider family. As non-Aboriginal people, our family unit has broken down quite a lot. They help us to see the gift of family and how the wider community is also our family, not just the nuclear family. It helps parents to see the need for our children to have skills to communicate with people from other backgrounds.

'One of the most powerful things is not what you do in public, but what parents say about Aboriginal people at the dinner table. That's the most significant thing that can happen for the future of our community.'

Mark said the experience had affected him personally. He has learned to have a greater respect for the land and, he said, on the spiritual level he has been opened up, due to the fact that Aboriginal people are 'very forgiving'.

Denise Champion also perceives a change in attitude in the town. For many years, Aboriginal people had been trying unsuccessfully to get the Aboriginal flag flown outside the civic centre. With the support of non-Aboriginal people, the flag is now flying high. If the experiences of Port Augusta sound trite in the context of powerful national debates on complex issues such as native title, think again. Concern for social justice has been shown to flow naturally from the relationships formed in the South Australian town.

In February, the Uniting Church organised a forum in Port Augusta involving Aboriginal people, pastoralists and other interested groups to discuss native title issues and the proposed World Heritage listing of the Lake Eyre Basin. Although not everybody agreed on all issues, Aboriginal people and pastoralists in particular were able to find common ground in their mutual pain about the loss of land and uncertainty about their future.

For Denise Champion, the crucial point is that people are listening to each other's concerns in a spirit of goodwill. 'People are listening. They recognise that there are enormous problems in the Aboriginal community; and a lot of that has come directly from losing their land and being disadvantaged. They are very willing to listen to our concerns.'

Reconciliation in Port Augusta is far from over. There may still be setbacks. However, community members are committed to talking with each other and maintaining their relationships. After all, they are becoming a family and no family is perfect.[19]

✠ COMMUNITY DEVELOPMENT MEANS SURVIVING IN A POLYETHNIC COMMUNITY: *'When you are right in it, you learn not to be afraid!'*

Not only do countries like 'white Australia' need to come to terms with our indigenous 'black history', but we also need to come to terms with our immigrant 'multicoloured future'. Ken Rolph, who resides in a multicultural Sydney suburb, tells us what it's really like, learning to live in a polyethnic community with people of all kinds, from all over the world:

When I walked around the corner and tripped over the goat, I realised that I had learnt something about multiculturalism.

I didn't immediately jump up and pen indignant letters to the *Bankstown Torch* about these dreadful foreigners and their habits. I got up, smiled at the goat's owners and continued on my way. The goat got up and went back to keeping the grass short.

It had a bag around its udder. One day, I intend to find out if the bag is to catch the precious milk or to keep the udder clean. But for now, I accept that if I rush around corners in my part of the world, I never know what I'm going to find.

The goat's owners had been sitting in the front yard,

drinking coffee with the relatives, just like back in the village. Some time later as I passed that way again, I saw that they had also learnt something about multiculturalism. The goat was tethered on a much shorter leash, so that it could not wander across the footpath. If your goat trips people up, there might be trouble.

Life in a multicultural area is full of tiny incidents like this. We live with a complexity that leaves us continually making minor adjustments and living with unanswered questions.

I have been living with these scenes for over five years, since I moved out to the southwestern area of Sydney, and have been putting together some new understandings from these experiences. Today, we have a debate over immigration, which has come up with obvious ideas. For example: migrants introduce complexity in areas where the people are already finding it hard to cope. But I find a lot of the discussion generalised and remote. Many people entering it lack an awareness of the daily texture of life in a multicultural area.

Do the following seem unusual to you?

* The local shopping centre has three video shops. One is Greek, one is Arabic and one Indochinese.

* Buddhist monks in robes walk to the railway station.

* The general store has cassettes with handwritten Arabic labels. Yashmaks are now part of official school uniform.

* Alongside the Mr Whippy van (selling ice cream) comes the Tio Miguel van selling tacos.

* School sport is cut back during Ramadan.

* Your kids want to know why they can't have rice and noodles like the other kids. And then they backchat you in Spanish, Korean or Arabic.

* Have you thought to look at the names of driving schools? Isn't that the first thing that a new ethnic minority does to establish itself in Australia — to start a driving school?

Around our way we have: Mario's Driving School (no prizes for guessing that one). There's Olympic, Champion and Andrew's, all with Greek subtitles. The Give Way Driving School has an Arabic translation. There's a Cedars of Lebanon Driving School, with the symbol just like you see on TV in Beirut. The Rio and Speedy Gonzalez schools are for South Americans. The newest ones are the Lam Sai, the Mandarin, the Mekong and the Freedom Driving School. Just lately, I have noticed Koala and Waratah Driving Schools. . .

Multiculturalism makes ethnic groups of us all and tempts us to simplify our identities. I have found it impossible to simplify my response to multiculturalism, because I have found that my expectations were usually wrong.

For instance, Antonio is in the maths group I take as a parent helper at the primary school. In the first term, he was Antonio. In second term we were doing polygons and he was excited to find that 'hexa-', 'penta-', and so on were Greek terms. But by the third term he was insisting on being called 'Tony'. At our last meeting, he was decked out in blue and white clothes and bunting (as were the rest of the group). His last words to me were, 'Are you for the Bulldogs (the local rugby league team who, by the way, won the Australian Rugby League Grand Final in 1995), Mr Rolph?'

The conventional assumption is that here is a young person between two cultures, possibly losing more than he is gaining. But he is just a person responding to his environment. There is only one world culture now, with local variants. The idea of pure ethnic groups is a figment of the imagination.

There are more things around which are made by combination of different cultures but belong to none, than there are pure cultural items.

Take the ham and pineapple pizza. This contemporary symbol of culture was condemned by a visiting group of Italian pizza specialists. The purist tradition didn't include ham and pineapple. Yet the people who wanted the ham and pineapple didn't traditionally eat pizza. What's worse, this product of the media-marketing complex comes frozen. It belongs to the new supermarket culture which is coming to dominate all previous ethnic cultures.

A church on Sydney's northside helped an Indochinese man rescue his wife from a Thai border refugee camp. They had arranged work and a home for the couple. But the wife was not happy with the new home. She said it was too far from McDonald's.

This new one world is smaller than we sometimes think. Another member of my little maths group, Nada, had to go back to Beirut. The family just went back to see how things were and to pick up grandpa, who had been shot in the arm. Nada's parents thought he would recover much better in Australia. These people are not migrating, they are commuting.

Some South Americans we know were discussing moving. They were either going to the next suburb, or back to South America.

The usual approach is to send one member of the family back home to see if the political or economic situation has improved. If it has, they go back. If it hasn't, they rescue more relatives and bring them out to lifeboat Australia.

It's all done by air travel. There's none of these long sea voyages, with tearful reunions on the dockside. Some of them don't even seem to sell their houses. The story is that the reason one of the local milk bars is always run by Greeks is that a certain village in Greece keeps sending people out for two year stints here. They open almost all the time and, that way, get enough money to retire in comfort back to the village, where life is cheaper. . .

And you thought it was only the wicked multinationals who thought of the whole world as their sphere of operation!

Living in a multicultural area is not for the complacent. At this point in the world's history, multiculturalism means living in the same suburb, or even the same street, as people whose compatriots are killing each other in some other part of the globe. And have been doing so since before Australia was established [as a nation]. This means living with a high level of paranoia, in an uncertain, changing world.

I'm often surprised that there isn't more violence than there is, given the fact that we've almost everyone who's ever hated anyone all living within reach of each other.

When we are sitting down to tea and we hear a loud noise and the kids argue about whether it is a car backfiring or gunshots, more often than not it's some ocker Australians driving around randomly shooting out car windscreens.

So we learn a little more how it is possible for people to remain in Beirut, Northern Ireland, or South American trouble spots. And we realise how relatively safe and peaceful it is living in Australia.

When you are right in it, you learn not to be afraid![20]

✠ COMMUNITY DEVELOPMENT MEANS THRIVING IN A POLYETHNIC COMMUNITY:
'We are the rainbow people of God.'

According to Desmond Tutu, not only do we need to survive in our polyethnic communities, but we also need to thrive in our polyethnic communities as 'the Rainbow People Of God'. We are a polyethnic family, living in a polyethnic community with a vision of all people thriving in a polyethnic world.

I am Anglo-Australian. I was born in England and migrated to Australia with my family as a child. My wife, Ange, is Greek-Australian. Her family migrated from Greece to Australia and she was born and brought up in a bi-cultural household. Our younger daughter, Navi, is Nepalese-Australian. She was born in Nepal before migrating to Australia. And our elder daughter, Evonne, is Indian-Australian. She was born in Australia, but was brought up in India, before returning as a bicultural child to Australia.

During the last twenty years, we have lived and worked not only in Australia but also in England, Holland, Germany, Kenya, Uganda, Sudan, Afghanistan, Pakistan, India, Nepal, Thailand, Singapore, Canada, the United States and New Zealand.

For more than ten years we were based in the cosmopolitan city of Delhi. The imperial splendour of Rajpath is superb. The quiet beauty of Lodhi Gardens is enchanting. And the hustle and bustle on Chandni Chowk is exciting. But it is the people, the millions of people who crowd into the city from all over India that make Delhi such a colourful place to live in. It is the meeting of Kashmiris, Punjabis and Rajasthanis, the Nagas, Mizos and Manipuris, the Biharis, Bengalis and Oriya; and the Telegus, Tamils and Malayalis, that made the poet Ghalib once describe Delhi as 'the soul in the body of the world'.

While we were there, we lived in an intentional polyethnic residential community, including twenty-one non-Indians and thirty-two Indians. Of the non-Indians, thirteen of us were from Australia, four from England, three from Canada and one from Germany. Of the Indians, sixteen were from Delhi itself, six from Punjab, five from Goa, three from Maharashtra, two from Tamil Nadu and one from Andhra Pradesh. Almost half of the marriages were inter-national, and almost all of the marriages, including our own, were cross-cultural. The complexity was further compounded by the fact that we were not only international and cross-cultural, but also multi-faith. Twenty-three of us were Christian, five Hindu, two humanist, one Muslim, one Buddhist and one Jain. At one stage or other, we all actually lived together in the same six-bedroomed house and absolutely loved it!

For the last ten years we have been based in Brisbane which, compared to Delhi, is like a country town. But we managed to settle in West End, which is the cosmopolitan centre of the city. Taking a stroll down Boundary Street you can taste Greek *souvlakia*, Turkish delight and Vietnamese sweet breads, or you can drop in at the Migrant Resource Centre for a cup of coffee with someone from any one of the fifty ethnic groups in the area, forty-one per cent of whom speak Greek, twenty-three per cent Vietnamese, twelve per cent Chinese and the rest a range of languages, including Arabic — and, of course, English of one kind or another.

While we are here, we live in an intentional polyethnic integral community, not apart from, but as a part of, our locality. The next door neighbours we are involved with include many migrants from England, Ireland, Greece, India and the Philippines. The neighbours scattered round the neighbourhood that we are

involved with include indigenous Aborigines and Islanders whom we do some community work with and
refugees from El Salvador, Eritrea, Bosnia, Afghanistan
and Vietnam whom we've also managed to settle in our
locality. We continue to live this way, because we love
it as a way of life.

Here are some of our tips for not merely surviving,
but really thriving, in a polyethnic community. . .

* *Meditate on the oneness of the human family.*
  There aren't many races; there is only one race.
  Beneath the differences we are all the same.
  The most personal feature is the most universal.
  We all want to love and be loved.
* *Celebrate heterogeneity rather than homogeneity.*
  There is one whole, but there are many parts.
  The differences may seem quite superficial, but
  they are actually quite significant. The universal
  is not uniform, but multiform. We all want to
  live different ways, not be forced to live the
  same way as everyone else.
* *Recognise the contradictions in our values.* We
  need to be aware of any egocenticity that could
  subvert our work for unity and any ethnocentricity that could subvert our work for diversity
  that may be operating unconsciously in the way
  that we live our lives.
* *Acknowledge the limitations in our knowledge.*
  We need to be aware of our ignorance. We all
  have blind spots which, by definition, we cannot
  see ourselves. So we need to listen to the feed-
  back that we get from others in order to see the
  way we live our lives as others see us.

* *Revel in the role of a learner at large.* To start with, we need to keep our mouths shut and our eyes and ears open. If we must speak, we need to ask open-ended questions rather than make statements that close down discussion. A closed person cannot learn from anyone, not even a dear friend. But an open person can learn from everyone, even a complete stranger.

* *Delight in the whole world as a teacher.* If we are willing to learn, the whole world will be willing to teach us. It can teach us not only a whole range of ways to talk, but also, with each new way of talking, can teach us a new way of thinking. Each new set of vocabulary gives us a new set of categories to be able to understand our world anew.

* *Relish developing another world view.* Our world view isn't the only world view. In spite of the propaganda of our various religions, none of us has a monopoly on verity. It can be really exciting to compare and contrast the vast array of perspectives that the world views of our numerous traditions provide.

* *Enjoy exploring the same world differently.* We need to take every chance we can get to look at the world through another's eyes. In spite of our fears, we need to have the courage to step out into the unknown with others as our guide. Then, we will be able to experience a myriad of unexpected wonders inherent in our otherwise predictable world.

* *Rejoice in the possibility of synthesis.* Together, we can work towards a community world — that

is, a unique combination of all our cultures, the best of all possible worlds: not single cropping, but companion planting; not agriculture, but permaculture; not ethnic cleansing, but inclusive living; not monoculture, but multiculture; not concrete jungle, but global village. We alone can do it, but we cannot do it alone.

* *Engage in the practice of* satya, ahimsa *and* tapasya. The first step towards a community world is *satya*. 'Satya' means seeking after the truth in every situation. Without such seeking, there can be no comprehension of the potential, let alone the realisation of the potential that is intrinsic to every situation.

The second step towards a community world is *ahimsa*. 'Ahimsa' means seeking a way forward together, with everyone who can help us, in a way that is not harmful to the welfare of anyone, whether they are part of the group helping us or not.

The third step towards a community world is *tapasya*. 'Tapasya' means seeking a way forward together and continuing to seek it until we find it; accepting the pain of the painstaking process as the price we are gladly willing to pay in order to find a way to become the 'rainbow people of God'.[21]

11

The political dimension of community development:

'A civilisation which is still to be created'

'AT THE PRESENT MOMENT,' SAYS Jacques Ellul, 'we are confronted with a choice — the "Brave New World" of Huxley, or a different civilisation, which we cannot yet describe because we do not know what it will be; it is still to be created.'[1]

The creation of this 'different civilisation' — what I call a 'community world' — is what the process of social transformation we know as 'community development' is all about. This process is essentially a political process, not in the sense that it projects our problems and the solution of our problems onto the state — quite the contrary — but rather in the sense that it involves people continually making corporate policy decisions, constantly deconstructing and reconstructing the nature of our common individual and collective lives.

The sociologist Talcott Parsons says: 'The political process is the process by which the necessary organisation [for making corporate policy decisions] is built up. . . the goals of action are determined and the resources requisite to it are mobilised.'[2] This may, or may not, have anything to do with the state.

But in order for true community development to take place, this process needs to be 'organised for the people, by the people themselves'. And it will be judged to have succeeded or failed 'by the practical demonstration in all feasible areas that the community [was able to] define its own needs and organise [its own] resources to satisfy them. . .'[3]

✠ MOVING BEYOND OUR IDEOLOGY: 'The agenda of love'

For communities to be free to define our own needs in our own terms and organise our own resources to satisfy them in our own way, the political process at the heart of community development must not be controlled by any ideology, not even a community development ideology.

An idea becomes an ideology when the following takes place:

1. *The end is all important.* The idea is the only thing that really matters.
2. *The means are implemented without restriction.* The methods are evaluated only in terms of the maximum effectiveness and efficiency of means for realising the end.
3. *The central idea distorts crucial values.* Notions such as truth and love and justice are slowly but surely coopted, perverted and misinterpreted as means to an end.
4. *The grand cause creates great conflict.* Any friend who is less than enthusiastic about our cause is

considered an enemy in the end and, in the meantime, any enemy of an enemy is considered a friend.

5. *The end justifies the means.* People are expected to continually and uncritically adjust to all the requirements of any means deemed 'necessary' to achieve the desired end, even to the extent of collaborating in the destruction of our own individual and collective lives 'for the good of the cause'.[4]

We need to always remember that. . . those who love community destroy community; only those who love people can create community.

Love is a sacrificial concern for the welfare of others. It is a concern that is not self-righteous, but self-forgetful in its concern for the welfare of others. It is not masochistic, but is willing to make significant sacrifices, spontaneously, to ensure the welfare of others which it seeks.

Love always works towards mutuality. Yet love requires sacrifice in order to create the possibility of reciprocity. Without sacrifice, there is no possibility of reciprocity at all.

Thus, though love always works towards mutuality, paradoxically its potential can only be realised in reciprocal relationships where concern for mutual advantage is not an issue that anyone would fight for, but one which everyone would equally joyfully sacrifice in the interest of the other.[5]

Love is seldom considered 'a political virtue'. But,

as Edgar Brook points out, 'the world languishes because love is being tried so little'. Hence, he joins his voice to the growing chorus of people around the world who call for love to be put onto the political agenda. 'It is imperative,' he cries, that love should not be left out of the process, but 'that it should be admitted to the field of politics. . .'[6]

If it were not only to be put onto our political agenda, but actually put on top of our political agenda, as the starting point for dealing with all the issues we need to deal with on our political agenda, it would profoundly affect the way we do politics.

First, love would remind us that politics is all about people — 'ordinary people and, for the most part, very ordinary people'.

Second, love would help us remember that the practice of due process in politics starts here and now with us. 'If I don't let it start in my own heart, I cannot expect it to start at all.'

Third, love would help us to make sure that we never forget that, while due process in politics may start with us, it can never be consummated without the full, free and frank participation of others, including all those who may oppose us. 'Everybody needs to be understood and involved in the negotiating process.'

Fourth, love would help us to continue to recognise the humanity of our opponents in the midst of disputes and to forgive the emnity that often erupts out of those unresolved disputes. As South African Michael Cassidy says, 'Unless we build [on the basis] of forgiveness, we will lose the day!'[7]

✠ MOVING TOWARDS OUR IDEALS:
'The struggle for justice'

Justice has no independent meaning apart from the meaning love imparts to it. Justice is the concrete manifestation of love in our political economy. Justice involves putting the people at the bottom of the heap on the top of our priorities and treating them in a way that will make them feel more loved and more able to love.

Love is the ideal. Justice is our attempt to realise that ideal in our community. At best, our realisation approximates our ideal. At worst, it parodies our ideal. The transcendent ideal of love constantly challenges our concrete attempts to realise that ideal in trying to do justice to disadvantaged groups of people, affirming any progress we may make and confronting any compromises we may make along the way.[8]

Love calls us to do justice through *emergency aid*, meeting other people's needs ourselves. 'Some of us avoid emergency aid because we don't want to share our resources to meet other people's needs. We will only be free to embrace emergency aid as an option if we are willing (as love always challenges us to be) to recognise that other people have as much right to what we have as we do ourselves.'[9]

Love calls us to do justice through *formative education*, training people to meet their own needs. 'A few of us avoid formative education because training others to meet their own needs involves a long term rather than short term commitment. We will only be free to embrace formative education as an option if we are prepared (as love always challenges us to be) to invest the same time equipping people with life-sustaining skills that others have invested in us.'[10]

Love calls us to do justice through *direct action*, opposing the groups who not only do not help, but actually hinder the process of people attempting to meet their own needs. 'A lot of us avoid direct action because we are afraid of conflict, preferring the support of the power brokers rather than risking their opposition by exposing their exploitation. We will only be free to embrace direct action as an option if we are ready (as love always challenges us to be) to stand for the oppressed against their oppressors, regardless of the consequences.'[11]

Love calls us to do justice through *model formation*, enabling people to develop a model of the way they want to meet their own needs with, or without, the support of the state. 'Many of us avoid model formation because we would prefer to put the onus for change onto the state, rather than the people, for change. We will only be free to really embrace model formation if we are convinced (as love always challenges us to be) that the only way for people to change their world is to do it themselves.'[12]

Love calls us to do justice through *community development*, enabling people to develop their community in terms of the model of community that they have developed themselves. 'Most of us avoid community development in practice, if not in theory, because we are wary about things getting out of hand — at least out of our hands. We will only be free to truly embrace community development if we are committed (as love always challenges us to be) to giving people a hand, to build a better world, without any strings attached.'[13]

✠ WORKING FOR LIBERTY AND EQUALITY AND DEMOCRACY:
'Doing the right thing by one another'

The world we envisage, a world in which justice is a way of life, can only be built on the basis of people working for liberty and equality in the context of consensual democratic communities.

In order to ensure justice, we need to practice the regulatory principles of liberty and equality. 'Both liberty and equality are regulative principles of justice. A more just order grants. . . liberty within a framework of increasing equality. But neither is an absolute social norm, neither is a constitutive principle of justice.

'Both are expressions of love finding embodiment in the structures of justice and, in turn, expressing within justice something of the tension between love and justice.'[14]

Rawls argues that to guarantee justice:

1. Each person is to have an equal right to the most extensive total system of equal liberties compatible with a similar system of liberty for all.
2. Social and economic inequalities are to be arranged so that they are both:
   (a) to the greatest benefit of the least advantaged, consistent with the just savings principle, and
   (b) attached to offices and positions open to all under conditions of fair equality of opportunity.[15]

Nielsen argues that in order to safeguard liberty from becoming an apology for social and economic inequalities in the name of some inalienable civil right, such as private property, we need to have an unequivocal commitment to work for 'equality of basic conditions for everyone':

> First, it means that everyone, as far as possible, should have equal life prospects;
>
> Second, there should be, where this is possible, an equality of access to equal resources over each person's life as a whole, though this should be qualified by people's varying needs. The intent is that this equal access to resources will prevent certain undesirable situations. It will avoid there being the sort of differences between people that allow some to be in a position of control to exploit others. It will protect against one person having power over other persons that does not rest on the revokable consent by those persons.
>
> In situations where it is not possible to distribute resources equally, where considerations of desert are not at issue, the first consideration should be distribution according to stringency of need, second [should be distribution] according to the strength of unmanipulated preferences, and third [should be distribution according to] lottery. . .[16]

My friend Allan Halladay, Senior Lecturer in Social Work and Social Policy at the University of Queensland, says that as far as he's concerned: 'There is no basic difference between Rawls' and Nielsen's first principles. Each of these first principles expresses the importance of the equality of self-respect. They both acknowledge the underlying importance of a social order where there is an equal respect for all persons.'

Allan says, 'The difference between Rawls and Nielsen comes in the second principle of justice. Rawls' second principle can be in conflict with his first. It could allow disparities of power, authority and autonomy which undermine self-respect. It suggests that those less well off should accept inequalities if it makes them better off in monetary terms. Nielsen's second principle, however, reinforces his first, insisting that, if the preservation of self-respect is to be the centrepoint of justice, there should be equal access to equal resources over each person's life as a whole.'[17]

While I agree with all this, I still have some reservations about the issue of justice being framed in terms of rights rather than in terms of what we used to call 'righteousness' or what we might now call 'rightness'. Though some might say the distinction is merely semantic, I would suggest the difference is very substantive indeed. When we talk about justice in terms of 'our right to have this and our right to have that', we tend to treat justice as if it were just another consumer product that is there for the taking in a consumer society like ours — if, that is, we have the money to buy it.

But justice is not a mass-produced, consumer product; it is a craft product, produced by the masses. Justice is not something, like a nice car, that we can aquire already made; it is, like a good friendship, something that we can only have if we make it ourselves. We don't get it by taking what we consider to be our rights without due regard for our responsibility to others. We get it by giving ourselves to doing what we know is 'the right thing' by one another.

Justice that preserves people's self-respect by doing 'the right thing' by one another is always going to be a struggle: a struggle to empower all those who, hitherto, have all too often been overpowered; a struggle to enable people from every strata of our society to move towards being less autocratic, more democratic and more able to actively seek and actually find the elusive synergy and serendipity of consensus through participatory processes of corporate decision-making in communities, large and small.

Reinhold Niebuhr reminds us that democracy is not a panacea. He describes it, rather ironically, as 'a method of finding proximate solutions for insoluble problems'. But, according to Niebuhr, democracy is nevertheless very important as a process in our struggle for justice because, as he says, '[our] capacity for justice makes democracy possible, but [our] capacity for injustice makes democracy imperative.' According to Niebuhr, 'The highest achievement of democratic societies [is] that they embody the principles of resistance to government with the principle of government itself.'[18]

Jacques Ellul warns us not to take any such achievements for granted. 'Experience has shown the state will only retreat when it meets an insurmountable obstacle. The obstacle can only be citizens organised independently of the state. But once organised, the citizens must possess a truly democratic attitude in order to depoliticise and repoliticise [our society in terms of community].'

'All this,' Ellul tells us, 'requires a profound change

in the citizen. It must be admitted that democracy is the exact opposite of our taste for tranquillity... As long as [we are] preoccupied only with [our] security and the stability of [our] life, we should have no illusions, we will certainly not find the civic virtue to make democracy come alive. . .

'Democracy,' Ellul tells us, 'becomes possible only through every citizen's will; it remakes itself every day, through every citizen. If we accept the view that democracy is a given fact, everything is lost. On the contrary, it must be understood that democracy can no longer be anything except will, conquest and creation. We must understand that democracy is always infinitely precarious and is mortally endangered by every new progress. It must be forever started again, reconstructed, begun again.[19]

✠ THE 'PEACE' PARADIGM — AN ALTERNATIVE MODEL OF COMMUNITY DEVELOPMENT:
Let's try another way altogether

As we consider how we might be able to start to reconstruct our society yet again, with due regard for the liberty, equality and democracy that we hold dear, we need to remember the mistakes we have made in the past so we don't repeat them in the future. Over the last fifty years around the world, we have implemented various economic, social and political models of reconstruction — invariably, with disastrous unintended consequences of one kind or another.

During the 50s and 60s, some of us began to focus our attention on GNP (gross national product) in the hope that, with modernisation and industrialisation, the political economy would take off and, as a result of the upturn, we would all be able to make so much money that, eventually, it would 'trickle down' from the top to the bottom of society, so that even the poorest of the poor among us would be able to meet their basic human needs.

Some political economies really took off, but the amount that actually trickled down as a result of the upturn was a lot less than anyone anticipated. In most places, the rich were better off, but the poor were worse off after their political economies took off than they were before.

So during the 60s and 70s, some of us began to focus our attention on BHN (basic human needs) in the hope that, through distribution and redistribution, we would be able to share and grow and grow and share the common wealth of the political economy as we went along, so that the rich would have less, the poor would have more and everybody would have enough to be able to meet their basic human needs.

Some political economies opted to share then grow and other political economies opted to grow then share. But regardless of where sharing came in the process, when it came time for sharing, very few of the rich were willing to share voluntarily with the poor. So in many places, ordinary people were no better off than before.

So during the 70s and 80s, some of us began to focus our attention on the NIEO (New International Economic Order) in the hope that, through liberation and revolution, we would be able to take charge of the political process and make changes in the economic order. These would ensure that the common wealth of the political economy would be shared equally with all so that everybody would be at liberty to meet their basic human needs.

Some political economies took charge of their own affairs and made changes — in some cases, quite significant changes — in the way they functioned. But, as often as not, those who took charge only made changes that suited them and served their vested interests. So in many places, ordinary people were worse off than before.

Because our leaders, who are rich rather than poor, see so much more potentional profit to be made in a take-off political economy, rather than a share and grow or grow and share political economy, they are doing their best to lead us back to the beginning of the cycle we have just come through. And because so many of us perceive ourselves as being worse off than we were before, many of us are willing to be led in the hope that, this time round, we will be able to catch more of the crumbs that fall from their table.

But we've been there and done that. It didn't work the first time we tried it. And it won't work the second time we try it. What we need to do is to try another model altogether.

Which brings us, at last, to the PEACE paradigm, an integrated model of development combining five facets: *Participatory politics* and *Equitable economics* with *Appropriate technnologies* in *Conscientised communities*, exercising ongoing *Environmental responsibilities*.

Of this paradigm, Toh Swee Hin says:

> The PEACE paradigm upholds development policies which are participatory with the [people who are] no longer powerless and [who are no longer] passively accepting of decisions dispensed from above by elites or experts.
>
> Participation allows the accumulated knowledge of the people to be tapped, rather than ignored, to the detriment of many modernisation schemes.
>
> Social, economic and political structures require radical transformation, so that societal resources are equitably distributed within and between nations.
>
> Technology has to be appropriate, optimising use of local human, material and cultural resources and capable of maximising economic benefits to the poor majorities.
>
> But at the same time, such development should harmonise with, not destroy the environment on which long-term human survival depends.
>
> Above all, 'PEACEful' development embodies the process of conscientisation, whereby the oppressed understand the political roots of their [oppression] and act to liberate themselves.[20]

It may help us understand the PEACE paradigm if we place it alongside the other models of development, so we can compare it and contrast it with the models of development we have tried so far.

Susan Black, in her groundbreaking thesis, appropriately entitled, *Digging in Our Own Backyard*, does this for us in the tables that are featured, in a modified form, on the next couple of pages:

TABLE I: Models of development

MODEL:	economic	social	political	holistic
TIME	50s, 60s	60s, 70s	70s, 80s	80s, 90s
PROBLEM	poverty	disadvantage	dependence	injustice
SOLUTION	modernisation	distribution	revolution	conscientisation
	industrialisation	redistribution	liberation	transformation
RESOLUTION	wealth	welfare	independence	justice
ISSUE	capital	access	power	love
EMPHASIS	GNP	BHN	NIEO	PEACE
POLITICS	executive	consultative	representative	participatory
ECONOMICS	entrepreneurial	liberal	national	equitable
CONCERNS	exploitation	patronisation	manipulation	nonrealisation

TABLE II: Comparing and contrasting models of development

MODEL:	Economic, social, political	holistic
ETHOS	material	spiritual
	competitive	cooperative
EMPHASIS	separate	integrated
	specialised	generalised
ECOLOGY	opportunistic	responsible
	exploitation	stewardship
ECONOMY	large-scale	small-scale
	growth orientation	equity orientation
POLITY	top down	bottom up
	imposing structures	participatory structures
SOCIETY	outside in	inside out
	centralised processes	decentralised processes
COMMUNITY	old style	new wave
	anachronistic nostalgia	postmodern paradigm

✠ PROMOTING 'PEACE' IN THE BIOSPHERIC COMMUNITY:
'Turn tears of rage to tears of laughter'

There is a myriad of new wave groups and organisations that have taken PEACE as their paradigm and are promoting the integrated holistic model of development as the only viable policy alternative for the future of the biospheric community.

For the last ten years I have been involved with one such network known as TEAR. TEAR (Australia) is a voluntary grassroots organisation of thousands of ordinary people scattered all around Australia who are committed to promoting participatory politics, equitable economics, appropriate technologies and environmental responsibilities in the context of a global association of local communities that are very determined to 'turn the tears of rage into tears of laughter'.

TEAR has no projects of its own. Rather, we respond to requests for support from communities which are initiating their own projects. In our cooperation with implementing groups and organisations, we aspire to equal partnerships based on mutual respect and trust. We gladly acknowledge that what we have learned about development we have largely learned from our partners and we seek to operate accordingly.

> *First*, we seek to reflect the sacrificial love
> exemplified in the life of Jesus of Nazareth;
> *Second*, we recognise that this love is to be reflected
> in work, not just for charity, but for change;
> *Third*, we realise the change we work for involves
> justice, not merely as an end, but as the means to
> the end;
> *Fourth*, we recognise this justice can only be justice
> if it is total justice — that is, justice for all;
> *Fifth*, we realise that the only way that there can be
> justice for all is if we all do all that we can to build
> a better world. . . both here and abroad.

In Brisbane, we meet regularly to encourage one another to do all that we can to build a better world, both here and abroad, by studying issues of justice together, sharing stories of how we try to deal with these issues in our own lives, participating in current campaigns for these concerns, and developing the capacity to support projects which address these at the grassroots.

One of the issues that some of us in West End have recently been particularly concerned about is the treatment of the people of East Timor, some of our nearest neighbours, who have been invaded by Indonesia who, in turn, has been aided and abetted by Australia.

Different people have protested against this injustice in a whole range of different ways. Bob, who lives across the road, spent a week camped outside Canungra, where the Australian army trains soldiers, including Indonesians, in the art of jungle warfare used by the Indonesians against the East Timorese. Jason, Manon and Paul dressed up in their best clothes and went into town to have long talks with the management of Petros about their oil explorations in the Timor Gap. And the rest of us drew up petitions, collected heaps of signatures on piles of paper and sent them with letters to the prime minister, objecting to Australia's apparent policy of trading 'blood for oil'.

But, as the human rights violations in East Timor have continued and wave upon wave of refugees arrive on our shores seeking sanctuary, only to be refused asylum by the government, a bunch of people at St Mary's, South Brisbane, decided it was time to stop leaving policy decisions to the politicians.

✠ THINKING GLOBALLY, ACTING LOCALLY: *'Developing sanctuary for East Timor in West End'*

Coralie Kingston, Ciaron O'Reilly and the congregation at St Mary's called on us to take the matter of extending sanctuary into our own hands. Late in 1995, the following article, written by Ciaron in his typically combative style, was published as a call to arms in our local *Neighbourhood News*:

St Mary's Catholic Church, South Brisbane, will declare itself a sanctuary for the 1300 Timorese facing deportation at the hands of the federal government. Foreign Affairs minister Gareth Evans recently announced that the government would be recommending to the Australian Refugee Review Tribunal rejection of refugee status to the Timorese presently seeking sanctuary in Australia.

The majority of the 1300 arrived in the past few years by means of overstaying visiting visas or making the perilous boat trip to Darwin. The Timorese are arguing that their lives and liberty are under threat from the Indonesian military occupying their country; with over 200 000 slain, they have ample evidence.

Evans doesn't make a counter argument to this claim; instead, he attempts to conjure a technicality. Fresh from the mid-year World Court hearings on the Timor Gap Treaty where his suited underlings argued Portugal no longer has any legal claim or responsibility in respect to East Timor, he tries the 'all Timorese are really Portuguese, so ship them to Europe' thrust.

Evans is attempting a shell game with the distinctions of 'nationality' and 'sovereignty' that is morally transparent and lacking in credibility.

As we approach the anniversaries of the 1991 Dili

Massacre (November 12) and the 1975 Indonesian Invasion of East Timor (December 7), relations are unusually estranged between the Suharto dictatorship and the syncophantic Evans/Keating administration. The Indonesian government is demanding some payback for the rejection of Dili massacre cheerleader, General Mantiri, as a marketable Ambassador to Australia. The Evans payback is the deportation of 1 300 Timorese from Australia.

Meanwhile, the streets of Dili experience the cycle of resistance and repression with reports of another two dead and 150 detained this past week. The latest roundup has included house-to-house arrests and the seizing of thirty youths gathered outside a Catholic school.

Sanctuary — the present

The threatened mass deportations is another face of Australia's contribution to the war on Timor. To remove a dissident expatriate community, many bearing the fresh scars of torture and loss of loved ones to a faraway continent is no small offering by Evans.

Indonesian foreign minister Alatas has expressed predictable excitement. The declaration of sanctuary of the church by St Mary's, South Brisbane, is also significant. To counter the government's threat of further exile with an offer of hospitality is a sign of hope for the Timorese.

Sanctuary — the past

The rediscovery of this ancient tradition and simple notion that sanctuaries should be sanctuaries is pregnant with possibility. The ancient notion that holy sites be regarded, by their very nature, as places of refuge is not uniquely Christian. Sanctuary was more or less formalised practice in Egypt, Syria, Greece and Rome. Political fugitives, debtors and slaves on the run all passed beyond the pale of revenge by making it into the precincts of a recognised shrine.

In the Christian tradition, sanctuary has its roots in the early pacifist church and its role as intermediary in disputes ('lest innocent blood be shed') as fugitives were protected, slaves interceded for and debtors sheltered until a bargain could be made with those seeking vengeance or forgiveness given.

Rediscovering the sanctuary as sanctuary has often been a 'confessional' clarifying moment in the history of the church. Its declaration celebrates the sovereignty of God (of peace, love, justice, life) in history, marking the limit of civil authority. It will indeed be a confessional moment for the Australian church in relation to its Timorese neighbours, who have experienced twenty years of genocide.

Also [it is] a confessional moment in relation to successive Australian governments that have actively and passively contributed to this genocide; a government that now stands poised to slam the door in the face of those who flee a situation it has helped construct — diplomatically, economically and mililarily; a Timorese people who offered sanctuary to Australian troops fleeing Japanese forces in the 1940s; a Timorese people who daily face the perils of offering sanctuary to those declared fugitive in their own homeland by a brutal military occupation force.

Although the function, practice and theology of sanctuary is not to be circumscribed by civil acknowledgement, in the history of the church, Christian sanctuary has enjoyed various seasons of legal recognition. The period and place where sanctuary was most formalised was medieval England, where for several centuries at any given time there were more than a thousand people under protection of the church's peace. The ecclesiastical turf was carefully set forth and elaborate procedures for the sanctuary seeker obtained.

There have bcen other occasions, however, when the sanctuary of the church has been swamped by the state.

In January 1933, the altar of Magdeburg Cathedral and many other churches in Germany were smothered in swastika flags. As American bombs rained on the children of Vietnam, Panama and Iraq, the stars and stripes could be found on altars throughout the United States.

For the most part, however, the practice of sanctuary has been fraught with risk. This has been the story from the underground railroad hiding escaped slaves to the martyrs of the French village of Le Chambon who secreted Jews in the 1940s to the 1980s movement responding to Central American refugees fleeing north from US-sponsored wars.

On October 28, 1991, Sabastiao Ranel, a Timorese student, was in the Motael church grounds when he was slain by Indonesian troops. By the time his November 12 funeral procession reached the Santa Cruz cemetery, it was transformed, by the same troops, into the bloodbath of the Dili massacre. Over 200 unarmed Timorese were butchered that day. Some of the survivors are now on Evans' deportation hit list.

Sanctuary — the future
The declaration of sanctuary by St Mary's is a step of faith and human solidarity. Where it will lead in terms of open confrontation with the Australian government and covert support of Timorese fugitives is an open-ended question. A time to be 'as wise as serpents and gentle as doves' it seems. It is an attempt to nonviolently confront our government's complicity in the war on the Timorese — a government that has trained their killers, stolen their oil and now slams the door on those who seek refuge.

It is time to say 'No!' It is hoped that more churches, institutions and communities around the country will also declare sanctuary and explore solidarity. West End would be an ideal community to take this on in terms of resources, safe houses, networks and skills in our community.[22]

When the day arrived, some 200 of us, Catholics and non-Catholics alike, gathered together to dedicate St Mary's Catholic Church as a centre for the sanctuary movement in our area. We recited an excerpt from the psalms that proclaimed the only hope that many of us feel we have in the midst of our despair:

> God will hide me in shelter
>   in the day of trouble:
> and conceal me under cover
>   of the Lord's tent,
> setting me high upon a rock.

And then we read the liturgy of sanctuary that had been written specially for the occasion:

> Our declaration of sanctuary is a clear 'No' to the government's recommendation to the Australian Refugee Review tribunal to deport 1 300 East Timorese refugees presently in Australia.
>
> It is a confessional statement that these East Timorese brothers and sisters have fled a genocide that our national government has been complicit in creating — diplomatically, economically and militarily.
>
> We make this declaration in the knowledge that the offer of sanctuary is firmly rooted in our Christian tradition and theology.
>
> We remember how 40 000 East Timorese were slain by the Japanese forces while offering sanctuary to Australian troops in World War Two.
>
> We are challenged by brothers and sisters in East Timor who daily risk life and liberty offering sanctuary to those declared fugitive in their own homeland.
>
> We undertake this non-violent step in faith as a prophetic challenge to our government to reverse its policy on these deportations and provide sanctuary.

Though this action may not provide full legal protection, we stand willing to offer practical support (through transport, shelter, security, etc) and solidarity with any East Timorese resisting these deportations.

Richard Waller of the *Courier Mail* filed his impressions of the service in the following report:

A Brisbane church yesterday declared itself a sanctuary for the 1300 Timorese refugees who currently face deportation from Australia by the federal government.

Congregation members say they are prepared to risk possible gaol terms.

In a symbolic gesture of human solidarity and support for the refugees, more than two hundred parishioners of St Mary's Catholic Church, South Brisbane, filed out of the 9.00 am service and joined hands in a line which encircled the building.

St Mary's Catholic community was part of a national Christian Sanctuary Network which took similar action around the country.

By making this statement, the Christian Sanctuary Network and its supporters would offer practical support to those refugees wishing to avoid deportation.

This would include some members offering their homes to shelter refugees from being caught by authorities — a criminal act which could attract a prison sentence up to six months.

St Mary's Catholic community spokesman, Dr Noel Preston, said the declaration of sanctuary was a clear rejection of the Australian government's recommendation to the Refugee Review Tribunal that the 1300 East Timorese be deported to Portugal (where those born before the Indonesian occupancy technically hold national status).

'Australia has within its existing laws the power to grant refugee status to the 1 300 on humanitarian grounds if it wants to,' Dr Preston said.[23]

For me, to be present at that service with a whole bunch of people I know from the neighbourhood who, in spite of their fears, were prepared to put the politics of love and justice into practice, by creating a sanctuary for our neighbours at the risk of being incarcerated themselves, was one of the most inspiring experiences of my life.

✠ THINKING LOCALLY, ACTING GLOBALLY: *Redeveloping the infrastructure in Mazar-i-Sharif*

However, we all know only too well that if we are actually going to be able to build a better world, we need to be able to do it, not only for other people here, but with other people abroad.

That is precisely the reason why, in TEAR, we continually encourage each other to consider the possibility of taking up the options that arise, from time to time, of going abroad to work with our partners in the majority world, through groups like Servants, Serve, Interserve and the Overseas Service Bureau. As I write, there are people we have sent that are at work with our partners in redeveloping the infrastructure for community development among the poorest of the poor in the squatter settlements of Manila, Phnom Phen, Bangkok, New Delhi and. . . Mazar-i-Sharif.

Most of us will have heard of major capital cities like Manila, Phnom Penh, Bangkok and New Delhi. But very few, if any of us, will have heard of Mazar-i-Sharif before. And I'm not too sure that even Brett Gresham and Ruth Harbison knew that much about Mazar-i-

Sharif before they got there — which is hardly surprising, since Mazar-i-Sharif, or 'Mazar' as it is affectionately known, is, apart from the bright blue mosque in the middle of it, a rather unremarkable little town located in one of the poorest parts of one of the poorest countries in the whole wide world.

After nearly twenty years of turmoil, Afghanistan is right at the bottom of the barrel when it comes to human development. In fact, the United Nations ranked it as 171 out of 173 countries, according to their criteria. In 1993, as a result of the war, out of a population of 17 million, 1.5 million had been killed, 2.5 million had been disabled and 6 million had been displaced. Even where a lot of the fighting has ceased, life expectancy, on average, is still only between forty and forty-two years at the most, due to both the short supply of the basic necessities people require for survival and the even shorter odds of, sooner or later, stepping on one of the ten million landmines that still litter the countryside.

According to Bruce Gibbs, the Executive Director of the International Assistance Mission whom I met a couple of months ago, the current situation remains confused. He says:

> Even though the Russians were driven out of Afghanistan some three or four years ago, since that time, sadly, the country has been involved in a civil war.
>
> Five or six factions are fighting for leadership of the country. As a result, in some locations the intensity of the warfare has not abated. In fact, it has increased.
>
> Some of Afghanistan's problems can be attributed to

the neighbouring nations who are supplying different factions with their war machines and the importance of this should not be underestimated.

The problem is that each of the faction leaders wants total control of the country. To achieve this, they form alliances of convenience to undermine whichever of the factions is strongest at the time.

In areas currently held by the government and its allies there is relative stability, but there remains much of the country that is still being contested.

From my own viewpoint, nothing has changed significantly other than that the government forces hold larger areas than they have in the past. People's lives have been devastated by the war. Hundreds of thousands of people have been forced out of their homes because of the destruction and their possessions looted. More than 3.5 million people are [still] displaced.

When we talk with people in the bazaars, it seems that there are very few whose families have not been affected in some way by the fighting. Most families have had at least one family member killed or seriously injured. There are already at least two million amputees. Certainly most have lost the meagre source of income they previously had.

Although reliable data is unavailable, there is every indication that, because of the loss of labour and capital and the disruption of trade and transport, economic production is lower now than fifteen years ago. The needs, therefore, of ordinary Afghans are immediate, immense and difficult to meet and the role of skilled expatriates [like Brett and Ruth] can be a vital one.[24]

After spending a few months of orientation in Pakistan, Brett and Ruth finally arrived in Afghanistan in September 1994. Their first task was to get a feel for Afghanistan, which is different from Australia where:

* When you're knee deep in mud, you're not in the middle of town.
* 'Bazaar' is an adjective, not a noun.
* Other people are strange and are stared at.
* 'TNT' is a courier company, not an explosive.
* You understand most, if not all, of what people are talking about.
* Tanks in the main street mean it's a parade.
* Shots in the day mean you're at a rifle range.
* Rockets at night mean you're at a fireworks display.
* Military helicopters don't hover, boneshaking, at TV aerial height.
* The amount of time since your last diarrhoea is measured in months or years, not hours or days. . .'

Their second task was to set up home in Mazar. Ruth said, 'I was told by at least three people not to cry when I see Mazar.'

Upon arriving in Mazar Brett wrote, saying, 'Well, imagine if you took an average outback Australian town, dropped in about 500 000 Afghans, ripped up the roads, plastered the houses with mud, pulled out [nearly all] of the trees and all of the grass, dumped a million tons of dust over the place and stuck a bright blue mosque, the size of the Sydney Opera House, in the middle of it. . . voilà Mazar':

Houses in Mazar are generally without internal plumbing, internal toilet, basic kitchen facilities, water tank or septic pit. In addition, ours lacked a water supply and a drainage system. [And the] yard looked like a bomb site.

We asked our landlord to help slow our house's gradual slide into the clay swamp. He was far too busy. He had at least one wife to patronise, a half-a-dozen kids to ignore, a war to run and cities to pillage. What's a bit of mould, he said. Fair enough, too, we thought.

Their third task was to learn Farsi, the language of poets and the language of the people of this part of the world:

The grammar is simple and the sound is sweet. Both of us learn Farsi more through relationships than from books, so being submerged in Farsi, we generally absorb new words with minimal pain. We've both now got passable, street level fluency in Farsi.

I [Brett] am currently learning to read a good book in local script and also translating a number of related studies.

I [Ruth] have started collecting and learning old folk sayings and songs. 'Chai na khorda jung na mesha!', 'You can't fight without a cuppa!'

Their fourth task was, with the help of their local partners, to find as many ways as they could to redevelop the infrastructure in the region for integrated holistic community development. In Australia, Brett was an engineer and Ruth was a nurse, so Brett began by drilling twenty-five wells in villages round the region and Ruth began by looking after the health of the staff working on this project. But it wasn't long before Brett and Ruth, in order to be available to do anything that needed to be done, found themselves doing things that they'd never done before:

'I am an engineer', I [Brett] said lamely. Still, due to lack of options when the previous director left suddenly, I became director of the Comprehensive Disabled Afghans Project, then regional director of Serve, with general oversight of policy, finances, personnel, liaison and all the projects in the region — including everything from improving water supply and basic sanitation to training people how to cope with their disabilities, learn new work skills and start new businesses.

I [Ruth] have become not only a health provider, but the health trainer for the whole of Serve, coordinating first aid and nutrition training for the field workers and overseeing the translation and printing of notes on these subjects.

In June 1995, just a little over nine months after their arrival in Afghanistan, Brett was asked to chair CAANN, the peak body that coordinates NGO activities throughout the northern regions of Afghanistan. Brett says: 'Our regional office has almost a hundred excellent and motivated staff, so my job is usually a joy.' And Ruth says: 'We are gradually developing a growing understanding of how to work closely and happily with Afghans.'[25]

Just how amazing an achievement this is can be best understood in terms of the story that one of the teams doing building projects in a nearby area told me during a recent visit:

The team had thrown themselves into their work with enormous enthusiasm, building hundreds, then thousands, of houses, clinics and schools all over the area. However, their demonstrable concern for widows and orphans was dreadfully, if not deliberately, misconstrued. One of the mullahs from a local mosque suggested that their motives might be suspect.

One day at Friday prayers, he told the gathered throng that they were only providing accommodation as an excuse to exploit the unprotected women and children who depended on them for their help.

The crowd went wild. They marched out of the mosque onto the streets, demanding vengeance at the top of their voices as they strode along the road to the team's office. They smashed through the gates into the factory, destroying everything they could lay their hands on until nothing that symbolised the team's effort was left standing.

When a member of the team turned up at the scene to see if there was anything he could salvage, he was driven off, wounded, under a hail of bullets, scarcely escaping with his life from the maelstrom of submachinegun fire.

After the dust settled, picking through the rubble of their broken dreams, the team was forced to face an awful decision. Should they give up or should they give it another go?

To give up would have been easy. They had every reason to. No-one, friend or foe, would have blamed them for packing their bags and making their way home. However, as hard as it seemed, they really felt they should try to give it another go. It was as if there was only one reason to do so, but it seemed to outweigh all the other reasons not to. It was a perfect opportunity for them to display the freedom of forgiveness towards people who had hitherto only known the bondage of endless cycles of revenge.

So the team decided to stay on, to start all over again, building a foundation for peace on the grounds for war.[26]

These Aussie expatriates and their Afghan partners show us that it is possible for us to begin to build a better world, not only here, but also abroad, even in some of what most of us would consider are all but impossible circumstances.

✠ PRACTISING 'PEACE' IN
THE BIOSPHERIC COMMUNITY:
'Work to improve the quality of life'

If we are to succeed in saving ourselves from destruction, we all need to join together to practise PEACE, only PEACE and nothing but PEACE. The kind of development that I would expect to emerge from the practice of PEACE would be:

> . . .a process by which the members of a society increase their personal and institutional capacities to mobilise and manage resources to produce [truly] sustainable and justly distributed improvements in their quality of life consistent with their own aspirations.[27]

> For most people this [may] seem obvious, hardly worth belabouring — until [you] realise that it bears almost nothing in common with the prevailing definitions that equate development either with industrialisation, or more broadly with increases in economic output.

> The above definition emphasises the *process* of development and its essential focus on personal and institutional capacity. It embodies the principles of justice, sustainability and inclusiveness. It acknowledges that the people themselves can define what they consider to be improvements in the quality of their lives. And [it] is grounded in a world that perceives earth to be a life-sustaining [planet] with a finite store of physical resources. Its only external and virtually inexhaustible resource is sunlight.

> Thus, the quality of life of its inhabitants depends on maintaining a proper balance between its solar energised regenerative systems, its resource stocks and the demands that its inhabitants place on these systems and resources.[28]

Anyone committed to the practice of PEACE should be aware that it is based upon the recognition of empirically verifiable facts and the realisation of profoundly significant values, and that our continuing practice of PEACE will very much depend on both our continuing appreciation of those facts and our continuing incorporation of those values, consciously, into our ordinary everyday lives.

The facts that need to inform our practice are that:

* The earth's physical resources are finite.
* The productive and recycling capacity of ecological systems can be enhanced through human intervention, but this enhancement cannot exceed certain natural limits.
* Governments by nature give priority to the interests of those who control power.
* Political and economic power are closely linked. Possession of either increases the holder's ability to exercise the other.
* Markets are important allocation mechanisms, but all markets are imperfect. By their nature, they give priority to the wants of the rich over the needs of the poor.
* Just, sustainable and inclusive communities are the essential foundation of a just, sustainable and inclusive global system.
* We need diversified local economies that give priority, in the allocation of available resources, to meeting the basic needs of community members. This, in turn, increases the security of individual communities — and the resilience and stability of the larger national and international economies.
* When the people control the local environmental resources on which their own and their children's

lives depend, they are more likely than absentee owners to exercise responsible stewardship.[29]

These values need to be reflected in our practice of these policies:

* All people should have the opportunity to produce a basic livelihood for themselves and their families.
* Current generations have no right to engage in levels of non-essential consumption that deprive future generations of the possibility of sustaining decent human living standards.
* Every individual has the right to be a productive contributing member of family, community and society.
* Control of productive assets should be broadly distributed within society.
* Sovereignty resides in the people. The authority of the state is granted by the people and therefore may be withdrawn by them.
* Local economies should be diversified and reasonably self-reliant in producing for basic needs.
* People have a right to a voice in making the decisions that influence their lives; decision-making should be as close to the level of individual, family and community as possible.
* Local decisions should reflect a global perspective and an acceptance of the rights and responsibilities of global citizenship.[30]

Everyone committed to the practice of PEACE should be aware that the holistic model of development, based on these facts and values, will differ quite markedly from all the economic, social and political models of development that have gone before, especially in terms of its policies. We need to practise policies from now on that will:

* Seek economic diversification at all levels of the economy, beginning with the rural household, to reduce dependence and vulnerability to the market shocks that result from excessive specialisation.

* Give priority in allocating local resources to the production of goods and services to meet the basic needs of the local population.

* Allocate a portion of surplus local productive capacity (beyond what is required to meet local basic needs) to produce goods and services for export to national or international markets.

* Strengthen broadly-based local ownership and control of resources by pursuing policies that: (a) allow communities substantial jurisdiction over their own primary resources; and (b) give individual producers control or ownership of their means of production. This would involve measures such as land reform, aquarian reform and policies favorable to locally-owned small farms and enterprises, member-controlled cooperatives and employee-owned corporations.

* Encourage the development of a dense mosaic of independent, politically conscious, voluntary and people's organisations that strengthen the direct participation of citizens in both local and national decision-making processes and provide essential training grounds in democratic citizenship.

* Develop strong, locally accountable, financed and democratically elected autonomous local governments that give residents a strong voice in local affairs.

* Establish transparency in public decision-making and strengthen communication links between people and government.

* Provide economic incentives that favour recovery and recycling over extraction and exploitation.
* Focus on the returns to household and community in choosing among investment options.
* Favour industrial investments that:
  (a) strengthen diversified small and intermediate scale production;
  (b) use environmentally sound resource-conserving, laborising technologies;
  (c) add value to local resources and products;
  (d) serve and enhance competitive efficiency within domestic markets; and
  (e) strengthen backward and forward linkages within the economy.
* Favour intensive, smallholder agriculture based on the use of high productivity, biointensive technologies.
* Give preference to advanced information-intensive technologies over those that are materials-intensive and resource-depleting.
* Give priority to the mobilisation of local resources, savings and social energy. Avoid dependency-creating debt financing, particularly foreign debt, except for clearly productive purposes that will generate the resources for repayment.
* Give high priority to investments in education that build the capacity of people to take charge of their own lives, communities and resources and to participate in local, national and international decision processes.
* Encourage an acceptance of shared responsibility for the well-being of all community members and a reverence for the connections between people and nature.[31]

The practice of PEACE isn't easy; it is often difficult. Yet, as Paulo Friere reminds us, slowly but surely, practice makes perfect:

As I conscientise myself,
I realise that my brothers and sisters
    who don't laugh,
    who don't sing,
    who don't love,
    who live oppressed, crushed and despised lives,
    are suffering
    because of some reality
    that is causing all this.
And at that point
I join in the action historically
    by loving genuinely,
    by having the courage
    to commit myself
    (which is no easy thing)
    or
    I end up with a sense of guilt
    because I am not doing
    what I know I should.
That guilt feeling rankles in me;
it demands (of me something).
I make contributions,
    hoping that way
    to buy peace.
But peace cannot be purchased;
    it is not for sale:
    peace has to be lived.
And I cannot live my peace
    without commitment to people,
    and my commitment to people can't exist
    without their liberation,
    and their liberation can't exist
    without the transformation
    of the structures
    that are dehumanising them.[32]

Part E: The journey

12

The spirituality of community:

'A community derives its coherence from the Creator'

IT'S ALL VERY WELL to talk about community development, but it's another thing to do it well.

Michael Kendrick says: 'We seem to have an ability as human beings to invest hope in whatever seems to be other than what we have right in front of us.' He contends that community needs to be seen as something that is right in front of us, warts and all. Unfortunately, 'right now community is made to look romantic. . . but community is not going to be able to escape the evils that human beings can do.'

He insists that 'we need to look closely at our idea of community and try to develop one that will stand the test of time; that is not just a fad, but will have real benefit for people. We need an idea of community that is based on a realistic vision of what human beings are like — people who are (quite often) not at their best. But we need to have ideals for community that challenge us to be our best. We need to cultivate in ourselves the desire to love one another [and] we need to encourage specific examples of mutual sacrifice and sharing.'[1]

The sociologist, Thomas Caplow, in his assessment of the utopian movements — community development is one of these — says that it is obvious that ordinary groups of people can take up the challenge of becoming what Kendrick calls human beings 'at their best' — human beings who not only 'love one another', but also 'lay down their lives for one another' in order to make their dreams of community come true. But, Caplow says, it is equally obvious that, while many can do so, very few do. Caplow asks himself the question that many of us ask when he enquires, 'Why, in the face of repeated demonstrations that segments of society are perfectible, is there so little interest in perfectionism?'

One answer to the question, Caplow says, might be the matter of scale. 'A utopia cannot be very large if its members are not to have competing affiliations. The utopian formula is applicable only to small settlements, although these may combine into larger federations.'

Another answer to the question, Caplow says, might be the matter of cost. 'The time and energy spent by the utopian organisation on its own maintenance is disproportionate to its resources. The rituals, the convocations, the ceremonies are all very costly.'

Still another answer to the question, Caplow says, might be the matter of efficiency. 'Aside from the direct costs of internal maintenance, utopian organisations tend to be inefficient because achievement is not stressed. The problem of maintaining voluntarism at very high levels takes precedence over problems related to achievement.'

But the answer to the question, underlying all the

rest, Caplow suggests, is a matter of faith. 'A utopian organisation needs an overwhelming incentive. It is misleading to discuss utopia in terms of structure alone. Their members are animated by a powerful faith. . .'[2]

Caplow is not alone in suggesting that our problems in society, and the possible resolution of those problems, are essentially matters of faith.

The philosopher, Jean Paul Sartre, argues that without faith there can be no values, and without values we do not even have a framework for recognising our problems, let alone resolving our problems. In *Existentialism and Humanism*, he wrote: 'The existentialist finds it extremely embarrassing that God does not exist, for there disappears with [God] all possibility of finding values in an intelligible heaven.'[3]

The existentialist, Albert Camus, argues that if there is no faith, there can be no hope for us and, if there is no hope for us, then we are all doomed to despair. 'Up till now, everyone derived their coherence from their Creator. But from the moment that [we] consecrate [our] rupture with God, [we] find [our]selves delivered over to the fleeting moment, to the passing day and the wasted sensibility.'[4]

Fritz Schumacher, the noted proponent of community development in the twentieth century, summed up our contemporary sense of 'wasted sensibility' by saying, simply, that it showed that 'the modern experiment to live without religion has failed'.

Schumacher believes that our only chance of any success in developing the communities we need for survival is by getting back into religion and reconnecting with others, through the Other, once again. According to Schumacher, our problems are not essentially political or economic. They are relational. The problems with our political economy are a consequence of the unresolved conflicts in our communities. According to Schumacher, there is no hope for community development unless we, individually and collectively, begin to deal with our alienation from God, from one another and from ourselves by rediscovering our capacity to:

1. 'act as spiritual beings — that is to say, to act in accordance with [our] moral impulses as human beings'.
2. 'act as social beings — that is to say, to act in accordance with [our] communal impulses as human beings'.
3. 'act as persons — that is to say, to act as autonomous centres of power and responsibility'.[5]

✠ THE PROBLEM WITH RELIGION: *'It can turn entire civilisations into cemeteries'*

Saul Alinsky, the community activist whom Jacques Maratain considered one of the few great men of our century, wrote in the preface of his infamous *Reveille for Radicals* that, as far as he was concerned, the main job of the community organiser was 'organising people so that they will have the power to realise those values of equality, justice, freedom and the preciousness of human life' that he identifies with 'Judeo-Christianity'.[6]

For many people, Judeo-Christianity is the 'gospel' and, for them, what Saul Alinsky says is 'good news'.

However, for many of us who have suffered at the hands of fundamentalists, what Saul Alinsky says is 'bad news'. I can almost hear the agony in the voice of Joachim Kahl, echoing in the groans of many people in my neighbourhood, when he cries out, in *The Misery of Christianity*, 'What to me is [Christianity] but the sado-masochistic glorification of pain?'[7]

Many studies in psychology and sociology would justify Kahl's complaint. They prove that many religious people are actually often less humanitarian, not more humanitarian, than their non-religious neighbours. Allport and Kramer have demonstrated that many religious people are more ethnocentric.[8]

Rokeach has demonstrated that many religious people are more dogmatic.[9]

Wright has demonstrated that many religious people are more judgmental.[10]

Stouffer has demonstrated that many religious people are less tolerant of political dissent.[11]

And Kilpatrick has demonstrated that many religious people are less charitable towards disreputable minorities.[12]

Richard Stellaway contends that 'religious belief has more frequently accommodated, rather than transformed society'.[13]

Take your average church (temple, mosque, synagogue or mandir), for example. 'A congregation may tolerate a minister's stand against injustice only for as long as the issue does not affect them personally. The more popular the congregation is, the less likely it is to advocate unpopular causes. The more established a

congregation is, the less likely it is to advocate change.
The more a congregation is seeking to establish itself in
a community (through recruiting members, raising funds
and building facilities), the less likely it is to take on
issues in the community that require the advocacy of
change.'[14]

Jacques Ellul has pointed out that 'whenever the
church has been in a position of power, it has regarded
freedom as an enemy'. He explains: 'If one turns to
history, it is surely apparent that Christians have more
often imposed restraints than championed liberty. Freedom finds little place in the church's history. It has been
a veritable catastrophe.'[15]

Take the history of my church in my country, for
example. According to social historian Brian Dickey,
'The history for evangelical Christians in welfare [in
Australia] has been conservative in most ways. The
recipients of aid have been treated [as] recipients of aid,
probably with a load of opprobrium thrown in, combined with a dash of social control.'[16]

The Australian commentator, Phillip Adams, speaks
for many cynical Australians in his acerbic but brilliant
critique of religion, appropriately entitled *Adams versus
God*. According to Adams: 'All religions are just a
psychological projection of an external father figure. . .
They are bedtime stories to ward off the darkness, to
soothe us in our fear of death.'

He finds a certain ambiguity in his attitude towards
religion. 'I can understand, and even respect, the yearn-
ings that produce religion, the troubled turbulent doubts
that people call faith. What I do find loathsome are the

internicene wars, the faction fighting that turns church into a charnal house. At its best, religion has lifted spirits and raised spires. At its worst, it has turned entire civilisations into cemeteries.'

It is his contention that: 'Religion is not the "opiate of the people". Opium suggests something soporific, numbing, dulling. Too often, religion has been the aphrodisiac of horror, a benzedrine for brutality.'

Of all religious groups, Adams considers the fundamentalists the worst, holding them accountable for the worst atrocities done in the name of religion. Fundamentalists are 'a humourless bunch' who see God as a grumpy old man. He contends that their churches are nothing but 'small totalitarian societies with a library of just one book'. The missionaries these churches send out practise 'a scorched earth policy' in their proselytisation, 'a cultural uprooting of local faiths from which many societies have never recovered'.

Phillip Adams concludes by saying, rather whimsically, but perhaps rather wistfully, too: 'If there was a God, I think he would dislike fundamentalists as much as I do.'[17]

✠ THE POTENTIAL OF RELIGION:
'It is a means of either enslavement or emancipation'

Aloysius Pieres says in his *Theology of Liberation* that: 'Every religion, Christianity included, is at once a sign and a countersign of the kingdom of God; that the revolutionary impetus launching a religion into existence is both fettered and fostered by the need for an ideological formulation; that its institutionalisation both constrains and conserves its liberative force; that religion, therefore, is a potential means of either enslavement or emancipation.'[18]

Many studies in psychology and sociology exemplify the point that Pieres is trying to make. They prove that while some religious people are actually often less humanitarian than their non-religious neighbours because of their religion, some religious people are actually often more humanitarian than their non-religious neighbours because of their religion.

Peter Glew-Crouch has shown in a recent study that the relationship between religious beliefs and humanitarian behaviour is not a simple linear one, but a more complicated curvilinear one, which no doubt when drawn would take the form of a bell graph. His study demonstrates that people who don't get into the ideology of an institutionalised religion are less likely to be prejudiced, for example, than those who do. But his study also demonstrates that people who get beyond the ideology of an institutionalised religion are less likely to be prejudiced than either of their religious, or their non-religious, neighbours.[19]

A review of the contemporary research on 'voluntarism' by David Gerard demonstrates that the most significant difference between those who are prepared to give themselves freely to work with others in the community and those who aren't is a degree of religious devotion to the Other that transcends their egocentricity.[20]

A review of the contemporary research on altruism

by Craig Seaton demonstrates that the most significant difference between those who are prepared to give their lives, sacrificially, to save the lives of others in the community and those who aren't is a degree of religious devotion to the Other that transcends their ethnocentricity.[21]

Scott Peck suggests that there are four distinct stages of growth in religion. The first stage is antisocial confusion. The second stage is institutional conformity. The third stage is individual nonconformity. And the fourth stage is communal spirituality.

For people who have been 'confused', no doubt the clarity of religious 'conformity', of one kind or another, can be quite helpful. But if people do not grow beyond acceptance of 'conformity' to a respect for 'nonconformity', they can get stuck at a stage of religious development where they get so locked into their dogma that they simply can't relate to an Other. Community development becomes a sheer impossibility. However, if people grow towards a stage of 'spirituality' where they acquire the maturity to be able to facilitate unity and diversity with an Other, regardless of dogma, religion can play a very creative role in community development.[22]

According to a survey conducted by S.J. Samartha, this type of spirituality is actually playing a vital part in much of the community development taking place in many of the new movements happening around the world today. 'One emphasis in all new movements,' Samartha says, 'is a more satisfying human life here and now. Another emphasis is the search for new forms of

community, partly as a protest against traditional, petri-
fied forms of community that stifled freedom and partly
because of the pressures of modern life that demand new
groupings and new relationships.'

'Seeking renewal,' Samartha says, 'movements of
innovation go back to the spiritual core. . . back to their
original resources. . . to discover a framework of meaning in which the person has a vocation to discover
community.'[23]

As the sociologist of religion, Oscar Maduro, says:
'The true role of religion is to enable people to transcend
the dominant ideologies of the day and to encourage the
people, so empowered, to criticise the *status quo*, catalyse
change in the system and create communities in which
they can overcome the evil with good.'[24]

✠ A ROLE FOR RELIGION:
'To create communities which overcome evil with good'

I think I learnt most about the role that religion can
play in the development of communities when I lived
in India.

As I've already said, Ange and I lived for many years
in a multifaith community, known as Aashiana.
Aashiana was a small group of some twenty to thirty
young people who had got together, from various religious backgrounds, to try to discern what it might mean
to practise the compassion of God, exemplified in the
life of Jesus of Nazareth, in New Delhi.

At the heart of our spirituality were six emphases
that were central to our apprehension of community:

☐ The *process* of prayer

Prayer, in Aashiana, was the process of 'developing an awareness of, and availability to, the Other'. It involved a conscious 'waiting upon the Other' and a 'willingness to yield to the Other'.

It was essentially a 'creative response to life in the light of the love of the Other'.

☐ The *place* of prayer

Prayer had an important place in the life we shared together. It was considered to be the centre of the community and the catalyst for community development: the still point around which the life of the community revolved; the point of integration where the conflicts in the community were resolved; the starting point at which people began to live again; and the point of departure from which people began to experiment and explore another way of living.

We emphasised the importance of prayer because we believed that community begins and ends with the Other and, in prayer, we could meet the Other who is the beginning and the end of the community development process.

It was in encounter with the Other that we believed that all that is good could be defined and affirmed, all that is evil could be exposed and opposed, and our task for the future outlined.

It was in encounter with the Other that we believed a vision of justice could be revealed and an infusion of grace could be realised.

It was in encounter with the Other that we believed

we could develop discernment in the midst of disorientation, energy when we had exhausted our ability, and endurance where we would have otherwise withdrawn.

It was in prayer, therefore, that we felt we could begin to engage, with the Other, in the struggle for the salvation of the world.

☐ The *inspiration* of prayer

It was in prayer that a vision for justice emerged. This is what I wrote elsewhere about this experience:

> It was a vision of *equality*, in which all the resources of the earth would be shared equally between all the people on earth regardless of nationality, colour, caste, class or creed.
>
> It was a vision of *equity*, in which even the most disadvantaged people would be able to meet their basic needs for good water, adequate food, sufficient clothing and secure accommodation, with dignity.
>
> It was a vision of a great society of small communities interdependently cooperating to practise political, socio-economic and personal righteousness and peace in every locality.[25]

And it was in prayer that we began to feel the inflow of an infusion of grace to enable us to realise our vision for justice:

> [It was] an infusion of grace that enabled us to begin to deal with the reality of our limitations and contradictions.
>
> [It was] an infusion of grace that enabled us to move beyond angry reactions to just actions that transcended those limitations and resolved those contradictions.

[It was] an infusion of grace that enabled us to
respond, if not always with courage, at least with
conviction, compassionately, constructively and pro-
ductively.[26]

We knew that there were many who pray but do
not act and many who act but do not pray. But it
seemed to us that such people had misunderstood the
meaning of both prayer and action.

Prayer, for us, was the inspiration for action.

When we prayed, we came into the presence of a Love
so profound that it challenged all our plans, opinions
and prejudices, and called us to a cause of pure compassion.

In the presence of that Love, we had to act with
love. Because to do anything else seemed utterly absurd.

In the presence of that Love, we were set free from
a preoccupation with meeting our needs for a vocation
of seeking peace on the basis of justice for all.[27]

Thus it was, through prayer, we developed a concern
for the people in our city. And it was, through prayer,
we developed a commitment to the people in the slums.
And it was, through prayer, we developed contact with
the Kanjars, the so-called 'Unclean Ones' that lived
across the road.

The Kanjars were a tribe of a thousand people who
migrated to the city in search of food during a time of
famine and ended up eking out an existence ever since
in one of the city's slums.

It was a very precarious existence. They lived in 200
little huts with thatch roofs, supported by bamboo poles,
that consistently failed to keep out inclement weather

— the cold in winter, the heat in summer or the rain in monsoon. Each hut housed a family of five or more — a grandparent, a couple of parents and two or three children in the space of a tent fit for two in a tight squeeze.

Around the huts, the dusty ground was covered with bits of trash, different kinds of refuse and faeces. Pigs rooted through the rubbish, searching for titbits of excrement to snaffle. The only water was a smelly, stagnant pool nearby that bred mosquitoes, carrying malaria round the settlement. There wasn't a single tap or pump that supplied any drinking water. If people wanted a drink, they had to beg for it.

They tried to survive on a diet of rotten fruit and vegetables that they scavenged from the waste bins in the neighbourhood. Disease was rampant. Death stalked the encampment. It seemed like someone died in the slum every week.

They lived with tremendous dignity. But behind the smiles, there were always tears. The joke was always on them. They were outcast, illiterate, illegal squatters, always being hassled by the public and harassed by the police.

We were determined to join them in their struggle for justice.[28]

◻ **The _pattern_ of prayer**

In our struggle with the Kanjars, we began to see that prayer was not just a means of doing justice, but that it was the _model_ for doing justice. To do justice to them, the process of community development needed to not only conform to the pattern of prayer, but actually become a form of prayer itself:

Community development is usually a form of intervention.

In any intervention, we tend to take on the concerns of others as our own. And we tend to depend on ourselves, and our capacity to help, to facilitate the resolution of the problems in the community.

This means we will only tend to work with people we think we can help and we will only work with them as long as our help is facilitating the resolution of the problems in the community.

If we had approached the Kanjars on these terms, we probably would have never started at all. But if by some strange turn of events we had, we certainly would not have stayed with the process very long because, as far as we were concerned, the situation was simply impossible.

It was only as our notion of community development was transformed in prayer — from an act of *intervention*, which depended on the expertise we had, into an act of *intercession*, which depended on the power God had to do something about the situation that we obviously could not do — that we were able to begin to engage in the struggle for justice alongside the Kanjars.

Right from the start, we realised that to do justice to them as people we would need to act with more regard for the process and less regard for the outcome.

We realised that if we acted with an eye on the outcome, we would tend to only select actions that were potentially successful and would tend to only concentrate on activities that would make us successful.

[This] seemed fair enough, till we realised that, in the process of focusing on success, we were most likely to exclude people from the project who were least likely to be successful; we were most likely to try to control the project and the people in the project for the sake of our success.

So, in order to avoid adding insult to injury, we tried to approach the process of community development with the Kanjars as we would approach prayer — that is, in a spirit of openness and responsiveness, being willing to do our bit, without any expectation of ever controlling the outcome.

When we began to visit the Kanjars, they were very suspicious. They had no visitors who were friends — no-one who just wanted to spend time with them, relate to them, talk with them, listen to them, or struggle with their concerns in an open-ended manner. The only visitors that ever made their way to the slums were politicians, who came looking for votes to collect at election time, or proselytizers, who came looking for souls to convert to their particular sect. So they were very suspicious of visitors who said they wanted to be their friends.

However, over innumerable cups of tea in the ensuing months, we were able to develop reciprocal relationships with real mutual regard. They were able to put us to the test, find us more or less trustworthy and transcend, if not suspend, their suspicions enough [for them] to be able to relate to us with a remarkable degree of vulnerability, which we did our best to reciprocate. So before the year was out, we were able to start to share our aspirations with one another.[29]

❐ The *power* of prayer

Hope of justice, for people without any hope of justice like the Kanjars, could not possibly develop on the basis of their experience. Their experience, characterised by a continual litany of one injustice after another, may make hope imperative, but it also makes it impossible. We all knew there was no 'quick fix' for the Kanjars.

The only hope they had was in the construction of an alternative future that would be in total contrast to their present situation and a total contradiction of their past history. But to be able to even begin to try to construct an alternative future, the people needed to discover the power to act against their conditioning, while the personal, social, cultural and political circumstances in which they were conditioned were still the dominant and dominating realities that circumscribed their lives.

And that they felt was, quite literally, beyond them. So the only hope of any hope for the Kanjars depended on their capacity to access a power beyond themselves:

> We were aware that there was a power that could be released in prayer that could be explained in terms of psychology and sociology.
>
> 'A self-therapy takes place,' Jacques Ellul explains. 'There is the giving up of anger and aggressiveness, a validation through responsibility and meditation, a recovery of balance through the rearranging of facts on successive levels as seen from a fresh outlook.'
>
> But we were also aware that there was a power that could be released in prayer that was beyond the capacity of contemporary psychology and sociology to explain. Ellul calls it 'the effectual, immediate presence of the wholly Other, the Transcendent, the Living One'.
>
> We knew that if we were to access enough power to break the bondage of our conditioning so that we would be free to think and talk and work towards an alternative future with the community, we not only needed as much self-therapy as we could get, but we also needed something 'wholly Other' than anything we had ever tried before.
>
> It was in the early days of our involvement with the Kanjars when it happened. . . The people were still quite nervous about any innovations. But, more out of desperation than anything else, they had decided to go ahead with a primary health program.
>
> They built a hut for a clinic and a medical student

volunteered to help the people with sanitation, nutrition and basic health care. For a while it seemed as if the program might not only empower the community to deal with their dysentery, but also with their despair.

But at a critical stage in the development of this program, a child fell seriously ill. She was brought to the clinic for help. But there was nothing that either the medical student or the other doctors she consulted could do to help. The diagnosis was tetanus. The prognosis was death.

We sensed that, if this child were to die, with it would die not only the hopes of the parents, but also the hopes of all the other parents who had hoped against hope that, at long last, their lives might be different.

So we did the only 'Other' thing we could do at the time — we called the community together for prayer.

Even though we all prayed for the child to live, I think all of us expected it to die. But it didn't. And that made all the difference — because it proved beyond doubt that things could be different. And that belief, that things could be different, unleashed the latent confidence in people that they could be different, in spite of their conditioning. And that confidence that they could be different became the foundation of all the work that the Kanjars have done to develop the community since that day.

I remember talking to Ramu, a Kanjar leader, before I left India. I asked him what he thought were the most significant changes that had taken place in the Kanjar community. I shall never forget what he said. He said: We have changed in many ways, *Daud bhai*:

* We believe God is for us. Not against us.
* Though we are little people, we are no longer afraid of big people. We are prepared to stand up for what is right — like the time we marched to the Office of

the Lieutenant Governor of New Delhi to demand
hamara [our own] land and *pukkha* [permanent] houses.
* We work things out better now in the community
council. We do not have as many fights. Remember the fights we used to have, when we used to
throw those big bricks at one another?
* These days us men spend less time taking drugs and
getting stoned. We work in the garbage recycling
co-op we have set up. We are able to bring in
enough money — two or three times more than we
used to get before — to meet more needs at home.
Our wives are happier. Our children are healthier.
And not so many of us die so young any more.
* Not everything is good. Many things are still bad.
But it's a whole lot better than it was before.[30]

☐ The *practice* of prayer

I have never forgotten the lessons I learnt in India about
the part that prayer can play in community development. And though it does not seem to come as easy in
Australia as it used to in India, I always try to remember
to put prayer at the heart of the process of whatever I'm
doing in the community I'm working with.

Let me suggest a few ways of praying that a lot of
people in our community, which is not particularly
religious, have found very helpful:

* *Be glad to be alive.* I try to make sure I get
enough sleep each night; that I can wake up
every morning, not groggy, not grumpy, but
glad to be alive. As I wake, I try to be aware
of the Life around me that is welling up within
me and give myself over to the joy of living.
* *Let the grudges go.* In order to prepare myself

for the day, I take a bit of time just to sense the tensions in my body that signal things I am uptight about. Usually these are grievances, real or perceived, of ways that people thwart my plans. I note the issues that they raise that I need to address. Then I let them go.

* *Let the love flow.* Once I let my grudges go, I can begin to let the love flow. I try to do this by bringing to mind all the people that I am connected to in the locality, then one by one picture their face, speak their name and pronounce a blessing upon each and every one of them, friend and foe alike.

* *Deliberate on the locality.* I often leave my house in a hurry and I'm on the move from morning to night. But at regular intervals throughout the day, I always take the time to stop, look and listen, to deliberate on the activities, conversations and undercurrents in the locality.

* *Meditate on the community.* Every now and again, I go up to the top of a hill which overlooks my locality to put that reality into a bit of perspective. I meditate on the community as it is and as it might be. I imagine all the things we could do to bring people in the neighbourhood together.

* *Contemplate responsibility.* Because there's so many things I *could* do, it's very difficult to figure out exactly what I *should* do. I am often confused. So I seek clarity by listening to the still small voice inside me. I keep listening until I

hear a word that is just right for me. Then I take that word to heart.

* *Discern a direction.* I take it to heart. But I don't go for it on my own. I run it by a group of people whose opinions I trust. And together we decide what we are going to do about it. I meet with a bunch of people in my neighbourhood each Monday morning, just to discern the direction we ought to take, on the basis of consensus.

* *Reflect on actions.* Even if I get the direction right, it doesn't mean I get the action right. I actually get it wrong far more often than I'd like to admit. So it's really important to be a part of a group that can help us evaluate our progress. I meet with a bunch of people in my neighbourhood each Wednesday morning to reflect on our actions.

* *Celebrate an achievement.* When I reflect on my actions, I am brought face-to-face with my failures as well as my successes. And if I'm not careful, I can let my failures discount my successes. It's really important to be a part of a group that can help us validate our progress, through success and failure. I meet with a bunch of people in my neighbourhood each Friday morning who celebrate any sort of achievement that any of us has managed to accomplish, no matter how big, or how small, it may be.

* *Consecrate the movement.* Every Sunday night, up to a hundred of us gather for community

worship. It's a time when a whole lot of us can get together, share our stories, confess our struggles, sing our songs of hope and despair and consecrate the movement, be it ever so faltering, towards the realisation of community in our ordinary everyday lives.

Every time we meet, a different person organises the liturgy. But barely a service goes by without someone using a prayer by Michael Leunig. Michael Leunig, Australia's foremost cartoonist, writes prayers for the *Sunday Age* as his contribution to what he calls 'this wonderful, free-form, do-it-yourself ritual of connection and transformation'.

So, it is probably fitting that we finish with a prayer by Michael Leunig that is a favourite of ours:

God help us to change.
To change ourselves,
    and to change our world.
To know the need for it.
To deal with the pain of it.
To feel the joy of it.
To undertake the journey
    without understanding the destination,
    the art of gentle revolution.[31]

Endnotes

Chapter 1
1. Hugh Mackay, *Reinventing Australia*, Angus and Robertson, 1993, p.3
2. 'God Help the Poor on the Dole', Sunshine Coast, Queensland
3. 'TV Reality', *Dolly*, July 1991
4. Penelope Russianoff, *Why Do I Think I am Nothing without a Man?*, Bantam, 1982, p.2
5. Ruth Stanley, 'Cruelty's Cost', unpublished poem, 1983
6. Anonymous, 'Daddy, Please Don't', unpublished poem, 1987
7. Tim Corney, 'Seeking Hope in the Ruins of Postmodernity', *Zadok Perspectives*, No. 49, July 1995, p.3. Used with permission.
8. Hugh Mackay, *Reinventing Australia*, Angus and Robertson, 1993, p.264
9. *Ibid*, p.271
10. *Ibid*, p.272
11. *Ibid*, p.285

Chapter 2
1. Lel Black, 'To See the Storyteller', *Network News*, Queensland Community Arts, first edition 1995, pp.8–9
2. Stephen Oates, *Let the Trumpet Sound*, New American Library, 1982, pp.260–262
3. *Ibid*, p.262
4. Anne Hope and Sally Timmel, *Training for Transformation*, Mambo Press, 1984, p.130
5. Emma Goldman in Conversation with Trevor Jordan
6. Colin Ward, *Utopia*, Penguin, 1974, p.82
7. Brian Mollison, *Introduction to Permaculture*, Tagari Publications, 1991, pp.169–170

8. Katrina Shields, *In the Tiger's Mouth*, Millenium Books, 1991, p.24
9. *Ibid*, p.24
10. Dave Andrews, *Can You Hear the Heartbeat?*, Hodder and Stoughton, 1989, p.xiii (edited)

Chapter 3

1. Colin Bell and Howard Newby, *Community Studies*, George Allen and Unwin, 1971, p.2
2. R. Williams, *Keywords: A Vocabulary of Culture and Society*, Fontana, 1976, p.66
3. L. Bryson and M. Mowbray, 'Community: The Spray-on Solution', *Australian Journal of Social Issues*, Vol.16, No.1, p.256
4. R. Nisbet, *The Sociological Tradition*, Heinemann, 1966, ch.3
5. Robert Bellah et al, *Habits of the Heart*, University of California Press, 1985, p.286
6. Gorody. Reference unknown.
7. Tim Corney, *Zadok Perspectives*
8. George A. Hillery, 'Definitions of Community: Areas of Agreement', *Rural Sociology*, No.20, 1955
9. David Clark, *Basic Communities*, SPCK, 1975, pp.4–5
10. Frederick Toennies, *Community and Society*, Harper, 1957, pp.12–29
11. John Cobb and Herman Daley, *For the Common Good*, Beacon Press, 1992, p.170
12. M. Scott Peck, *The Different Drum*, Rider and Co., 1988, p.59
13. Luther Smith, *Intimacy and Mission*, Herald Press, 1994, pp.98–100
14. Henri Nouwen, *Reaching Out*, Doubleday, 1975, pp.48–51
15. Jean Vanier, *Community and Growth*, St Paul, 1989, pp.31–32
16. M. Scott Peck, *The Different Drum*, Rider, 1988, pp.61–62
17. Jean Vanier, *ibid*, pp.20–22
18. John Cobb and Herman Daley, *ibid*, p.172
19. M. Scott Peck, *ibid*, p.63
20. A. Etzioni, *The Spirit of Community*, Simon and Schuster, 1993, pp.144–147
21. Anonymous

Chapter 4

1. Michael Kendrick, 'Community Living', *Interaction*, National Council on Intellectual Disability, Canada, 1989, p.20
2. George Lovell, *The Church and Community Development*, Grail, 1980, p.20

3. Tony Kelly, and Sandra Sewell, *People Working Together* (Vol.2), Boolarong, 1986, pp.5-17
4. Digby Hannah, 'Upside Down Camps', *Zadok Perspectives*, No.48, March 1995, pp.10–12. Used with permission.
5. *The Program for Personal Growth*, Grow (International), Canberra, p.5
6. 'Free and Whole Together', *Input,* Grow (International), Canberra, Vol.6, No.4, October 1992, pp.1–2 (quote edited slightly)
7. 'Mary and the Caring and Sharing Community', *Grow Comes of Age*, C. Keogh (ed.), Grow, Sydney, 1979, p.40, pp.118–120 (quote edited slightly)
8. *The Program of Growth to Maturity*, Grow, Canberra, 1957, p.79
9. Noritta Morseu Diop, *The Bristol Street Household*, unpublished paper, Brisbane, 1992, p.1 (quote edited slightly)
10. Jason McLeod, *Bristol Street*, unpublished paper, Brisbane, 1993, pp.1–10 (quote edited slightly)
11. Jim Dowling, 'Ten Years of the Catholic Worker in Brisbane', *Dayspring*, Summer, 1993-1994, pp.3–5 (quote edited slightly)
12. George Lovell, *The Church and Community Development*, Grail, 1980, p.2
13. George Lovell, *ibid*, p.2
14. M. Scott Peck, *The Different Drum*, Rider, 1987, pp.86ff

Chapter 5

1. Alan Twelvetrees, *Community Work*, MacMillan, 1982, p.112 (quote abbreviated slightly)
2. L. Bryson, & M. Mowbray, 'Community: The Spray-on Solution', *Australian Journal of Social Issues*, 1981, Vol.16, No.1, p.258
3. Michael Kendrick, *op.cit.*, p.21
4. John McKnight, 'Regenerating Community', p.9
5. M. Scott Peck, *The People of the Lie*, Simon & Schuster, 1985, p.229
6. Michael Kendrick, *op.cit.*, p.20
7. *Ibid*, p.21
8. *Ibid*, p.22 (quote abbreviated slightly)
9. *Ibid*, p.22 (quote abbreviated slightly)
10. *Ibid*, p.22 (quote abbreviated slightly)
11. *Ibid*, p.22 (quote abbreviated slightly)
12. Trisha Vanderwall, 'Broken Hearts, Broken Minds', *On Being*, 1991, Vol.18, No.7, p.12
13. P. Hammond, 'Ward 10B', *Courier Mail*, 27 February 1991, p.3, 9, 12

14. 'House of Horrors', *Sixty Minutes*, Channel 9, 20 December 1990
15. Charles Elliot, *Comfortable Compassion*, Hodder & Stoughton, 1987, p.126
16. *Ibid*, p.126
17. Robert Chambers, *Rural Development*, Longmans, 1983, p.210
18. *Ibid*, p.217 (quote abbreviated slightly)
19. George Foster, *Traditional Societies and Technological Change*, Harper & Row, 1973, p.178
20. *Ibid*, p.178
21. *Ibid*, p.178
22. M. Scott Peck, *op.cit*, p.216
23. *Ibid*, p.216
24. Gene Sharp, *Power and Struggle*, Porter Sargent, 1973, p.9
25. *Ibid*, pp.9-10
26. *Ibid*, pp.11 and 12
27. *Ibid*, pp.18-24
28. *Ibid*, pp.25-32
29. *Ibid*, p.25 (quote abbreviated slightly)
30. *Ibid*, p.32
31. *Ibid*, p.36
32. Charles Elliot, *op.cit*, p.129
33. *Ibid*, p.31
34. Robert Chambers, *op.cit.*, p.211
35. *Ibid*, p.215
36. *Ibid*, p.215 (quote abbreviated slightly)
37. George Foster, *op.cit., p.150*
38. M. Scott Peck, *op.cit.*, p.215
39. *Ibid*, p.215
40. *Ibid*, p.215

Chapter 6

1. J. Wagner, *The Search for Signs of Intelligent Life in the Universe*, Harper & Row, 1985
2. Tom Hampson and Loretta Whalen, *Tales of the Heart*, Friendship Press, 1991
3. Lyle Schaller, *The Change Agent*, Abingdon Press, 1986, p.11
4. Michael Kendrick, *op.cit*, p.19
5. Lyle Schaller, *op.cit.*, p.118
6. T. Batten, *Communities and their Development*, OUP, 1957, pp.20–23
7. Lyle Schaller, pp.169–171
8. T. Batten, *op.cit*, p.185

9. Wolf Wolfensberger, 'Social Role Valorisation', *Mental Retardation*, Vol.21, No.6, 1983, pp.27–29
10. F. and J. Panckhurst, *Evaluation, Standards and Accreditation for Government Subsidised Services for Handicapped People*, F. & E. Schonnel Centre, Brisbane, 1982
11. *Ibid*
12. Jean Vanier, *The Challenge of L'Arche*, Dartman, Longman and Todd, 1982, p.2
13. *Ibid*, pp.259–260 (edited)
14. J. O'Brien, 'Discovering Community', *Changing Patterns in Residential Services for Persons with Mental Disabilities*, Presidents Committee on Mental Retardation, Washington, 1987, p.34
15. Jean Vanier, *op.cit*, pp.259–260
16. Robert Greenleaf, *Servant Leadership*, St Pauls, p.237
17. *Ibid*, p.237
18. *Ibid*, p.50
19. Alan Twelvetrees, *op.cit.*, p.58
20. Lyle Schaller, *op.cit*, p.61–62 (quote abbreviated slightly)
21. *Ibid*, p.175 (quote abbreviated slightly)
22. *Ibid*, p.175
23. Charles Elliot, *op.cit*, p.153–154

Chapter 7

1. Australian Government Social Work Commission, *Community Development Controversies and Issues*, 1975
2. Adapted from *Community Development in Queensland*, QCOSS
3. Adapted from *Community Development in Queensland*, QCOSS
4. Fred Milson, *Introduction to Community*, Rutledge Kegan Pond, 1973
5. Rahindrinath Tagore, quoted in lecture by Tony Kelly, 1923
6. Henry Bugbee, *The Inward Meaning*, Harper & Row, 1976, p.155
7. T. Hampson, and L. Whalen, *op.cit.*, p.170
8. Parker Palmer, *To Know as we are Known*, Harper, 1993, p.X
9. T. Hampson, and L. Whalen, *op.cit.*, p.193
10. Parker Palmer, *op.cit*, pp.xiii–xv. Used with permission.
11. *Ibid*, pp.7–8
12. *Ibid*, pp.30–32
13. Thich Nhat Hanh, 'Please Call Me By My True Name', in *Being Peace*, Parallax Press
14. Trevor Jordan, *Social Ethics and the Justice System*, QUP, 1993, Pt 2, p.1
15. Amitai Etzioni, *op.cit*, p.31

16. *Ibid*, p.13
17. *Ibid*, p.31
18. *Ibid*, p.35
19. *Ibid*, p.30
20. *Ibid*, p.36
21. Robert Fulgham, 'We Learned it all in Kindergarten', *Kansas City Times*, September 17, 1984
22. D. Hardman, 'Not with my Daughter you Don't!', *Social Work*, Vol.20, No.4, Nat. Assoc. of Social Workers, July 1975, pp.278–285
23. Stephen Covey, *The Seven Habits of Effective People*, The Business Library, 1994, pp.34–35
24. A. Etzioni, *ibid*, pp.98 and 99
25. Beverly Wildung Harrison, *Making the Connections: Essays in Feminist Social Ethics*, Carol S. Robb (ed.), Beacon Press, 1985, p.250
26. Karen Lebacqz, 'Pain and Pedagogy', in *Education for Citizenship and Discipleship*, Mary C. Buys (ed.), The Pilgrim Press, 1989, p.173
27. *Ibid*, p.170
28. Paulo Friere, in *Walk in My Shoes*, ABA, 1977, p.92
29. Stephen Covey, *op.cit.*, p.46
30. *Ibid*, p.317

Chapter 8

1. *Encyclopedia of Religious Quotations*, F. Mead (ed.), Peter Davis, 1965, p.400
2. Ved Mehta, *Mahatma Gandhi and his Apostles*, Penguin, 1977, p.46
3. Stephen Covey, *op.cit.*, pp.69–70
4. *Ibid*, pp.69–70
5. *Ibid*, p.71
6. *Ibid*, p.72
7. Katherine Spink, *A Chain of Love*, SPCK, 1984, p.3
8. Malcolm Muggeridge, *Something Beautiful for God*, Collins, 1971, pp.19–22
9. Carl Jung, *Collected Works*, Princeton University Press, 1967, vol.17, ch.vii, pp.167–187
10. Ange Andrews, 'Who of you will join me?', *Dayspring*
11. Stephen Covey, *op.cit.*, p.128
12. Carl Jung, *op.cit.*, pp.167–187
13. Stephen Covey, *op.cit*, p.108
14. Carl Jung, *op.cit.*, pp.167–187

15. W. Bryan, *Preventing Burnout in the Public Interest Community*, Northern Rockies Action Group Paper, NRAG, Vol.3, No.3, 1980
16. Katrina Shields, *In the Tiger's Mouth*, Millennium, 1991, p.124
17. Dave Andrews, *op.cit.*, p.32
18. Stephen Covey, *op.cit.*, pp.81-85
19. Art Gish, *Living in Christian Community*, Albatross, 1979, pp.47-54
20. Peter Westoby, *Waiting in Line*, QCT, 1994, pp.13-24

Chapter 9

1. Fran Peavey, *Heart Politics*, New Society Publishers, 1986, p.1
2. Mike Riddell, *Godzone*, Lion, 1992, p.15
3. Gerard Dowling, *Frameworks*, unpublished paper, 1989, p.19
4. Fran Peavey, *op.cit.*, pp.142-147
5. B. Entwhistle, *Making Cities Work*, Hope Publishing, 1990, pp.xi-xiv, pp.60-88. Used with permission.
6. Stephen Covey, *op.cit.*, pp.49-51
7. Stephen Covey, *op.cit.*, pp.150-155
8. J. Rothman, *Planning and Organising for Social Change*, Columbia University Press, 1974
9. R. Chambers, *Rural Development*, Longman, 1983, p.173ff
10. *Ibid*
11. *Ibid*
12. Robert Greenleaf, *op.cit.*, p.294
13. T. Kelly and S. Sewell, *With Head Heart and Hand*, Boolarong, 1988, p.60
14. Stephen Covey, *op.cit.*, p.258
15. A. and W. Howard, *Exploring the Road Less Travelled*, Rider, 1985, p.80
16. Jean Vanier, *op.cit.*, p.17
17. M. Scott Peck, *A World Waiting to be Born*, Bantam, 1993, pp.290-291
18. Stephen Covey, *op.cit.*, pp.262-263
19. *Ibid*, p.263

Chapter 10

1. I. Brown, *Understanding Other Cultures*, 1963
2. Frederick Toennies, *Community and Society*, Harper, 1957, pp.12-29

3. John Cobb and Herman Daley, *For the Common Good*, Beacon Press, p.170
4. Hugh MacKay, *op.cit.*, pp.155–156
5. adapted from R. Linton, 'A Hundred Per Cent American', *The American Mercury*, Vol.40 (1937), pp.427–429
6. Hugh MacKay, *op.cit*, p.160
7. James Jupp and M. Kabala, *The Politics of Immigration*, Bureau of Immigration Research, 1993, pp.18–19
8. Pat Dodson, *Aboriginal and Torres Strait Islander People and Multiculturalism*, QUT, Brisbane, 23/8/93, pp.9–10
9. *The Cultured Pearl*, J. Houston (ed.), JBCE, 1986, p.229
10. Australian Council on Population and Ethnic Affairs, *Multiculturalism for all Australians*, Australian Government Printing Service, 1982
11. B. Chambers, and J. Pettman, *Anti-Racism*, Australian Government Printing Service, 1986, p.26
12. Fred Hollows, *An Autobiography*, Kerr Publishing, 1991, pp.259, 87–90, 100–101. Used with permission.
13. Nimmi Hutnik, Ethnic Minority Identity, OUP, 1991
14. S. Hitchings, 'Mandawuy Yinupingu', in *Australian Left Review*, June 1992, p.3
15. Mandawuy Yinupingu, 'The Yothu Yindi Family', *BIPR Bulletin*, April 1992, pp.26–27
16. S. Hitchings, *op.cit.*, p.3
17. Mandawuy Yingupingu, *op.cit.*, pp.26–27
18. D. Washington, 'Living Together', *On Being*, Melbourne, May 1995, p.22
19. D. Washington, *ibid*, pp.21–24
20 *Green Shoots in the Concrete*, Peter Kaldor et al (eds), Scaffolding, 1985, pp.63–67
21. These terms are in Hindi. We learnt to take these steps in India.

Chapter 11

1. Jacques Ellul, *The Presence of the Kingdom*, Seabury, 1967, p.42
2. *Encyclopaedia Britannica*, University of Chicago, 1975, Vol.14, p.697
3. Fred Milson, *op.cit.*
4. Bob Goudzwaard, *Idols of Our Time*, IVP, Downers Grove, 1981, p.23
5. G. Harland, *The Thought of Reinhold Niebuhr*, OUP, 1960, pp.5–10
6. Michael Cassidy, *The Politics of Love*, Hodder and Stoughton, 1991, p.124

7. *Ibid*, pp.125–135
8. G. Harland, *op.cit.*, pp.20–25
9. Dave Andrews, *op.cit.*, p.27
10. *Ibid*, p.27
11. *Ibid*, p.28
12. *Ibid*, p.28
13. *Ibid*, p.28
14. G. Harland, *The Thought of Reinhold Niebuhr*, OUP, p.56
15. J. Rawls, *A Theory of Justice*, Harvard University Press, 1971, p.302
16. Allan Halladay, *Confronting Disadvantage with the Context of Social Justice*, University of Queensland, 1986, p.14
17. *Ibid*
18. *Ibid*, p.164
19. Jacques Ellul, *The Political Illusion*, A.A. Knopf, 1967, pp.224–236
20. *Teaching Geography for a Better World*, J. Fien and Gerber (eds), Australian Geography Teachers Association, Jacaranda Press, 1986, p.153
21. Susan Black, *Digging in Our Own Backyard*, Social Work Department, University of Queensland, 1987, pp.55–56
22. Ciaron O'Reilly, 'Local Church to Declare Sanctuary. . .', *Neighbourhood News*, Issue No.28, November 1995, p.15
23. Richard Waller, 'Church Offers Sanctuary for East Timor Refugees', *Courier Mail*, 6 November 1995
24. Bruce Gibbs, 'It doesn't come much harder', *Target*, TEAR Australia, Melbourne, No.4, 1995, pp.2–3
25. Brett Gresham and Ruth Hearbinson, Personal Letters and Published Quotes, 'But I'm an Engineer!', *Target*, ibid, pp.9–11
26. Dave Andrews, 'What Christlikeness is All About', *On Being*
27. David Korton, *Getting into the 21st Century*, Kumarian Press, 1990, p.67
28. *Ibid*, pp.67–68
29. *Ibid*, p.68 (quote slightly edited)
30. *Ibid*, p.69
31. *Ibid*, pp.69–70
32. *Walk in My Shoes*, ABA, Melbourne, 1977, p.92

Chapter 12

1. Michael Kendrick, 'Community Living', *Interaction* 3, Vol.3, Canada, 1989, p.20–24
2. Thomas Caplow, *Principles of Organisations*, Harcourt, Brace, 1964, p.315
3. Jean Paul Sartre, *Existentialism and Humanism*, 1948, p.33

4. Albert Camus, *The Rebel*. Reference unknown.
5. Fritz Schumacher, *Guide for the Perplexed*, 1980, pp.115–116
6. Saul Alinsky, *Reveille for Radicals*, Vintage, 1969, p.xiv
7. Joachim Kahl, *The Misery of Christianity*, Penguin, 1971
8. P. Allport and B. Kramer, 'Some Roots of Prejudice', *Journal of Psychology*, 1946, 22, pp.9–39
9. Rokeach, M., *The Open and Closed Mind*, Basic Books, 1960
10. D. Wright, *Psychology and Moral Behaviour*, Penguin, 1971
11. S.A. Stouffer, *Communism, Conformity and Civil Liberties*, Doubleday, 1955
12. Peter Glew-Crouch, *Religion and Helping Behaviour*, University of Tasmania, 1989
13. R. Stellaway, 'Religion', *Christian Perspectives of Sociology*, Zondervan, 1982, p.254
14. *Ibid*, p.255
15. Jacques Ellul, *The Ethics of Freedom*, Eerdmans, 1967, pp.88-90
16. Brian Dickey, *Evangelicals and Welfare*, Zadok, 1989
17. Phillip Adams, *Adams Versus God*, Nelson, 1985, pp.10–25
18. Aloysius Pieres, *Theology of Liberation in Asia*, Orbis, 1989
19. Peter Glew-Crouch, *Religion and Helping Behaviour*, unpublished thesis, 1989, pp.2 and 23
20. David Gerard, 'What makes a Volunteer?', *New Society*, Vol.74, Nov. 1985, pp.236-238
21. Craig Seaton, *Altruism and Activism*, Trinity Western Langley, 1990, p.12
22. M. Scott Peck, *The Different Drum*, Rider, 1987, p.188
23. S.J. Samartha, 'Mission and Movements of Innovation', *Mission Trends*, No.3, Paulist Press, p.239
24. Otto Maduro, *Religion and Social Conflicts*, Orbis, 1982, pp.115–120
25. Dave Andrews, *Aashiana*, thesis, University of Queensland, Brisbane
26. *Ibid*
27. *Ibid*
28. *Ibid*
29. *Ibid*
30. *Ibid*
31. Michael Leunig, *A Common Prayer*, Collins Dove, 1990